THE MORAL LIFE

Obligation and Affirmation

Tony L. Moyers

University Press of America,® Inc.
Lanham · Boulder · New York · Toronto · Plymouth, UK

Library of Congress Control Number: 2011929056
ISBN: 978-0-7618-5557-6 (paperback : alk. paper)
eISBN: 978-0-7618-5558-3

♾™ The paper used in this publication meets the minimum
requirements of American National Standard for Information
Sciences—Permanence of Paper for Printed Library Materials,
ANSI Z39.48-1992

Contents

Preface

Several important questions surface in this study. Why should we be moral? How do we know what is right and wrong? Is there an absolute universal set of moral principles binding on every society and every age? If so, how can we discover what they are? Are moral principles important for atheists or agnostics? These are just a few of the questions that face us. These are interesting and important questions.

Before beginning, however, I need to make some of my intentions clear. In this book, I introduce a number of different viewpoints. I do not claim to be neutral on these topics. Yet, my purpose is not to persuade but to inform and stimulate thought. I try to present the reader with a clear and understandable account so he or she can reflect upon the viewpoints and make sense of them. Making sense of information is often a challenging job, but it can be rewarding.

I work under the assumption that we are all different to some degree. While we all have things in common, we understand and value things differently. What counts, however, is what we do with our abilities. We make sense of the world and the things we see and read in different ways. We all have different life stories. No matter how similar we are, we never have the exact same set of life experiences or thoughts. Individuals and events have affected and touched our lives in particular ways. In short, this situation affects how we see the world.

Additionally, an individual's personality can have an influence on understanding. An emotional or sensitive individual may respond and value things differently than one who lacks these qualities. Therefore, the response of one person may not be better or worse than the response of another, only different.

In summary, we live our lives out of a different set of life experiences. The differences and the different perspectives make life interesting and enriching. Differences increase our understanding and appreciating of ourselves and others. I do not desire to paint everything with a single brush. I value diversity. There may be many ways of doing the right thing, not just one.

Innovation often is the result of diversity. How to relate fairly and justly toward others is one of the most difficult issues facing humanity. Do we attempt to provide justice on a societal level or on an individual level or both? To what extent, if any, are we obligated to sacrifice our interests to help others? How far do I go to help a hurting neighbor? On the other hand, is it society's responsibility to help individuals in need? These are real practical questions.

Moreover, does an ethic require calculations? Is an act good if it helps 51% of the people affected? Is an ethic a matter of something that can be quantified? Alternatively, should we act from a sense of duty to do the right thing? If so, where does that sense of duty come from? Is it based on reason, feelings, an inner voice, or God? Does that inner voice call us to listen to our better nature?

I would just note that this book has taken shape over years of teaching a course on moral values. Since students could take the class as a philosophy or sociology, this book covers both areas. The title for the first edition of the book published in 1996 is *Wanderings: Exploring Moral Landscapes Past and Present*. The change of the title to *The Moral Life: Obligation and Affirmation* results from the significant changes made to this edition. I have not changed my mind as much as I have focused my thoughts in a more definite direction. Also, I have reorganized many parts of this edition. I have also updated and added a number of new topics.

Acknowledgments

I want to express my deepest thanks and gratitude for the diligent work of my wife, Ruth Moyers. She has spent a great deal of time editing the work in both the first edition of this book and this one as well. She has provided frequent encouragement, suggestions, and careful proofreading of this text. I am grateful to late Dr. Curtis Coleman for giving me the opportunity to teach a course on moral values from which this book emerges. Many students have also contributed by their questions and comments, which have helped me to clarify, refine, and smooth out many places in the text. I am appreciative of one student in particular, Kathy Petersen, for her assistance in proofing the early drafts of the first edition. I am also grateful to two good friends and colleagues Dr. Clarence Johnson and Dr. Robert A. White. Dr. Johnson's proofreading of the manuscript, and his suggestions have been particularly helpful. Discussions and conversations with Dr. White have supplied me with kind words and much encouragement along the way.

Chapter One
Diversity of Moral Thought

Morals and a sense of obligation are necessary ingredients for life to flourish. Nevertheless, there are various views on what is moral as well as how we can determine what our moral obligations are. This book is largely descriptive in that it seeks to describe a number of different views on morality or ethics past and present, which should provide the reader with a general view of the subject matter. I describe this subject from a several different disciplines. The question that runs throughout, however, concerns the possibility of ethics. Can ethics as defined by societies or philosophers or politicians or whomever provide a safe guide for human thought and action? If it cannot do so, then what is our alternative to ethics? Discussion of premodern, modern, and postmodern thought throughout allows me to draw some conclusions in the last chapter. I would not want to provide those here since I do not wish to unduly influence the reader at the very beginning. One of my goals is to spur the reader to reflect and think. I would like to challenge the reader to come up with her or his own solutions or at least to consider various possibilities. I simply say for the moment that what is moral cannot be defined absolutely nor can it be a matter of precise calculation. Morality is not calculus. I do not think the answer to our moral dilemmas or questions reside in the power of reason or calculation. Both may be tools to help guide us in difficult situations, but they cannot provide us with final and absolute answers to all our moral questions.

It is a safe assumption that some sort of moral values have existed in all societies from the beginnings of human history. These moral values differ from culture to culture or tribe to tribe. Nevertheless, there are moral values that people believe to be essential for the ongoing of a productive society. For this reason, moral values fulfill some of the same roles as law and tradition. They seek to control or discourage some kinds of behavior while encouraging other types. Since it is not possible to determine the origins of these values with certainty, we can begin where we are by acknowledging that moral values exist and have played and continues to play an important role in societies.

Therefore, we need morals of some sort. One cannot separate oneself from a moral realm. The exact nature of this moral realm is a matter of dispute. Morals are a pragmatic fixture of social life. These moral values share a social component and perhaps a component that is not social. The social and nonsocial elements are subjects discussed in various places below.

In the following pages, I examine different approaches. I try to describe these views. Many modern writers seek to discover and argue for a universal set of moral principles that provide a guide for everyone. Others may see moral values as a necessary part of society, but they may not be looking for universal principles. They may simply desire a set of moral values that fit their particular society. Others may question the whole enterprise of philosophical ethics in an attempt to foster a moral perspective that values pluralism and diversity.

In the last few years, we have been moving in the direction of postmodern thought, which has major implications for traditional ethical theories. Postmodern thought does not consider the discovery of moral certainty possible. I believe there is a need for a book that explains values and ethics in a postmodern context that is easily accessible to readers outside the fields of religion, literature, or philosophy. Nevertheless, to understand a postmodern ethical perspective, one also needs to understand something of the long story of morals and how they have functioned in different cultures over the years. Many of the books, essays, or articles about postmodernism presuppose a level of comprehension and understanding that is not common knowledge. A general postmodern attitude toward ethics is widespread in contemporary society, and yet many people do not recognize, know, or appreciate the reasons for the shifts in moral thinking over the past fifty years. I attempt to clarify and simplify this area of thought as much as possible so readers and students can clearly understand the options before them. The contents of this book offer a basic insight and outline to help readers follow and understand current thinking about moral values.

I must confess before continuing that I am neither an ethicist nor a philosopher. A significant degree of my doctoral work is in biblical studies. There are those better qualified to write a book on moral values. However, the same intellectual movements that have influenced religious studies in general and biblical studies in particular apply to the subject of morals. Both areas must deal with modern and postmodern thought, issues of gender, ethnicity, and class within a pluralistic social environment. It is no longer possible for one or two models to dominate these fields of study. In addition, the factors that lead to the explosion of different perspectives on biblical literature are also responsible for the loss of confidence in moral absolutes. While the desire for moral absolutes may persist for many people in today's society, the ability to establish such absolutes is unrealistic.

This book entails a long narrative that does not attempt to be exhaustive. Rather than trying to say a little about a great number of people and approaches, this story is selective. It attempts to discuss some of the most significant ideas, traditions, peoples, and scholars that have contributed to human understanding of morals and ethics. The goal of this description is to discuss these ideas, peoples, and scholars in order to obtain an understanding of current notions about moral values and to see how values might continue to play an important role in a pluralistic world.

OUTLINE OF THE BOOK

In this book, I am attempting to provide information about moral values from several different perspectives. This work covers as many different views as possible, but it gives added weight to views that have often been ignored or avoided. For instance, I have incorporated the insights of Friedrich Nietzsche. Nietzsche has written a great deal about morality and values. His work is perhaps one of the most important for pushing the discussion of values and ethics beyond the narrow interests of traditional ethical approaches. As a result, I have incorporated a number of quotations along the way. Quotations can do more than just recite the ideas of others. They are also capable of stimulating the reader's curiosity by providing him or her with a sample of a writer's ideas, and they may even entice one to read some of these works.

A major goal of this undertaking is to examine what academic and common people past and present have thought and said about what is good and bad as well as what is acceptable and unacceptable behavior. In this respect, I have looked at moral values from a theoretical and practical perspective. On the theoretical side, I have examined several philosophical positions relating to ethics such as egoism, utilitarianism, relativism, and absolutism. From a practical viewpoint, the following pages have considered how people and societies think and feel about particular ethical issues.

This book should illustrate just how important moral values are for any society. I also note how values change as the needs of a particular society change. Overall, this material attempts to describe the moral attitudes of people and societies both in the past and present.

To accomplish these and other goals, this study encompasses the following elements. The next two chapters examine the social function of morals and their nature. It considers how one acquires morals and ethics. This examination defines morals and ethics in relation to other phenomena such as religion and law. In chapter four, the focus is on the historical development of moral thinking and behavior in ancient Israel and ancient Greece. These two societies continue to have a significant influence on modern and postmodern thought through the Greek philosophers and the Judeo-Christian traditions. Chapter five examines the thought of several individuals who have contributed to our modern view of morals and ethics. This modern view derives in large part from the Enlightenment worldview that stresses reason and rationality as the way to Truth. Moreover, it accepts the view that a human being can be a neutral or objective subject capable of discovering universal and timeless Truths. The following chapter looks at the movement toward postmodernism. Postmodern thinkers say that human beings can only be neutral and objective to a limited degree. For them, truth is relative to a location and relevant to a particular time in history.

From this background material, our study moves on in chapter seven to note how societies and their values have evolved and how this evolution has changed the way we understand and perceive our world. The changes illustrate how our value systems have developed and continue to develop over time. Anyone can see the change by just comparing television programs from the 1950's and 1960's with current ones. In addition, issues such as employment practices, education, and family values describe these changes. Accompanying these changes, we also discuss the nature of culture and relativism.

Chapter eight focuses primarily on the personal or psychological aspect of ethics or moral values. This discussion leads to a difficult question: Should ethics be solely a personal consideration or should they be related to the social world or both? We also consider the relationship between morality and moral development in relation to gender. Does gender have any affect on one's moral reasoning and development?

Chapter nine continues the line of thought introduced in chapters five and six. Whereas chapters five and six examine moral systems of thought that inform modern and postmodern theory, chapter nine investigates modern and postmodern ethics as well as an ethic of care that does not fit fully in either category. Chapter ten focuses on the nature of morality and gender looking at issues of power and control in relation to sexual equality. Can we have equality and at the same time value the differences between the sexes? In the final chapter, I sketch my own perspective on ethics and obligation for readers' consideration.

It is my hope that the book leads the reader to reflect on what is at stake and what constitutes a responsible approach to the issues we face. I am not attempting to convert the reader to a particular view. Nevertheless, I want to stress the importance of moral action. Different views can inform us about our options and what is important. My own views on this particular subject have developed out of my study and reflections on this topic over the last twenty years. The effort has been rewarding, fruitful, and worth the effort. It is also important. I believe two things are at stake. First, what will our lives be like? Will we take moral concerns of fairness and justice seriously or not? Second, will the society of which we belong take these things seriously? The answers determine the nature and direction of our future.

Finally, this study of moral values is interdisciplinary. It incorporates the fields of sociology, philosophy, anthropology, psychology, and religion. These disciplines take up the issue of morals and ethics on occasion. For sociology, psychology, and anthropology, the field of ethics is primarily a descriptive discipline. Philosophy and religion are more than descriptive since they often seek to establish rules of behavior. The following investigation of moral values considers the descriptive and abstract natures of moral thinking and behavior.

Chapter Two
Social Function and Nature of Morality

Working Definition of Ethics and Morals

To be moral, correct, ethical means to obey an age-old law or tradition. Whether one submits to it gladly or with difficulty makes no difference; [it is] enough that one submits (Nietzsche 1984, 66)

The word *ethics* comes from the Greek word *éthos*. Éthos means character or custom. Therefore, the meaning of the word ethics suggests that it relates to what a society customarily does or sanctions. To be more specific, *ethics* is a "body of values by which a culture understands and interprets itself with regard to what is good and bad" (Scott 1990, 4). These ethics or values provide a picture of what a society deems to be appropriate and inappropriate. In this sense, we should not sharply distinguish between *ethics* and morals because both terms refer to a body of principles, which are guides for human conduct and value judgments (Scott 1990, 4).

The English word *moral* comes from the Latin word *mores*. This word also derives its meaning from the idea of custom. Some ethicists try to distinguish between morals and ethics. Philosophers tend to think of ethics as a philosophical inquiry into what is good or bad. Ethics in this sense is an attempt to establish and justify a certain set of norms defining how one ought to live. However, in everyday language, we use these two words interchangeably. Both words have an intimate connection with custom, which is generally an authoritative norm of conduct for a society. In general, I use the two terms as synonyms except in those cases where I am discussing particular ethical systems or ethicists.

SOCIAL FUNCTION OF MORAL VALUES

Moral values are essential for society. We can safely assume that morals have played an important role in societal life ever since people began living together in communities. We begin our story with societies of the past.

Moral values differ from society to society, but the role they play generally allows people to live together in community. Moral values, therefore, have a pragmatic value. They are the glue that can bind people together providing a common purpose, identity, and sense of direction. They provide structure and guidelines. This structure would typically be functional for most people although it may be dysfunctional for some. Nevertheless, the pragmatic nature of moral values is important for societies then and now.

Looking at how a particular society's morals function can help one understand that society better. However, we cannot discover the origin of moral values for a society. Views of right and wrong have always been present regardless of their origin. It seems more helpful to examine how these values have functioned in particular societies. The social function of morals for a society does not necessarily tell us anything about their origins.

In premodern societies, moral values are predominantly social in nature.[1] Right and wrong behavior refers to the kind of behavior a society considers helpful or harmful to the larger group. Morality defines the limits or boundaries of legitimate thought and action. These values provide a certain amount of stability for society.

Every society follows a set of customs, values, and beliefs. These values provide guidelines for behavior; they tell people what is acceptable and unacceptable. Consequently, some customs have a moral quality, and this quality provides societies with a stability and common identity. Moral customs tell us how to act.[2] They also provide one with an identity as part of a particular group. They know what is expected of them. Most cultures foster values and traditions that reveal something about who they are and what they seek to accomplish. These values offer reasons for acting in ways that reflect favorably upon one's community. Moral values, therefore, are largely responsible for making an orderly life possible.

This description suggests that moral customs are pragmatic. They serve an important purpose. They may sometimes survive even after their value for a society has diminished or faded altogether. Some moral customs may over time cease to serve an important role at all. Others may evolve and change as society changes.

Besides customs, moral values are also intimately connected to sacred traditions. Sacred traditions have developed in numerous ways. They may begin as oral stories. Individuals and groups keep them alive through the process of telling and retelling. The community can transmit important values through the medium of stories. Some ethicists believe that stories or narratives are in fact the best way to communicate values. One cannot underestimate the importance of this medium for communicating values important to the group. These stories play an important role in the socialization of children and adolescents. In some past cultures, an individual or group of individuals would write their stories down. Some of this literature in the Ancient Near East probably goes through an oral stage before passing over into written texts. This process would be true for some of the texts in the Bible. Jesus' stories are communicated over many years before they are written down. The earliest written Gospel in the New Testament dates at least 35 to 40 years after Jesus' death.

In other cultures, stories continued to thrive as an oral art form. One generation passed them down orally to the next through the art of storytelling. Among the Plains Indians, for instance, legends told orally belonged to specific individuals. These individuals had the responsibility of selecting a new owner to whom they could entrust the story. This person was responsible for the preservation of these stories (Lankford 1987, 46-47).

Customs and sacred traditions provide instructions for daily living. These traditions can become an important source for a society's moral values. As these customs or traditions become widely accepted, they become part of the taken-for-granted world. Individuals of a society often accept and internalize them to the degree that they would not question their validity. Everyone simply knows that it is desirable to conform and bad not to conform.

These moral customs and sacred traditions endure as long as they maintain their legitimacy for the community. Political or economic changes in a society can produce changes and transformations in a society's value system. The process whereby societies become more pluralistic or more diverse leads to a natural evolution. As these societies become more diverse, values must be able to appeal to a wider audience. If they cannot, they are in danger of losing their hold or legitimacy on people. As diversity increases, it becomes more difficult for values to maintain their importance for society.

Jürgen Habermas provides a description of societal evolution. He defines societies as "primitive, traditional, or modern." Evolution implies progress. Clearly, he thinks that the modern society is superior to the one based on authority or tradition. The triggering mechanism that leads to evolutionary change is conflict or crisis. When a crisis occurs, a system can lose its legitimacy. In the case of "primitive societies" relying primarily on kinship ties, outside influences introduce possible threats. These influences can pressure a "primitive society" and could eventually destroy it. This occurrence could lead to the next type of societal evolution, which he calls a "traditional society."

A traditional society bases its legitimacy on authority and tradition. According to Habermas, sacred traditions and divine authority provide legitimation for particular morals in so-called "primitive" and "traditional societies." Nevertheless, as the complexity of the society progresses, these traditions and authorities can lose their appeal. Consequently, the legitimation of moral values has to take place differently. In modern societies, the basis for legitimation is reason and rationality (Habermas 1975).

While much of Habermas' description of societal evolution seems like good solid common sense, one might question his assumption that the modern view is the best and highest stage in the evolutionary process. If we view evolution and progress as synonyms, then we would view postmodernism as better than modernism. While postmodernism has certain advantages over modernism, postmodern thought would reject the notion of continual and steady progress toward an ideal. Moreover, we should note that even in modern society, we could find plenty of examples of small and large groups operating on authoritative or traditional levels. Many Christian groups appeal to the Bible above all else. Certain societies may still be governed by a political or religious system that dictates every aspect of a society's existence. If we ignore his association of evolution with progress, then his views are helpful in a general way. Evolution means change. Change is inevitable, but it may not be change that leads to a higher level of thought, awareness, or concept of justice and morality. Taken as a description of societal evolution, his views help us understand why and how societies change.

A similar view occurs in the work of Peter L. Berger and his description of plausibility structures. His concept has the advantage of not describing change in terms of progress. When things lose plausibility for a group or individual, they lose their legitimacy.[3] When one loses faith in God, for example, religion loses its grip on that person. Alternatively, when the government loses plausibility, one might join a revolution.

Moral values change as society changes. Herbert Spencer says that as societies evolve they become more complex. This complexity results in *differentiation* (Spencer 1971, 71-80). Differentiation refers to a process whereby individuals or groups take on certain roles. These roles set them apart from others individuals in the group. An example would be the division of labor. People learn how to do specific jobs that differentiate them from other people. So, as complexity increases people become more dependent on others. For example, one may have to depend on someone else to provide a service that he or she cannot provide for himself or herself. For this reason, social integration becomes more difficult for a society as it becomes more diverse.

Émile Durkheim looks at social integration in terms of "*mechanical*" and "*organic solidarity.*" *Mechanical solidarity* exists in premodern times. It refers to the strong sense of unity existing in a simple society. This unity rests upon public opinion and morality present in the group. In this type of society, values are well integrated into the *collective conscience*. The collective conscience includes a common set of values, ideals, and expectations. The collective conscience is stronger in premodern societies than it is now, since a past society would exhibit more unity among its members.

This unity, however, diminishes as the population grows and as societies become more diverse. This process in turn leads to an increasing *division of labor*. At this point, the integration of individuals becomes a problem. In short, societies tend to become more complex as they develop and adapt to changing conditions. As conditions change significantly over time, a society moves from mechanical solidarity to organic solidarity where unity is more of a problem (Durkheim 1933, 70-110 and 152-164).

Organic solidarity is a form of integration typical of industrial societies. It focuses on the lack of self-sufficiency and an individual's dependency on other people. It is a reciprocal situation. The city dweller makes farm implements. The farmer uses the implements to grow his or her crops. The city dweller needs products grown by the farmer. Neither can survive without the other.

Moreover, the unity of public opinion and morality tends to break down or diminish as diversity increases. In modern terms, the increase of diversity can cause trouble for the larger society. Shared values help integrate the individual into the larger society. This integration becomes more difficult as society becomes more diverse.

As societies become more complex and diverse, values often clash creating tension and disunity. In such instances, moral values may only bring unity for a particular group of people related by location or common interests. For instance, agreement on a national level is more difficult than agreement in a small homogeneous community. This process creates differences, and these differences may lead to disunity in a society.

To illustrate this point, we can go back to the views of Habermas. Habermas maintains that as religion moves away from myths and legends to a more philosophical orientation, it changes. Religion becomes more like philosophy, and it must provide rational justification for its beliefs. Simply appealing to tradition or some religious authority is less appealing in modern societies. Instead of basing religion on tradition or authority, modern societies tend to justify religion more on *reason and rationality.* Theological liberalism takes exactly this route. It bases belief and thinking on reason and experience. Fundamentalism, however, emerges as a movement that opposes this liberal approach to rationality. Instead of dying out, this controversy continues a hundred years later with no signs of coming to an end. In short, plurality and diversity work against homogeneity and unity.

Returning to premodern societies, one can best understand moral values within a community context. Things change somewhat with the Greek tradition, which tends to place more importance on the individual. The emphasis on rationality and the human endeavor to find the truth is central for some Greek philosophers. Human beings use reason to discover what is right and wrong. Socrates and Plato assume that correct knowledge leads to correct or moral action. From this standpoint, the individual is capable of knowing and doing what is moral. Good actions derive from the individual's correct knowledge. A person's vices come from his or her own ignorance. Here the individual rather than society is the focal point. Moral values serve the larger society. Plato's book, *The Republic*, focuses on discovering how to organize a society to create a just order. Specifically, Plato's vision calls for an ideal society where moral values lead to a well-ordered and structured world.

This trend toward individualism and the use of reason for defining values continued into the modern period through the Renaissance (ca. 14th and 17th centuries) and Enlightenment (ca. 18th century). The Renaissance revolted against the narrowness and otherworldliness of the Middle Ages, which it followed historically. Both the Renaissance and Enlightenment expressed confidence in human ability to find Truth through reason. Modern views, following the ideals of the Enlightenment, exhibited a faith in human ability to solve problems through reason and science. Accordingly, most ethical perspectives steeped in the Enlightenment tradition stressed the importance of individual reason as a tool for discovering and distinguishing moral from immoral.

Religion and religious ethics before the Renaissance depended primarily on a vertical authority. Divine revelation through nature, written Scriptures, priests, or other religious leaders was the only adequate means for distinguishing moral conduct and thought from the immoral. Modern ethicists and many liberal religious thinkers, on the other hand, appropriated much of the Enlightenment perspective and attempted to legitimize moral values by means of reason and experience.

In summary, moral values serve much the same function today as always; they support and uphold a certain worldview. This worldview provides support for a given social stability. Morals may sometimes lead to laws that make for a safer life or they may discourage behavior that would disrupt and endanger societal order.

Nevertheless, moral values today do not have the same reach as they had several years ago. Today's societies are more diverse, which means that there is no one set of values. Our values have several possible sources of legitimation. For some people, the Bible or some other Scripture may be the basis for morality. For others, some special tradition or some philosophical notion of fairness or justice may legitimate values. For others, it may be a sense of obligation or duty. Regardless, moral values continue to give guidance for behavior. They can provide and give meaning for one's life. Group values offer its members a common identity from which to live their lives. Values can even help one to understand himself or herself as a participant in some greater plan.

MORAL VALUES: A FORM OF COERCIVE POWER

Another important aspect of moral values concerns their coercive force. Morals have control because people view them as legitimate. The control may be beneficial to society as a whole but not necessarily so. Karl Marx maintains that the oppressors or those who own the means of production use religion as a way of keeping people subdued and in their place. Religion is used by those who have power to keep the poor and oppressed under their control. The owners of the means of production use religion to keep people docile. Religion keeps people looking up to heaven rather than mobilizing forces to challenge and change the injustices of this world. Politicians, religious leaders, as well as secular leaders may often appeal to shared morals to promote their own secret agenda. Consequently, it is important for people in any given society to recognize how individuals use morals to compel conformity.

Therefore, issues of power, authority, control, and legitimacy are related to the study of morality. Some societies are simply more egalitarian than others. In many societies, morals can contribute to one's social or economic status. In any society, there are those individuals, such as political leaders, who have the respect of the people and thus possess more authority. Political or religious leaders might influence others to conform to their values and norms, which may or may not be in the other individual's best interests.

Morality and Authority

We can now move on to the issue of authority. Why do things have authority? Sociologist Max Weber identifies three types of authority: traditional authority, charismatic authority, and rational-legal authority (Weber 1971, 169-179). Things have authority over us because we recognize their legitimacy. Rational-legal authority would have more widespread appeal than the others because it can impose penalties for breaking laws. Traditional authority and charisma authority may be more limited. For instance, certain religious traditions are authoritative for specific Christian denominations. Charismatic authority is important in a church where members expect their minister and other leaders to possess charismatic qualities.

These different types of authority support moral values in different contexts. In a traditional setting, moral values would appeal to important traditions. The work of professional ethicists, on the other hand, would likely find ethical rules or principles backed by reason authoritative. Whenever moral values are widely recognized, they have considerable influence. These moral values not only have power, but they possess authority as well.

Informed individuals and societies are obstructions to those who wish to use moral values as a means of manipulating and controlling. Skillful manipulators know how to get a certain result. They use such things as common customs, traditions, fear, scripture, anxiety, or statistics to gain the upper hand over others. In the vast majority of cases, these manipulators are not even aware of what they are doing. Political or religious leaders, for instance, simply know what to say or do to gain support. To some extent, most human beings seek either consciously or unconsciously to manipulate situations to their own advantage. In the former case where one consciously seeks to manipulate others, he or she might intentionally withhold key information. In this way, the manipulator would be insincere or dishonest, playing a part to gain support.

Appeal to religious values, patriotism, loyalty to one's group can be rather effective ways of persuading people to support a particular agenda. The individual, however, can take responsibility. The individual can judge whether he or she should yield to such influences. By adopting an attitude of cautiousness and suspicion, one should be able to make decisions that are more responsible. Only by maintaining a sense of individuality can one decide to give or withhold support.

In short, moral values can actually work against the individual. Often we feel guilty for not yielding to the call of patriotism or some other common value. We may not protest our government's activities because we would feel like a traitor. Politicians may use this fear against us. Therefore, the politician can use certain values as tools for enlisting the support of others. Politicians or other leaders can use morals because people recognize their authority.

Authority, according Weber, refers to the right of a person or thing to be recognized as legitimate by the larger society. This legitimacy bestows something or someone with a sort of legitimate power. Power by itself lacks authority. A thief may have the power to take one's wallet, but he or she does not have any legitimate right to do so.[4]

This point is important. Moral values do not have any power of their own. Their power comes from the fact that people recognize them as having a claim on their lives. This authority shapes the perceptions of the wider society. Blindly accepting and following the values, customs, and traditions of others can make one a prisoner of society.

Morality and Ideology

Ideology is another important aspect of this discussion. Ideology refers to a group of related ideas or philosophies that have power to mold and shape people's lives. Leaders and institutions often use ideology to maintain or overturn the status quo. One could use political ideologies, for instance, to justify wars, tax cuts, gay rights, or any number of other agendas.

Marx saw ideology as negative. Ideology is a tool that allows the powerful to force powerless individuals to conform to their wishes. However, ideology can also serve positive purposes as well. Political policies and ideologies can improve and enrich the lives of people. Religious ideologies can give meaning to life that makes one feel more complete. Yet, politics and religion can use its legitimacy for questionable purposes. Religion, for instance, can redirect an individual's concern away from a better life in this world to a concern for the next world or the life after this one. Alternatively, it could redirect a person's concern for others to a concern for one's own personal salvation.

Morality and Rhetoric

Consequently, ideology is a set of ideas that promote a particular worldview. Rhetoric refers to the power of persuasion. More specifically, it refers to the skillful use of oral and written communication to persuade others of a particular viewpoint. If ideology did not draw upon the services of rhetoric, ideology would be ineffective and insignificant.

People use language to justify ideologies, customs, religion, moral values, political doctrines, or economic philosophies. We might say that rhetoric is a morally neutral technique since one can use it for either worthy or unworthy purposes. The use of rhetoric to convince someone of a particular point by misrepresenting the facts raises moral considerations. To make one's argument seem more convincing than it is, one often stretches the truth or leaves out key bits of information. One may be arguing for something that is virtuous, but how one makes that argument is of moral concern.

In Plato's dialogues, there is a distinction between two types of rhetoric. One type, as represented by Gorgias, sees rhetoric as a means to an end. The end is the satisfying of one's needs. The person who masters the art of rhetoric has a great advantage over others. The rhetorician might be able to persuade others to further his or her own agenda. According to these dialogues, Socrates distinguishes this type of persuasion from one in which an individual offers reasons for retaining certain beliefs or ideas. This type of individual can offer a skillfully reasoned and convincing account of why we should embrace certain beliefs (MacIntyre 1966, 26-27). We might describe rhetoric in the first sense as a dishonest attempt to gain support. The motives of this individual are morally questionable. Perhaps, the first type of person who comes to mind is the politician. In the second instance, the individual is acting in good faith. In fairness, one might wonder if anyone can totally resist the urge to make an argument sound better than it is or to revert to silence at key places. Often it is what goes unsaid that is most important.

One could go so far as to say that we are expected to be a little dishonest. Do we tell a prospective buyer everything that is wrong with our house or do we avoid over emphasizing its positive points. Many of us may feel a tinge of guilt for making something sound better than it is. Therefore, the temptation to deceive is great. We all know this. The old adage "buyers beware" warns us to suspect the motives and words of others.

In summary, authority, power, legitimacy, ideology, and rhetoric strongly influence us, and they often govern human interaction. It is important for us to acknowledge the relationship that exists between these forces and standard morality since these forces can limit one's ability to make responsible choices.

Some might argue that we really do not have a choice. All our actions including our moral ones are determined by genetics and social upbringing. According to this view, one can never act freely. Our decisions would be predetermined by nature or socialization. Yet is this argument true? Do we not have the freedom to make choices? If we do not have freedom, we are just prisoners of our social environment or our biology or our genetics. In such a circumstance, would we be responsible for the choices we make? On the other hand, would they be choices at all? Instead, one would follow his or her social, biological, or genetic programming.

FREEDOM AND MORAL RESPONSIBILITY

Are we free to make decisions? The debate over whether an individual is able to make free choices is a long and complex one. At this point, I limit the discussion to a few key points. The focus of our examination relates to an individual's relation to the larger society. More specifically, it examines how social and personal factors combine to affect human choice.

One of the most important issues confronting the subject of morality is *free will*. How could we hold people responsible for their actions if they do not have free will? If a husband murders his wife because she annoys him, can we blame the husband? Most would be quick to respond with a yes. However, could the husband be completely at the mercy of forces beyond his control? What if the husband does not have a choice or free will, is he responsible for his actions? Is he responsible if his behavior is completely controlled by unseen forces, the home environment, or his genetic makeup? Is he *morally* responsible, if his behavior is determined? Moreover, if this is the case, what should society do? Is it morally just or fair to punish one who could not have done otherwise?

Most people assume that human beings are free to make choices about what they do. Typically, the mother who has to decide between going to see her child in a piano recital or making a business meeting believes that she is deciding between two options. Yet, what if she only imagines she is making a choice? Suppose social, psychological, or biological factors determine her choice before hand.

On the other hand, it is natural for us to look for causes that explain human behavior. We assume that the social environment, biology, foods we eat, and even our genetic makeup can greatly influence human thought and behavior. With this belief, humans can explain why Jack is a serial killer and why John is abusive husband. We generally believe that such actions are not entirely free and that we can help the person if we can discover what went wrong. The result is that most people accept a common sense view that we are free and that we are slaves to other forces.

Several religious and scientific thinkers argue that human behavior is determined. From a religious or theological point of view, there are those who argue that God has predetermined everything. All things happen as they do because of the divine will. The theological positions of such Christians as Saint Augustine, John Calvin, and others support the notion that God has preordained everything. There are also passages in the Quran (i.e., Islamic Scripture) that stress Allah's foreknowledge and control (Noss 2008, 554-555).

Additionally, some psychologists believe that various external stimuli combine to determine behavior. From the standpoint of behavioral psychology, we can understand human behavior on the stimulus-response-reinforcement model. This model also relates to the notion of cause and effect. A particular stimulus causes a predictable response. Moreover, one must admit that there is a good bit of evidence to support the notion that human behavior is predictable. We could perhaps compare this view of human behavior to a trained animal where we give a command (i.e., stimulus) and receive a certain expected response. As we shall see later, this model of human behavior is too limited.

There are many other thinkers religious and otherwise who support the view that human beings are capable of making choices. Existentialists such as Søren Kierkegaard or Jean-Paul Satre recognize influences that might imprison us, but they maintain that we are free and responsible agents. Following Kierkegaard, existentialism puts emphasis on the individual confronting the decisions of life. Kierkegaard is not concerned about humanity in general but individuals in their concrete life situations. One must make decisions without assurances since our knowledge is limited. Decisions are required precisely because we are not privy to all the necessary information and knowledge. So we must decide. Without freedom, there would be no real decision.

Writers such as Kierkegaard, Martin Heidegger, Satre, Simone de Beauvoir, Nietzsche, and Berger note that people often just follow the crowd. People often hide in the crowd and relinquish their freedom. By just doing what others expect, we fail to live authentic lives. Heidegger, for example, describes this hiding in the crowd as bowing to *Das Man*, an anonymous "one" or "they" (Berger 1963, 146-148). We simply do what "they" say or expect. We live in accordance with what they expect, and we remain unaware of our options.

For example, a young white woman living in a Southern State during the 1960's falls in love with a young Afro-American. She would no doubt become painfully aware of what it would cost her to follow her heart and disregard societal expectations. On the other hand, if she follows normal expectations, she could avoid trouble. The authentic life can only be lived when one lives as an individual who makes decisions for himself or herself and accepts the consequences of those decisions.

To have some freedom would at minimum mean that we would be aware of various expectations and influences that shape our behavior. The problem is that we can never be aware of all these influences. Nevertheless, awareness and an open mind can provide a person with more possible options.

Habits, impulses, and compulsions also severely curtail one's freedom. At best, we have potential freedom and this freedom is never absolute. Human freedom is always a matter of degree. Yet, without some freedom, real decisions and personal responsibility for our actions would be impossible. Without freedom, we might hold the murderer responsible in a legal sense, but morally we could not.

Having potential freedom carries with it certain implications. French existentialist, Simone De Beauvoir contends in her book, *The Ethics of Ambiguity* that human beings are free, but she qualifies this freedom by describing the forces that work to limit or quell that freedom. She says that:

> The child's situation is characterized by finding himself cast into a universe which he has not helped established, which has been fashioned without him, and which appears to him as an absolute to which he can only submit. In his eyes, human inventions, words, customs, and values are given facts (De Beauvoir 1994, 35).

Taking this statement as a starting point, I pose this question: Are we captives of society?[5] Are we captives to customs, habits, morals, and traditions? Uncritically following certain customs or traditions is to be a passive slave to these customs and traditions. Nietzsche says that "when men determine between moral and immoral, good and evil, the basic opposition [is] . . . adherence to a tradition or law [i.e., good] and release from it [i.e., evil]" (Nietzsche 1984, 66). Blind obedience to custom, then, robs one of his or her ability to make real decisions.

De Beauvoir calls such a person "sub-human." By this statement, she only means that freedom distinguishes us from the other objects in the universe. She is not devaluing the worth and dignity of such persons. Most of us could be called sub-human at times since we often do not exercise our freedom and simply do what others expect.

Before continuing, I would illustrate the importance and terror of being free. To be free to any degree, one must have certain awareness and be able to make a decision between competing options. I begin with terror of freedom. Everyone is painfully familiar with the obedience the masses gave to Adolf Hitler. A German soldier is given an order to kill an innocent person. What should he do? The soldier can obey or disobey. Even though disobeying may lead to his own death, he still has that option. So what should he do? Another horror presents itself in stories from people who join cults. Charismatic leaders such as Jim Jones have ordered people to commit suicide. Imagine being in a group where the leader tells everyone the world is about to end and orders them to take up arms against outsiders. Do they have a choice?

It is frightening that many people seem to follow a leader and take orders without question. Some experiments have demonstrated that under the right conditions average people take orders from an authority figure even to the point of endangering the lives of other people.

In Stanley Milgram's experiment, subjects thought that they were helping people improve their memories by administering electrical shocks for each wrong answer given to a particular question. With each incorrect answer, the amount of electrical shock increased. The subject of the experiment did not know that in reality there were no electrical shocks being given. Milgram found in this particular experiment on conformity that the majority of subjects, about two-thirds (twenty-six subjects out of forty), were willing to give potentially lethal electrical shocks to strangers if commanded to do so by an authority figure. They did so even when the person who was supposedly receiving the electrical shock begged for the subject in the experiment to stop. There were several variations of the experiment. The first experiment (the "Remote Feedback" variation) clearly demonstrated that the majority of people were prone to follow the commands of an authority figure. The other subjects who refused to go all the way to 450 volts still felt uneasy about not continuing the experiment.[6]

Therefore, we can say that we have potential freedom. Being aware of how individuals and social situations influence our behavior could have a liberating effect. Yet, one must still be willing to exercise freedom. Individuals must be able to make choices or decisions based on the available information. Only then can one really speak of choices and freedom in any meaningful way. Nietzsche eloquently expresses the importance of individuals thinking for themselves when he says,

> We may always infer that a civilization is really high when powerful and domi-
> neering natures [like Plato] have little influence and create only sects. This ap-
> plies also to the various arts and the field of knowledge. Where someone rules,
> there are masses; and where we find masses we also find a need to be enslaved.

Where men are enslaved, there are few individuals, and these [individuals] are opposed by herd instincts and conscience (Nietzsche 1974, 195-196).

Nietzsche is not discussing individual freedom in this passage, but his reference to the rulers who enslave makes the same point I am stressing. Mere conformity to any group leads to imprisonment or enslavement.

In this chapter, I have examined different aspects of morals and ethics. Morals and ethics are necessary for stable societies. Yet, they can play a positive or negative role in society. They can make orderly life possible. On the other hand, they can function to curtail individuality forcing one's thoughts and actions into a confined space. It is not a matter of morals being good or bad. They can produce good and bad. For this last statement to make sense to some people, I would just say that morals do not always equate to good in the sense I am using it in this chapter. Morals and ethics refer to what a society accepts or rejects. Some communities and societies have engaged in practices others would call immoral. What is considered moral for one person or community may be considered immoral by another.

The last part of this chapter addresses the importance of thinking for oneself. I have argued that human beings have a measure of free will. As a result, we are morally responsible for our actions and decisions. Blindly following the dictates of society is dangerous. Being a moral person goes far beyond just following the rules of ethicists or societies. The remainder of this book describes both ethics in the social sense of what society expects from the individual as well as the views of philosophers and others who attempt to determine and instruct others in what morals require of individuals and societies. The next chapter focuses on how one knows and comes to possess morals.

NOTES

1. I am defining premodern societies as all societies from 3,000 B.C.E. up to the industrial age where there is a sharp increase in the division of labor. Before 3,000 B.C.E, we could describe human societies as hunter-gather and horticulturist societies (Lorber 1994, 123-143).

2. Customs are not necessarily moral. Morals and ethics refer to what is customarily done or what people generally approve. Some customs, however, might fall more under the category of folkways, which refers to things that are expected but not necessarily ranked on a moral scale.

3. Habermas refers to the point where something is in danger of losing legitimation as a legitimation crisis.

4. See Max Weber 1962, 71-73, 117-118.

5. Compare to Peter L. Berger 1963, 93-150.

6. For more details and a discussion of these experiments, see Warren Cohen 1995, 157-197. Stanley Milgram performed this experiment in 1961.

Chapter Three
Finding and Acquiring Morals

In the midst of all the doubts which we have discussed for four thousand years in four thousand ways, the safest course is to do nothing against one's conscience. With this secret, we can enjoy life and have no fear from death. (Voltair 1919, 232)

Being clear about what is and what is not a matter of ethics or morals is necessary. Such distinctions allow us to gain a better understanding of morality and to focus attention in areas that provide for a broad discussion and description of the subject matter.

How can we distinguish between moral and nonmoral aspects of life? Graham Sumner distinguishes between *folkways and mores*. Folkways are rules one should follow as a matter of good manners. These rules, however, do not reach the level of *mores* or morals. Folkways might include such things as eating with a knife and fork, driving on the right or left side of the street depending upon the country, or greeting another person with a handshake. However, some expected actions are more central to the survival of the community, and as a result, they obtain a higher level of importance.

Societies may come to associate some of these folkways with what they believe to be true and right. As a result, they take on a higher status; they become *mores*. They encourage some actions and forbid others as immoral (Sumner 1975, 82-88). *Mores* may consist of such things as inappropriate dress or language. In addition, folkways are more open to change while *mores* typically are more entrenched in society resisting change.

Modern ethicists attempt to distinguish clearly between moral and nonmoral guides for behavior. They differentiate between such things as morals and etiquette or morals and laws. Moral standards typically reflect what a society deems to be binding on the group and individual.

In modern societies, for example, we often create a code of ethical behavior. Professional ethics may fall somewhere between etiquette and law. These codes are created to govern the conduct of individuals in a particular professional environment. These codes are to inform the individual about the type of behavior expected in his or her profession. Today, many businesses have developed policies about such things as drug testing and sexual harassment. In some cases, the ethical codes are vague and general. In other cases, the codes have to be more stringent and binding. The Catholic priest, for example, upon hearing up the confession of a murderer is not free to share that information with the police.

All societies have formal and informal standards of behavior, and they expect members to conform to these standards. Some moral philosophers or ethicists have tried to formulate moral standards that are universal and absolute. At minimum, one could describe ethics as standards that prevent unjustified harm to others.[1]

Reason is an essential tool for defining moral guidelines even if it is not foolproof. Many ethicists agree that moral guidelines depend upon the adequacy of the reasons given for their support (Shaw 1993, 4). For these ethicists, the source of legitimation is not found in the community. Rather, it is located in the abstract process of rational analysis.

We might pause and inquire whether one is better than the other? Should morals be legitimated by means of reason and rationality or by the views common in society? I would not argue for either one to the exclusion of the other. Reason is important. Nevertheless, can it provide us with absolute moral standards? The views of society are also important. Many people may assume that reason is better because of its association with being objective. They might argue that by using reason one could conceivably develop an ethic binding upon all people regardless of where they live. Still, reason can never be totally objective, and our reasoning skills always depend on our own presuppositions and assumptions. Assumptions may guide our reason, and we may not even be aware of our most basic assumptions. Reason may be an important tool for developing pragmatic ethical guidelines, but it is a limited tool. Should we, on the other hand, just accept the existing moral standards of the larger community? I do not think either extreme is tenable alone. Now I begin this chapter by discussing important distinctions between morality and related areas.

MORALS, ETIQUETTE, AND LAWS

It is rather common for people to think of manners or law in the same way as they think about morals. Special codes of conduct, known as etiquette, insist that certain types of behavior are inappropriate. Etiquette would be similar to folkways. Many types of conduct are impolite. However, it does not follow that these types of behaviors are immoral. For instance, a person eating with his or her fingers may be rude, but he or she is not necessarily breaking any moral standard.

Similarly, there is a difference between *morals and law*. This difference is somewhat more complex. In Greek, ethics or *éthos* can refer to character, custom, or habit. More specifically, however, *éthos* can denote customs or habits associated with a particular geographical location or region. *Éthos* has a regional character; one's *éthos* is connected to where one lives. When a person grows up in a particular *éthos*, he or she is not likely to accept another way of being. Moreover, there is a close connection between the notion of *éthos* as custom and as a location. People in a particular location tend to follow a particular set of values or customs peculiar to that area.

Law, on the other hand, comes from the Greek word *nómos*. Law seeks to extend its reach beyond small communities or regions. It attempts to control unruly force. In the process, communities or tribes can lose control if they do not resist. Conflict between peoples with different customs or ethics creates an attraction or appeal for universal laws backed by prescribed sanctions.

As societies develop, law creates distance between oneself and the other person. According to Zygmunt Bauman, proximity is the place of closeness where morality resides. Distance, on the other hand, is the "realm of estrangement and the Law. Between the self and other, there was to be distance structured solely by legal rules" (Bauman 1993, 83). Bauman is here talking about modern thinkers who plan modern life in a way that creates distance between people. It also stresses universality and society in the abstract. Bauman's discussion of postmodern ethics returns to the place of the individual in relation to the Other.[2] It is a place he calls the moral party of two.[3] This description of the difference between law and morality points to a continued tension between the two concepts.

According to Charles E. Scott, stubbornness accompanies *éthos*. To overcome stubbornness and regional quarreling, there is a need for rules or laws so that different locales can be brought under control or held to a common standard. These rules or laws produce or impose a timeless and universal order. Scott concludes that "our desire for universal laws and values and a changeless basis for them arises out of human's clinging to security and familiarity in the face of displacing and threatening differences" (Scott 1990, 144-146).

Therefore, from this description, it is easy to see how *éthos* differs from law. We can see that there is a connection between ethics and law, but they are not identical. Laws require conformity, and they punish offenders. Ethics may also require conformity, but the reach of its power may extend no further than the tribe. Often ethics and laws are in tension. Simply put, laws are those norms recognized as legitimate by the larger society. They would be able to control a number of smaller communities or local groups. These laws tend to uphold order in the larger society, and they quell or diminish the differences associated with particular localities. Ethics as described by Scott has to do with the character or custom of a given society.

It is also important to recognize that law is insufficient as a guide to moral behavior. It can govern our behavior as does ethics, but saying an act is illegal does not settle the issue of morality. In some sense, laws and ethics should remain separate; a society needs the tension. The tension would mean that humans should not merely accept laws without question. A society's *éthos* or *mores* precede laws in an evolutionary sense. Some set of binding rules recognized by a society are always necessary. However, situations where local practices disagree with certain state or federal laws can still present possible sources of tension.

For instance, some might question the fairness of laws prohibiting polygamy for those particular areas of the country that favor or support such practices based on their own religious beliefs. Alternatively, should prostitution be illegal? Should the state be able to tell one what he or she can do with his or her own body? It seems, therefore, that the legality of an action does not mean that the action is morally right. Polygamy may be illegal but some Mormons and Arabs believe it is moral. Prostitution is illegal in most places, but some might argue that individuals have the right to use their bodies as they wish. Others may say that even if abortion is legal, it is not moral. As a result, conformity to law is not sufficient for moral conduct. Martin Luther King, Jr., maintains that breaking an unjust law may be justifiable as long as it does not entail violence. Probably no one in the modern era has expressed this point more eloquently than he has.

RELIGION AND MORALITY

Can we separate religion from morality? Perhaps it would be best to begin by defining religion. There are many different definitions. It suffices here to use the definition offered by Ronald L. Johnstone. He says, "Religion is a set of beliefs and rituals by which a group of people seek to understand, explain, and deal with a world of complexity, uncertainty, and mystery, by identifying a sacred canopy of explanation and reassurance under which to live (Johnstone 2007, 14). Morality is a part of religion. It is part of the beliefs and practices of a faith. However, there is much more to religion than just morals. In certain cases, one could even argue that ethics could challenge certain religious beliefs and practices.

Is morality dependent on religion for its validity? There is a close connection between morality and religion. Particular religious traditions, sacred writings, and teachings provide their faithful with a worldview. This worldview may very well provide moral guidelines for one's everyday activities.

Because of this connection, many people take it for granted that morality depends upon religion. They think that without religion there would be no morality. From their point of view, both religion and morality depend primarily upon authority from above. Worshippers can justify their religious practices and beliefs because of divine authority. Ivan Karamazov (a character in Fydor Dostoevsky's novel the *Brothers Karamazov*) says in effect that if there is no God then everything is permissible. This statement goes back to the issue of origins or source. Is God or the gods the only source of all morals? On a pragmatic level, however, this statement is not true.

Ethics and morals do not have to depend upon sacred traditions or written laws. For some, ethics depend primarily on reason and rationality (Sinnott-Armstrong 2009). For example, the German philosopher, Immanuel Kant, justifies moral principles solely based on pure practical reason and not on any type of religious authority. From this perspective, religion is not necessary to establish the existence of universal and absolute moral and ethical standards. Furthermore, for Kant, moral laws[4] are binding. We have a moral duty to obey them. Reason, therefore, overtakes religious authority as the legitimating factor.

Some people might object and say that without religion there would be no reason to act morally. One might argue that acting morally prevents punishment in the afterlife and leads to eternal happiness. Yet, this is not the *only reason* for behaving morally. Many people act morally out of habit. Others may act morally to gain the approval of peers, avoid the pains of conscience, or escape some sort of punishment in this life. In short, there are several reasons why one might behave in a normally expected manner (Shaw 1993, 8).

Upon asking students, why one should act morally, I have received all the above answers and more. The view that we should act morally to escape punishment in the afterlife is clearly not the primary reason given for acting morally. Almost everyone, including the atheist, recognizes the need for one to act morally.

Others may say that only religion can give us sufficient moral guidance. Yet, the moral teachings of the world's great religions are rather general. We must use reason to determine the exact meaning of these teachings.

> For example, the Bible says, "Thou shalt not kill." Yet Christians disagree among themselves over the morality of fighting in wars, of capital punishment, of killing in self-defense, of slaughtering animals, of abortion and euthanasia, and of allowing foreigners to die from famine because we have not provided them with food as we could have. The Bible does not give unambiguous answers to these moral problems. So, even believers must engage in moral philosophy if they are to have intelligent answers (Shaw 1993, 8).

In short, morality may have close connections or ties to religion, but it is not necessarily dependent upon religion for its validity.

On a personal level, there may be those for whom morality depends solely upon religion for its validity. While religion may be enough to legitimate moral values for some people, it is not sufficient on a large scale. Religion cannot legitimate moral values on a larger scale since we come from different religious backgrounds and different perspectives within the same religion or from no religious background at all. For instance, in the Christian religion, there are different denominations that disagree strongly over certain issues. Some denominations are rather rigid in what they define as moral behavior, whereas others are much more tolerant. Morals that are dependent upon some specific religious tradition would have limited appeal for the broader public who do not recognize the claims of that religious tradition. So, is it desirable or justifiable to insist that the members of a given society follow morals associated with a particular religious tradition in such a pluralistic environment?

Most religions recognize to some degree the role of human reason in describing and determining right and wrong. In this respect, the use of reason and experience to justify morals can appeal to a wider audience. Reason may produce some moral principles that Christian, Hindu, agnostic, or atheist can generally agree upon. Focusing on religion alone, however, may yield little agreement.

VALUES AND FACT

A further distinction commonly made is between value judgments and facts. In contrast to value judgments, facts are those things we can verify. Many people simply assume that the values they hold are indisputable facts. Philosophers and others, however, distinguish between areas where one can have certain knowledge and areas characterized by values. David Hume, an English philosopher, defines this distinction as is/ought. In scientific terms, one can verify a fact through scientific method or observation. From this perspective, only statements that can be proven are facts. Facts would be those things that one could repeatedly duplicate or confirm through measurements and experiments under controlled conditions. Alternatively, it might refer to things that happen. If I say that Jane cheats on her test because I saw her looking at a paper with cheat notes, then this statement would be open to possible confirmation and would be a statement one might be able to confirm. What if I had say, Jane ought not to cheat on tests. This statement is different. I am making a value statement rather than a factual one. It is my view that she acts immorally by doing this.

Consequently, moral values are not facts. Philosophers known as *logical positivists* have argued that only verifiable statements are meaningful. This view would mean that values have no meaning. Saying that Jane ought not to cheat on exams is a meaningless statement. On the other hand, telling the teacher that I saw Jane cheat, and that she has cheat notes in her purse is a statement open to verification. Therefore, the latter is a meaningful statement. Morals or ethics correspond to the former statement—she ought not to cheat. Saying that it is wrong to steal is meaningless according to the logical positive because one cannot prove that is wrong to steal.[5] However, the very statement that only facts or "empirically verifiable statements are meaningful" is itself a problem since it is not open to verification. One cannot verify that only these types of statements have meaning and so the statement itself is a value judgment (Lawson 1985, 19).

In my view, moral values are extremely important. They are also meaningful to human societies even if they cannot be proven in a factual manner. While we may be unable to prove moral judgments, we can still evaluate values in part based on our experience and current understandings of supposed facts.

Consideration of moral issues is essential for a society. In our modern technological society, for instance, it is not enough that we can do something. We often need to stop and consider if we ought to do it. In Dan Brown's novel, *Angels and Demons*, a scientist, who is also a Catholic priest, learns how to produce a sizeable amount of anti-matter, which could produce an incredible amount of energy. While this scientist/priest sees its great potential for the service of humankind, the novel shows how it is used for evil purposes. Moral questions, therefore, are essential for society. Just because we are able to achieve something does not mean we should do it.

Moral values can also motivate people to work for the betterment of others. Scientists have personal commitments that affect their work. They are no different than anyone else. Their values and personal views always threaten their objectivity, but those same values may motivate them to work hard on projects that make life better.

Our interests and values can play a very positive role for society. Our interests prompt us to work in a particular area. For example, the environmentalist may have strong feelings about protecting the environment. This commitment may even affect his or her work at times. This concern for the environment may make it impossible for him or her to be totally objective. Yet, it may be this environmentalist's convictions and interests that leads to breakthroughs that improve the quality of life for everyone. Moral values, therefore, are indispensable for human existence.

In short, facts are those phenomena that one can verify whereas values are those things that a person deems to be either good or bad. Neither facts nor values can offer much help by themselves. By themselves, they provide a limited view. Even together, they do not solve all of our problems, but they provide a more complete view of the world. While individual facts by themselves may not get us too far, one's value system may help us interpret known facts in ways that provide some guidance for our lives.[6]

There is also a great diversity of values present among different people. Because we are all individuals with different experiences, our personal interpretation of the world is likely to differ in some respects from one individual to another. Different views occur to some extent because we all value different things. A person living in modern Western society may value various technologies and the changes they bring about in society. Other societies that value simple life may fear technology and change. They may prefer to resist modern technology. In this case, it is not a question of right or wrong but preference.

To this point, we have distinguished moral values from etiquette, law, religion, and fact. In the remainder of this chapter, I focus on the process by which we acquire our values. Our discussion shows the importance of socialization in the development of our conscience. I begin by examining how people come to adopt certain moral values.

THE ACQUISITION OF MORAL PERSPECTIVES

Most people at some time in their lives reflect on moral principles and on what moral standards seem justifiable. The moral views of individuals serve as their guides. When a moral principle is part of a person's moral viewpoint, that principle is a source of strong motivation. Furthermore, a person tends to feel guilty when his or her own conduct violates the values of his or her own reference group. A person also tends to disapprove of others whose behavior conflicts with those values. So how do we acquire morals in the first place? Moreover, why do people act in accordance with these morals?

Primary and Secondary Socialization

People acquire a moral perspective through the socialization process, which is in fact a life long process. Sociologists have broken down this process into primary and secondary socialization. As young children, we internalize the objectified world. The *objectified world* consists of those things we commonly take-for-granted. This common-taken-for-granted-world confronts us daily; it is a world we cannot ignore; it exists apart from us. This world includes fixed ideas about politics, religion, education, morality, and customs, which are taken-for-granted by the members of a society. These fixed ideas constitute a significant part of our objective reality; this objective reality is the reality that confronts us in our daily lives.

For example, most children after a certain age know that society does not condone stealing. They learn this through being scolded for taking something from someone else or seeing other children punished for this act. They learn that it is a bad thing to take their playmates crayons or toy cars. Therefore, we pass this world on to our offspring by means of parental guidance, adult supervision, teacher-pupil relationships, and other social settings that influence the child.

To internalize something is more than just to be influenced by it. Internalizing involves making the objectified world our own world. Often this internalization can be so complete that much of the objectified world that governs our lives goes unnoticed. This world always has an influence on people. Once this world is fully our own, we often act and react based on unconscious impulses. When we internalize the objectified world, we make the objective reality our own subjective reality.

Competition, for example, in athletic events or in the workplace is so much a part of our way of life that we cannot imagine how to live without it. This need to compete controls our lives, and it has a great impact on the way we see ourselves and others. If we do not go on to understand how the objectified world influences our own lives, we may end up limiting our vision and our options (Berger 1963, 66-92).

This acquisition of moral perspectives is helpful and dangerous. The danger comes when one blindly follows. Formal teaching and informal experience could cause a child who is sensitive to the needs of others including cute little animals to become cold and callous. Knowing how the objectified world affects us, therefore, is the first step toward acquiring some measure of freedom. Awareness diminishes the sway of cultural values.

Externalization allows individuals the opportunity to change their world. Humans, at least to some extent, have freedom. Human beings are not simply passive beings. We can make a difference. Reform movements stress this idea. Human beings can add to the existing or objectified world in various ways. Invention is a good example. Computers have changed the entire objectified world. They have vastly increased the pace of scientific development. This technology has changed our world. We can find an ethical example of externalization in the message of King. The call for equality and justice for all changed the objective or existing worldview (Berger and Luckmann 1966). Such new ideas change the world, and they serve to shape the *conscience* of following generations.

Socialization does not end at some definite age. The experience of being influenced continues throughout life. Primary socialization is probably stronger than secondary socialization. Nevertheless, we encounter people and ideas along life's journey that may change us and our views. Education is a process of *resocialization* in many ways. If the process of education is done properly, a person begins to integrate new ideas and consider his or her beliefs and views in light of new information. One never breaks away from these various forces. However, as we broaden our perspectives, we also increase the possibility of making better moral decisions. American psychologist William James made a distinction between what he called first and secondhand religion. This distinction applies to morals as well. Firsthand religion, or in this context morality, is the ideal because it is authentic. In terms of morality, I would use the term firsthand to refer to the act of making conscious decisions about what we believe or accept as morally binding. It is where we struggle with choices and embrace our role as moral decision makers. Secondhand morality might refer to what we have inherited from others. We adopt it without critical reflection.

In the end, however, we are never completely free of secondhand views on religion and morality. Open-minded individuals are always in the process of developing their own views and ideas. On the other hand, we are never able to be entirely independent either. Outside influences shape us and our identity.

Intuition and Conscience

Conscience is at least in part a product of the socialization process. As a result, can it really steer one in the right direction? In the classic children's novel, *The Adventures of Pinocchio*, the fairy comes to grant the wish of Gepetto who is Pinocchio's creator. Gepetto wants a little boy. The fairy comes to Gepetto as he is sleeping and transforms Pinocchio from a wooden puppet into a living boy. The fairy instructs Pinocchio that he should always do what is right. Pinocchio asks, how do I know what is right? The fairy replies that he should let his conscience be his guide. Yet, does our conscience always tell us when something is wrong? Is our conscience a completely reliable guide? What exactly is our conscience? Is it the same thing as intuition? What is intuition? Are these two concepts related?

There are ethical systems based on intuition. These systems rest on the notion that one should consult one's conscience to determine what is right or wrong (e.g., Joseph Butler). Ethicist G. E. Moore goes so far as to say that intuitionism is the only satisfactory moral theory. He concludes that moral truths are self evident and discoverable through reflection (Pojman 1990, 143-144).[7]

We often think of these terms, intuition and conscience, as interchangeable, which is the case in *ethical intuitionism*. This type of intuition asserts that "human beings have a special faculty (for instance, conscience) that is able to make valid moral judgments or [it] somehow just 'knows' what is true or right" (Honer and Hunt 1978, 243). Yet, is *ethical intuition* the same thing as *conscience*? People have defined intuition in different ways. From a psychological perspective, intuition is a "direct and immediate perception, judgment or knowledge, arrived at without prior conscious cogitation or reflective thinking" (Wolman 1973, 203). Human conscience, on the other hand, is largely a product of social learning.

Is intuition an adequate guide for making moral decisions or judgments? How could one ever verify that intuition provides a solid basis for action? Those who appeal to intuition as the way of knowing or obtaining knowledge are "subject to criticism on the grounds that . . . [intuition] is not always consistent." Different people have rather different intuitions. When this occurs, how can we choose between two conflicting intuitions? In addition, not everyone claims to have intuition. So, how can one insist on using intuition as an ethical system? Consequently, we cannot trust intuition as a way of knowing right from wrong (Honer and Hunt 1978, 84, 116). Besides, intuitions can be about anything. We may feel that we should not go on a trip or have a bad feeling about taking a job. Conscience, on the other hand, is specifically related to moral concerns.

Different View of Conscience

There are several different views on conscience. Some believe we are born with a conscience. Others consider conscience as a development of human evolution. Perhaps, the majority see conscience as part of the socialization process. It emerges as children learn what others consider right and wrong. Another possibility is that socialization and social conscience are only part of the story. Could there be something more, something similar to the notion of a moral intuition? We can now consider these possibilities in the thought of several different individuals.

Joseph Butler

Is our conscience a sufficient moral guide? What exactly is conscience? Different thinkers have defined the term "*conscience*" in different ways. Joseph Butler (1692-1752), a bishop in the Church of England and a moral philosopher, says that human beings have an innate ability to know what is right and what is wrong. He identifies conscience as the mechanism that makes it possible for us to know what is required. Conscience, then, is our moral guide. Therefore, he does not understand conscience as a product of social learning. We possess a conscience, and, as a result, we are moral creatures. Butler stresses that conscience is a principle of reflection. Upon reflection, we can know what is right. In this way, human conscience is an instrument that can either approve or disprove of human thoughts or actions (Butler 1964, 201). It follows from this view that human beings have no excuse for doing what is wrong.

Charles Darwin and Conscience

Evolutionary and social scientific views of ethics rejected this conception of an innate conscience. Charles Darwin (1809-1882), an English naturalist, was most widely known for his ideas on human evolution found in his book, *The Descent of Man* written in 1871. His views on human evolution made him an enemy of fundamentalist Christians. Interestingly enough, Darwin studied theology at Cambridge University and obtained a degree from there in 1831.

Darwin maintains that conscience emerges in human evolution. For him, conscience is a product or creation of *social instincts*. He bases his view of conscience on biological evolution. Darwin explains human behavior on the premise that human beings are animals, and they share characteristics with other animals. Conscience, according to Darwin, is the most important distinction between human beings and the other animals. He argues that human beings often act out of instinct or more specifically conscience. Conscience is about group survival. Conscience keeps humans acting in ways that preserve the well-being of the group.

What is at stake is the survival of the species. He rejects the view that human beings act out of a desire for happiness. Conscience is not about securing one's own pleasure or happiness. Instead, he contends that human beings often act

> 'impulsively, that is from instinct or long habit, without any consciousness of pleasure.' A man will endure fire and extreme peril to rescue a fellow creature, and even will die for another person; such behavior cannot be properly regarded as aimed at pleasure. . . . Man's motivation is not pleasure, but impulsive power, instinctive behavior, a deeply implanted social instinct. According to the doctrine of natural selection, social instincts have 'been developed for the general good rather than for the general happiness of the species.' By the general good [Darwin means] . . . 'rearing of the greatest number of individuals in full vigor and health, with all their faculties perfect,' under the prevailing conditions (Sahakian 1974, 143-144).

Accordingly, it is not happiness that conscience promotes but survival. This survival also explains why human beings are group oriented. We do not seek the survival of everyone but just those who can help us survive. Devotion to one's group then is part of conscience. Nevertheless, this devotion or feeling of obligation is not always successful. Often we ignore this sense of obligation, which results in guilt.

According to Darwin, we acquire virtues and social instincts, which in turn stimulate admirable actions. We acquire these virtues and social instincts through the process of natural selection. The more permanent social instincts dominate the less permanent ones. As a result, one might feel an obligation to comply with one instinctive desire instead of another. One may likewise feel a sense of guilt or regret at giving in to the urge for self-preservation instead of risking one's own life for the sake of the other persons in the group. The individual may even feel regret if circumstances push him or her to steal food to avoid starvation. Social instinct in the form of conscience can produce a sense of guilt in the individual who engages in anti-social behavior due to his or her desire for self-preservation, lust, or revenge. Darwin's conclusions end on a positive note.

> At the moment of an action, man will no doubt be apt to follow the stronger impulse; and though this may occasionally prompt him to the noblest deeds, it will more commonly lead him to gratify his own desires at the expense of other men. But after their gratification when past and weaker impressions are judged by the ever-enduring social instinct, and by his deep regard for the good opinion of his fellows, retribution will surely come. He will then feel remorse, repentance, regret, or shame. . . . He will consequently resolve more or less firmly to act differently for the future; and this is conscience; for conscience looks backwards, and serves as a guide for the future (Sahakian 1974, 144).[8]

According to this view, altruistic behavior is not doomed and may one day rule over selfish or narcissistic conduct (Sahakian 1974, 144).

Sigmund Freud and Conscience

A more recent approach comes from the famous psychologist, Sigmund Freud (1856-1939). He provides a somewhat different account of conscience. He explains conscience in terms of the "*superego*." Freud divides the person into three parts: the id, the ego and the superego. The *id* is the most primitive stage. It is the blind, irrational, and brutish part of the human psyche. It demands immediate gratification. The id is the asocial, egoistic force within all of us. The transformation of these impulses into socially acceptable actions requires us to control or "repress" the pleasure-seeking demands of the id. The *superego,* therefore, consists of the acquired ethical and moral standards of the community.

The superego, therefore, is what we usually call conscience. It is in the superego that the sociological significance of Freudian thought appears. The superego is a product of the community and its concerns. The third part of the person is the ego. The *ego* is the part of us that experiences reality and integrates the conflicting demands of the superego and the id. The ego must adapt to the desires of the id, and it involves the moral censorship of the superego as well. The ego, then, can redirect the impulses of the id in a socially acceptable way so one can achieve a measure of self-gratification. One always follows his or her impulses when the id rules. This is true even when the impulses are entirely unacceptable. If the superego completely dominates, one might always sacrifice his or her own good for the desires of others. The ego is an intermediary between the id and superego. The superego over time becomes the child's conscience and moral sense (Cuzzort and King 1989, 105).

We can easily describe this process in a common everyday life. The child operating before the development of the superego may see a toy that belongs to another child and take it. He or she has no conscience, so the child is in a pre-moral stage. At this stage, the child would not feel remorse. As the child grows and learns that taking something from someone else is wrong, things change. For instance, Tom sees that his friend John has a nice iPod. Tom wants an iPod of his own, but his parents will not buy it for him and he does not have the money. He could seize an opportune moment and take it. Yet, what happens if Tom takes such a course of action? His conscience or superego may bother him. His ego would warn him against such an action since the consequences of being caught would be bad. Tom may even feel that stealing the iPod is wrong regardless of the consequences. The ego may step in and help Tom think of alternatives. Perhaps, he could find a job or save his or her allowance.

For Freud, the ego operates in the private area of one's life where he or she considers his or her options apart from outside influences. The private self, therefore, is free from the controlling influence of the social world. The sociologist George Herbert Mead, however, does not recognize any private moments. The social world is part of every thought and action.

George Herbert Mead and Conscience

George Herbert Mead (1863-1931) is an American philosopher and social psychologist. He defines conscience as a *social force*, which arises out of one's social training or upbringing. Our conscience can coerce and even frustrate the more primitive or biologically grounded impulses. For both Mead and Freud, "social conscience" (Mead) or the "superego" (Freud) can suppress the biological urges and physical demands in their forcefulness. For Mead, "social conscience" is a coercive force. This social force exerts pressure on individuals from their childhood to adulthood through the influence of parents, schools, religion, significant other, generalized others, and other public institutions (Cuzzort and King 1989, 128-129).[9] This process does not leave any private space free of the social forces that influence one's actions. The process of socialization forms this social conscience.

Mead and other social psychologists explain the force of socialization by saying that when we wonder if we should do something such as cheat on a test, we go through possible outcomes. This act is a social experience because we consider our options in relation to how others will see us. This process sounds like Freud's superego and ego, but it is different. For Mead, there is never a private space, or in other words, there is no solitary ego only the social self. Society is always in my most private moments. The generalized other is always present with me calling me to account for my actions and thoughts. I know what is expected and not doing that causes discomfort. The generalized other is not just one's conscience since it can extend well beyond moral expectations. How one maintains his or her property (which is typically a nonmoral consideration) is influenced by a generalized other as well as how one treats his or her neighbor (which is often a moral consideration).

Zygmunt Bauman and Conscience

A more recent discussion of conscience comes from Bauman. Bauman is Emeritus Professor of sociology at Leeds University in England. He writes about conscience in his book on postmodern ethics.

Bauman carefully distinguishes between conscience as a product of social learning as proposed by Mead, and *moral conscience*. Moral conscience does not derive from the socialization process. According to Bauman, the *moral conscience* arouses a *"moral impulse"* in human beings, which also serves as the basis for *"moral responsibility"* (Bauman 1993, 249). The moral impulse is the ground[10] on which the moral self stands (Bauman 1993, 62).

Conscience, as described by the social sciences, derives from the social self (i.e., the socialized self) whereas the moral impulse resides in the moral self. The moral self is a self without a firm foundation (Baumann 1993, 62). The moral self is not built upon any ethical system of thought. Bauman recognizes that most of what we typically call conscience develops during our upbringing. Conscience from this viewpoint, therefore, is a social product as Mead contends. Conscience provides guidance in the form of socially conventional norms. The social-self with its conscience develops in interaction with its world. On this account, conscience is nothing more than a reflection of society and its norms and expectations. In turn, guilt and reservations do not mean that we have done anything wrong, but that we have gone against the norm.

The *moral self* is rather different from the social-self. The moral self refers to a self that precedes social interaction (Bauman 1993, 71-75). The moral self is at home in the party of two, the other and me. True *moral impulses* exist before the desire to follow rules or social norms. Philosophical ethics tries to replace the need for *moral impulse* with procedures, rules, or guidelines supported solely by reason and rationality (Bauman 1993, 82-109).

The sociological approach, on the other hand, assumes that our conscience (a product of social learning) provides the self with what it needs for a moral life. It furnishes conventional norms to guide one's behavior. Bauman rejects both rules and social conventions as the basis for ethics. We do not have any rules or guidelines to tell us how to be responsible for others. Rules and social norms offer us comfort; they attempt to inform us about what others expect from us. I can say, "I did my duty" or "I did what the rules said that I should do." Additionally, I could say, "I did everything that could rightfully be expected of me." Moral impulse, on the other hand, offers no such comfort. The moral self who acts from moral impulse never knows if he or she has done exactly the right thing (offering the proper needed assistance), or if he or she has done too much (e.g., interfering).

Caring for the other carries with it certain risks. These risks involve one person imposing his or her will on another. We can do this with the best of intentions. My interpretation or understanding of how to act for the other can lead to an imposition of my understanding or will on the other. There is often a fine line between caring for another or imposing our will on another. Additionally, the act performed on behalf of the other can endanger the freedom of the other (Bauman 1993, 88-98).

Suppose John feels his best friend has a drinking problem. He must decide whether to confront his friend about this perceived problem. If he does and his friend ignores his advice, John might have to decide whether to push the issue further. John's friend probably thinks that he can handle his drinking and does not need any help. If John does not pursue it, he may be letting his friend down, but if he does, he would be intruding upon his friend's privacy. John must struggle with this decision; no rules or conventions can settle the issue. Bauman thinks that we hide behind social conventions and rules, which have kept us from following our "moral impulse."

The moral self is most at home in one on one (face-to-face) interaction (a party of two). Face-to-face refers to one's interaction with another self apart from any mask or persona (Bauman 1993, 71-75). This means that the moral self is responsible for the other without regard to the role he or she may play. I am responsible to Nancy not because she is president of a large company, but because she is another self. Therefore, the cradle of the moral self is in face-to-face interactions.

In looking at these different views of conscience, we can see similarities and differences. All but Butler sees a social component involved in what we call conscience. Bauman has similarities to Butler in that both of them see a conscience independent of the socialization. Nevertheless, they are also different. For Butler, conscience is sufficient to tell us what to do; Bauman bases moral acts on moral impulses that do not tell us exactly what to do. For Bauman, there is no certainty. Bauman's views also recognize the social side. What we might generally think of as conscience consists of what we have learned in the socialization process.

We may conclude that conscience is primarily a product of the socialization process. Various social forces converge to form an individual's conscience as the growing child internalizes societal values that are part of our objectified world. In other words, our conscience develops from within our particular social environments. Yet is there anything beyond this social conscience? Is Bauman correct?

Moreover, we must note that at best our social conscience is only a *partially reliable guide*. It may disturb us even when we are doing the right thing. For instance, we may do the right thing, but our actions adversely affect some friends and family. In so doing, we may even feel guilty over doing what we believe to be right. Just because we feel guilty does not mean that what we are doing is wrong. Consider the following example. Should Jack go to the hospital and stay with a sick mother or attend an important business meeting? The business meeting would take him out of town for two days. Jack reasons that his mother is in stable condition and that the business meeting is extremely important. Family and friends, however, expect him to be with his mother, and they think that he is being selfish by putting his interests ahead of his mother's well-being. Jack agonizes over this decision, but decides that it is more important for him to attend the meeting. He feels that he has made the right decision since he feels that missing the meeting could have adversely affected his job, which could also harm his family. Yet, he feels bad about disappointing family and friends and possibly even his mother. He may have made the correct decision, but his conscience still hurts. If, however, he stays with his mother he would still feel guilty for missing a meeting that he feels is essential for him to attend.

Bauman's description of this situation adds other important aspects. In his view, something more than social conscience is created through the socialization process. There is a moral conscience or impulse as well. It may tell us that we have an obligation to help another person even if it means sacrificing our own interests. While we cannot prove that a moral impulse exists, it seems reasonable. Social forces determine the social conscience. It is not always reliable since it largely reflects how we are raised. The social conscience does not always prepare one to deal with conflicting feelings of obligation. One may have a keen sense of fairness or justice that comes from a moral conscience. However, as Bauman points out, moral impulses often leave us in a quandary. Often making moral decisions is agonizing because our options are not clear and the situation reflects considerable ambiguity. Social expectations or universal rules may miss the mark of particular situations.

Ethics in general and Bauman's ethic in particular, raises another concern. How far do we have to go to satisfy our moral responsibility or moral obligations? Can we blame an individual for not risking his or her life to save another person's life? There may be some obligation for professionals such as police officers to engage in some risky behavior on behalf of others, but what about citizens who do not belong to such professions? In short, are there things that go beyond moral obligation?

LIMITS TO ONE'S MORAL OBLIGATION?

Is it possible to go beyond the call of moral duty? Such acts, if they exist at all, are referred to as supererogatory acts. Supererogatory acts require one to distinguish between one's moral obligations and those acts that go beyond obligation if an act can in fact exceed one's obligation. Human beings often perform acts that are morally praiseworthy such as putting their own life at risk to save another person. However, one may ask whether we really have any moral obligation to put our lives at risk in this manner. Less drastically, there are those who have given their lives in the service of others. We may see the acts of such individuals as going beyond ordinary expectations. *Supererogatory acts*, therefore, are those acts that go beyond one's moral obligation. They are excessive acts, acts of heroes and saints who put others first.

Consequently, one cannot easily define the limits of moral obligation. Bauman's notion of moral uncertainty seems to be an unavoidable aspect of trying to decide what to do. Could it be that most acts, which entail sacrificing one's own interests or safety for another, fit this category? Again, one must wonder if we can really ease our conscience by saying some things are beyond moral obligation. Did King have a moral obligation to put his life at risk to lead the Civil Rights Movement? Do we have a moral obligation to give most of what we have to the poor? Should one have an obligation to risk his or her life to save an old man in a burning building? What if the person was a baby rather than an old man, would it matter? One could lengthen this list a great deal and in so doing become somewhat unsettled. Our socially produced conscience probably tells us we cannot be expected to sacrifice ourselves for strangers. This voice of conscience may not be able to extinguish the voice of the heart.

MORAL DILEMMAS

To make matters more complex, people sometimes find themselves in situations where there does not seem to be a correct moral response at all. One encounters an extreme example of this in the novel, *Sophie's Choice*. In this novel, William Styron tells an amazing story of a Polish immigrant, Sophie Zawistowski. In this novel, Sophie becomes a prisoner in a Nazi concentration camp. In this place, she is faced with an impossible decision. A Nazi officer made her choose which one of her children would live and which one would be killed. If she refuses to choose, both will be killed. In short, she would have to live with the choice of choosing one child over the other or allowing both to die. So what should she do? Is there a correct choice? Would people consider her immoral regardless of the choice she makes? This moral dilemma is an inhuman and monstrous situation where right and wrong looses its punch, where it is meaningless. Making a choice would mean living with guilt forever. There are other situations less horrific where harm occurs to someone regardless of the choice one makes. Particular situations, therefore, create a problem for making moral choices.

SITUATIONAL ETHICS

Before concluding this chapter, one other type of ethic deserves mentioning in this context. A situational type of ethic recognizes that morality depends upon the situation. Often moral situations are ambiguous and require one to make decisions. Anglican theologian, Joseph Fletcher, proposes an ethic based on the Christian principle of love. The moral obligations we have depend upon the situation we find ourselves in. The principle for making decisions in these situations is to "do the loving thing." Love takes the place of law. Fletchers says

> Christian situation ethics reduces law from statutory system of rules to the love canon alone. For this reason, Jesus was ready without hesitation to ignore the obligations of Sabbath observance, to do forbidden work on the seventh day. . . . In exactly the same way Paul could eat his food kosher or not, simply depending on whether in any situation it is edifying (upbuilding) for others (1 Cor. 10:23-26) (Fletcher 1966, 69).

On this basis, could doing the loving thing cause one to take a life? Many people across the world would say yes because they advocate euthanasia as the loving and caring thing to do for a person in certain situations. For them, the quality of life is more of a concern than the length of life, and they may view the needless prolonging of life as uncaring and unloving. This type of ethic is another perspective one can use to make ethical decisions, but it is not foolproof. It would not really help us in the example above. In Sophie's case, she has no option that one could describe as a loving act.

CONCLUSION

In this chapter, we have distinguished between moral and nonmoral aspects of life. Additionally, we have examined how these moral values relate to the socialization process and to our concept of conscience. In the next chapter, we will examine ethics from two different cultures that still have a major influence on contemporary society. I begin with moral thought based on Jewish writings (the Hebrew Bible or Old Testament and the New Testament).[11] I touch on ideas and influences from other cultures in the Ancient Near East that help shape and influence moral thought from a Jewish perspective. The other important influence on modern Western thought comes from the Greeks. Philosophy and ethics in the Enlightenment and beyond draw upon the Greeks as a major source for their thought. Later on in this book, I discuss John Caputo's book, *Against Ethics*, which draws upon both traditions and coins the term "jewgreek."

NOTES

1. For an extended discussion of this thought, see Sinnott-Armstrong 2009, 57-89.

2. The practice of capitalizing "Other" is common in postmodern ethics.

3. Later in the book, he does discuss morality beyond the party of two.

4. For Kant, the moral law is binding on everyone. It does not derive from God. Even God is subject to the moral law.

5. An advocate of this view is A. J. Ayer. Ayer contends that one cannot verify ethics or values. Ethics are expressions of emotions according to Ayer (Ayer 1946).

6. There is at least one sense in which values are factual. When one says that an act is either right or wrong, he or she is referring to a particular value system that judges the act as either right or wrong. In this sense, values are not facts. However, what people do about their beliefs is observable and is, therefore, factual. We may observe the act of John telling on Jane for cheating on the test because he strongly believes in honesty.

7. For additional information about intuitionism, see William K. Frankena 1973, 102-105.

8. Sahakian is quoting from Charles Darwin's *The Descent of Man*.

9. Additionally, see George Herbert Mead 1934.

10. He argues that no modern philosopher would consider this a foundation since it is too weak and would not support their ethical systems.

11. The New Testament is part of the Judeo-Christian tradition. There is only one possible non-Jewish author in the New Testament.

Chapter Four

Jewish and Greek Moral Perspectives

HEBREW MORAL THOUGHT

The ancient Israelites were both similar and different from her neighbors in the Ancient Near East. Other societies in this region had a significant influence on Hebrew or Jewish[1] thought and belief. One commonality for these societies in the Ancient Near East was their concern for social order.

Ancient societies, perhaps more than current ones, tended to view the world in religious terms. In these societies, order was essential for a people's survival as in any society regardless of time. Order and chaos represented two contrasting realities. When there were problems in a society, its inhabitants needed to know why these problems occurred. By determining why something bad happened, they might be able to prevent it from happening again. For instance, ancient societies saw the occurrence of a devastating disease as punishment by the gods for some inappropriate behavior. Additionally, they attempted to identify and eliminate the behavior responsible for the trouble so they could avoid further problems. They also made offerings to the gods to appease them or to receive forgiveness from them.[2]

In short, an orderly society depended upon the conduct or behavior of its members. In the Ancient Near East, the ancient Egyptians and ancient Israelites associated order primarily with good behavior or correct observance of procedure. On the other hand, they associated chaos with bad behavior or the failure to follow correct procedure. They supposed that bad behavior unleashed a force that could destroy a community. Subsequently, they had to deal with this potential problem.

For example, Genesis 1 tells how God tames the waters and brings them under divine control. The water, as a force of nature, struggles to exceed its boundaries.[3] The forces of chaos are always a potential threat. In the Hebrew Bible or Old Testament, human disobedience occurs after creation, and it leads to the flood. God brings about the flood as a punishment because of the people's disobedience. Without the protection of God or gods, humans are at the mercy of natural forces far more powerful than themselves.

For the societies in the Ancient Near East, right or moral conduct is essential for survival and for an orderly life. From the perspective of ancient Egyptians, ethics means acting in accordance with the principle of *maat*. For ancient Israel, one should obey God's laws. In this context, the relationship between the natural and supernatural worlds is of utmost seriousness. Society cannot tolerate misconduct for the results of it can bring disaster.[4]

Nevertheless, the people in ancient Egypt, ancient Israel, and ancient Mesopotamia came to question the belief that acting morally ensures order and justice in society. Unlike ancient Egypt, ancient Israel and others in the Ancient Near East had no strong belief in an after-life that could justify the wrongs suffered in this life. Therefore, the Sumerian writing entitled "I Will Praise the Lord of Wisdom," and the biblical book of Job struggled with the problem of innocent suffering.

Other writings in the Hebrew Bible question the traditional view of rewards and punishments. They raise the question of theodicy. Theodicy refers to an attempt to justify the actions of the gods or God. How does one uphold the view of a righteous God in the face of undeserved suffering?

This same question also haunts the modern world. The belief that moral conduct leads to reward and bad conduct leads to punishment survives today. In religious form, it survives in the notion of retribution. Retribution means repaying bad for bad and good for good. Many Christians believe that people pay for their sins; they pay now or some time in the future or even in the next world. Even today, many people attribute disasters and their harmful effects on people as divine punishment. Some people still believe hurricanes, tornadoes, foreclosures, or death is the result of a person's sinfulness.

ETHICS OF ANCIENT ISRAEL

A description of morals or ethics in ancient Israelite society is a complex task. Our sources for describing and understanding such morals can include archaeology, various nonbiblical texts from the Ancient Near East, and biblical texts. From these sources, one cannot derive one unified ethic, but a wide variety of different ethical perspectives (Wilson, Robert R. 1994, 61-62). A full discussion of such perspectives goes well beyond the scope of this book. I briefly discuss five of these perspectives. The first three relate to the three divisions of the Hebrew Bible or *Tanach*. *Tanach* stands for the three divisions of the Hebrew Bible: Law (*torah*), Prophets (*nevim*), and Writings (*kethuvim*). The forth and fifth come from the teachings of Jesus and the Apostle Paul.

One simply cannot assume that the morals expressed in certain written texts reflect the actual morals or ethical views of all ancient Israelites. Written texts in ancient Israel came from the elites and many of the stories are about the elites or members of that society's upper echelons. We cannot be sure about the views of the common people,[5] but scholars continue to spend a great deal of time and energy trying to recover as much as possible. This investigation is important. This section, however, focuses on the official religion of ancient Israel, which reflects the interests of the male elites (Haas 1994, 154-155). I take this route because this view shapes much of Western religious culture.

In ancient Israel, one's behavior leads to reward or punishment. This view occurs throughout the Hebrew Bible or *Tanach*. All three divisions of the Hebrew Bible contain texts that maintain this view. This view of reward and punishment is also called into question. The Books of Job and Ecclesiastes deal with the failure of this reward and punishment system. The acceptance and rejection of this view remain in tension within the pages of the Hebrew Bible.

Torah

Torah means law and instruction. It is the Hebrew title for the first five books of the Hebrew Bible. Law is similar to morals in some ways, but there is a difference as well. The word ethics comes from the Greek word *éthos*. That word occurs in late Jewish writings and in the New Testament. When it occurs in the New Revised Standard Version,[6] it is translated as custom. In some instances, it has a moral tone while in other places it denotes what is typical without any moral overtone. 2 Maccabees 13:4, a late Jewish text, says:

> But the King of kings[7] aroused the anger of Antiochus against the scoundrel [the Jewish high priest Menelaus]; and when Lysias informed him that this man was to blame for all the trouble, he ordered them to take him to Beroea and to put him to death by the method which is the custom (*éthos*) in that place (NRSV).

In this context, the *éthos* is connected to a legal and moral offense. It refers to the type of punishment prescribed for a certain moral and legal offence. It is not custom in the sense of acceptable human behavior.

The Greek translation of the Hebrew Bible known as the Septuagint does not have the word *éthos*.[8] There are Hebrew words that convey a similar notion. Words such as good, righteous, just, honor all convey the view of what is customarily approved of by ancient Israelite society and God. Such words as bad, evil, wicked, transgression or violence refer to types of behavior and thoughts opposed by God and God's people.

Good and bad acts are described in many different ways in the Hebrew Bible as well as in the New Testament. What the monarchy in ancient Israel might view as good may be seen as bad by other segments of society. Yet within particular groups based on class or gender, there is a common set of things viewed as good or bad. It seems clear that the notion of *éthos* is present in Jewish thought, and it is not necessarily synonymous with law. There are acceptable and unacceptable thoughts and behavior in the Hebrew Bible that are not covered in the legal codes directly. In many cases, good refers to things more generally related to character and custom. Not all laws or customs discussed in Jewish literature would fall under what we today might describe as moral.

Creation and Flood Stories

Genesis 1 tells how God created the heavens and the earth. "In the beginning when God created the heavens and the earth, the earth was a formless void and darkness covered the face of the deep." The story tells how God brought order out of disorder. This story is similar to other creation stories in the Ancient Near East. The Hebrew word for the "deep" (*tehom*) relates to the Babylonian goddess *Tiamat*.[9] Tiamat is the Babylonian goddess of chaos. In some sources, Tiamat leads the forces of chaos against the forces of light and order. The Genesis 1 story echoes much that is in the Babylonian creation stories.

The Babylonian creation story tells how the world came into being with the defeat of Tiamat by the hands of the Babylonian god *Marduk*. Marduk with the help of another god *Ea* creates human beings to serve the needs of the gods. Marduk creates human beings out of the blood of *Kingu*. Kingu is another Babylonian god, and he is responsible for the uprising in the first place. Kingu, the second husband of Tiamat, helps her fight against Marduk.[10] Marduk successfully restores order by defeating Tiamat who represents the forces of chaos. One account tells how Marduk defeats Tiamat and uses her body to make life on earth possible. He divides her body into two parts or canopies. He uses one of the canopies to hold back the waters above the earth. He employs the second one to cover the waters below the earth allowing dry land to appear.[11]

Even after creation, waters pose a threat to humanity. Waters are unruly and chaotic; some power or force has to keep the unruly waters under control. The gods are the only ones who can keep these forces in check. In Genesis 1, God (*Elohim*) is in control of all natural forces including the waters.

Genesis 1 recounts the story of how God overcomes the powers of the deep and creates an orderly world. Later, the people's disobedience threatens the established order. In Genesis 6-8, we have the story of the flood. God punishes the people's sins by destroying the world with a great flood. In the flood account, chaos (i.e., the flood) comes about because of the people's sins. Order becomes chaos. God again subdues the unruly forces and reestablishes order. In the Hebrew faith, the way to maintain order is to live according to the laws and moral codes. If the people fail to do so, punishment becomes a real threat.

Keeping the Torah or Law

For the ancient Israelites, keeping the law or the torah is essential. The community who lives by and obeys the laws could expect good things. Law breaking, however, presents a threat to the individual and community. One individual breaking the law may harm the entire community. The ancient Israelites have a way of taking care of mistakes. When one becomes ritually unclean due to some wrongdoing, the community has to do something about that person's sin. Becoming unclean may or may not be a moral issue from our modern point of view. Eating certain foods may make one unclean in that society. However, many things can make one unclean, and these wrong doings are breaches of moral and legal codes in ancient Israelite society. The notion that individual wrongdoing can adversely affect the entire community is evident in the Hebrew Bible. Putting a sinful or unclean individual outside the community of faith is a safeguard for others in the community. Allowing immoral people to remain in the midst of the community could lead to the loss of divine presence and protection (e.g., Ezekiel 10:1-22 and 11:22-25).

When people sin or do something wrong, the priests are the legitimate authorities to take care of this problem. That is why the ancient Israelites need the sacrificial system; the priests perform certain rituals and make sacrifices that provide the individual with a way back to the community of faith. In this way, the individual is not abandoned. When the individual becomes clean again, he can reenter the community without endangering it. Rituals and sacrifices, therefore, are important mechanisms; they help to maintain an orderly society.

Deuteronomy 28 illustrates in part how the law and morals function. In this passage, Moses says that if one obeys the law rewards or blessings will follow. If, on the other hand, one disobeys the law the result will be bad for the person. The Deuteronomistic History (Joshua, Judges, 1 and 2 Samuel, and 1 and 2 Kings)[12] continues this line of thought. One can find this same view throughout much of the Hebrew Bible.

Hebrew Prophets

Even the Hebrew prophets accept as fact the belief that the LORD (Yahweh)[13] punishes disobedience. For example, the prophet Jeremiah becomes unpopular with the people when he proclaims that Yahweh would use the Babylonians to punish the people for their sins and would allow these same Babylonians to destroy Jerusalem (e.g., Jeremiah 20:4). Jeremiah's prophecy becomes a reality in 586 B.C.E. In this particular historical context, the Bible says that the deity of the ancient Israelites uses a foreign nation to carry out the destruction and punish of the people because of their disobedience.

There were many prophets in the Ancient Near East in general and ancient Israel in particular. Some of them were considered illegitimate or false prophets. A prophet who simply told the king what he wanted to hear would be considered a false prophet. A common theme in the prophetic texts called upon people to repent. The prophets called people to account for a number of offences. From a moral perspective, issues of social justice were prominent. Oppressing the poor and needy was unjust and immoral; it was connected to false worship in the Book of Amos. In Amos, one's motive was connected to moral actions. While some people went through the motions of worship, their motives became clear as they left the sacred ceremonies to go about their normal routines. These normal routines included cheating and oppressing the poor and needy. The situation was so bad that the wealthy could not wait for special religious days such as the Sabbath and new moon to be over where they could return to business as usual. In Amos 8:5-6, the following description was provided.

> When will the new moon be over so that we may sell grain; and the sabbath, so that we may offer wheat for sale? We will make the ephah small and the shekel great, and practice deceit with false balances, buying the poor for silver and the needy for a pair of sandals, and selling the sweepings of the wheat.

Generally, God warns the people through the prophets about a number of moral issues. Through the prophetic word, God warns the people and gives them a chance to turn away from their wrongdoings. A positive response by the people can avert God's judgment or punishment. Disobedient conduct has consequences. Even the punishment has a positive intent. These consequences typically affect a group or nation and not just single individuals. The prophetic warnings are pleas for people to change, and the punishment is an attempt to make things right.[14]

Wisdom Ethics

I have discussed how the creation story, the flood stories, the law, and the prophetic texts had important implications for human welfare. The same was true for wisdom texts. The sages or wise individuals based their wisdom primarily on experience (Crenshaw 2010, 12-16). The principle that ruled everything was

> subject to God's will. . . . The Lord of the universe always spoke the final word. No concept of order held that sovereign will in subjection. . . . At the same time, they believed that God did not exercise the right of veto arbitrarily, and thus the wise confidently endeavored to discover the principle by which they should live (Crenshaw 2010, 61).

The sages *wise* observe that certain behaviors bring fortune while others disaster. By this kind of observation, the wisdom writers believe that one could discover the embedded truth in all reality. It is the responsibility of human beings to search for that insight and thus to learn to live in harmony with it. Being wise means discovering the principles and proper conduct that secure one's welfare. The universe itself depends upon appropriate human conduct. This conclusion is pragmatic. Other parts of the Hebrew Bible view reward and punishment as the result of keeping or breaking the covenant or law. These sages observe nature and behavior. They conclude that proper conduct results in the happiness or the good of an individual or group. Bad things occur because of misconduct (Crenshaw 2010, 12-13). That is the way of God's created order.

The sage in Proverbs 6:6-11 observes the ant and through observation draws conclusions for human well-being. The story provides a moral lesson. This sage contrasts what he or she has learned by observing the ant with what happens to the lazy person who exhibits the opposite characteristics of the ant. The sage instructs one as follows:

Go to the ant, you lazybones; consider its ways, and be wise. Without having any chief or officer or ruler, it prepares its food in summer, and gathers its sustenance in harvest. How long will you lie there, O lazybones? When will you rise from your sleep? A little sleep, a little slumber, a little folding of the hands to rest, and poverty will come upon you like a robber, and want, like an armed warrior.

In other places, the sage speaks as a parent to a son. In Proverbs 1:8-19 the father instructs the son:

Hear, my child, your father's instruction, and do not reject your mother's teaching; for they are a fair garland for your head, and pendants for your neck. My child, if sinners entice you, do not consent. If they say, "Come with us, let us lie in wait for blood; let us wantonly ambush the innocent; like Sheol let us swallow them alive and whole, like those who go down to the Pit. We shall find all kinds of costly things; we shall fill our houses with booty. Throw in your lot among us; we will all have one purse"—my child, do not walk in their way, keep your foot from their paths; for their feet run to evil, and they hurry to shed blood. For in vain is the net baited while the bird is looking on; yet they lie in wait -- to kill themselves! and set an ambush—for their own lives! Such is the end of all who are greedy for gain; it takes away the life of its possessors.

In both cases, the sage instructs another individual. The idea is that certain behaviors such as laziness or violence naturally lead to destruction while their opposites have good consequences.

Therefore, Hebrew wisdom assumes that human actions have universal implications. God creates the universe orderly and leaves humans to survive on their own. Their survival depends on their own observational skills. Survival depends on learning the lessons of experience. Those who use their intelligence to discover the secrets of the universe and live by those secrets fare well, but those who do not suffer serious consequences. Wisdom, therefore, comes to assume a code of ethics (Crenshaw 2010, 8-11).

In the biblical book of Job, a list of offenses includes external deeds and inner disposition. Orthodox wisdom writers teach that the good life comes to those who live in harmony with this code of ethics. The orthodox view that suffering results from sin often occurs in the Hebrew Bible, and the book of Job struggles against such a view. Job, for instance, maintains his innocence in spite of his suffering. The orthodox view that suffering results from sin continues to have a wide appeal. The message of Job struggles against such a view.

Belief in reward and punishment is still alive today. In some Christian traditions today, it is popular to assert that individual suffering results from a person's misdeeds. On the other hand, it is common to hear how God blesses those who do his will. Many people interpret the word "bless" to mean gaining financial or other material rewards.

The belief that there is a connection between what a person does and what happens to that person is a common view in the Ancient Near East. It is the orthodox view in ancient Israelite wisdom literature. In Hebrew thought, wisdom takes on feminine characteristics. One secures one's well-being by living in accordance with her instruction. There is also Lady Folly. Following Lady Folly leads to destruction. The ancient Egyptian goddess *Maat* plays a similar role in Egyptian culture. Egyptologist H. Frankfort concludes that the Egyptian term "maat" designates *truth, order, and justice. Maat* highlights several opposites: order versus disorder, truth versus falsehood, and right conduct versus wrong conduct. The creator replaces disorder and falsehood with order and truth. Additionally, the gods and pharaohs must live in accordance with *maat*. To live in harmony with *maat* entails living a life of truth and justice resulting in rewards (Frankfort 1961, 53-56). For the Egyptians, living an unjust life leads to punishment, and this punishment can occur either in this life or next.[15]

In the Egyptian judgment, the sun god, *Re* weighed a person's heart, which for the Egyptians, was the seat of the conscience. If the virtues of one's life outweighed the faults, then he or she could join the gods. If, on the other hand, the faults outweighed the virtues, the individual received punishment (Wilson, John A. 1951, 119-120). According to one view, a strange creature destroyed the soul. Another one said that the soul was "thrown into a fiery hell, where it is punished severely" (Noss 1974, 44). Consequently, the threat of punishment after this life was a motivational force for acting according to the principle of *maat*.

This view of reward and punishment is not limited to the Ancient Near East. The caste system of India works on the belief that if an individual wants to improve his or her place in subsequent reincarnations that person has to be faithful in executing the duties associated with his or her caste. *Karma,* for instance, is the law that causes good to be rewarded and bad to be punished. Hinduism ties this notion to *samsara* (i.e., the circle of rebirths). Together *karma-samsara* means that one's position in a subsequent life depends on what one does in this life. Therefore, *karma-samsara* legitimates one's current social status in Hindu society; any suffering a person endures is one's own fault (Weber 1964, 42-43; Berger 1969, 65-68).

It is quite common for people across the ages to assume that morality is reciprocal in nature. People want to believe that their good deeds will be rewarded. Even today, people generally believe that moral behavior pays off. For many, the reason for doing good things is to receive a reward (i.e., heaven) and to avoid punishment (i.e., hell). However, the person who truly acts out of love and concern for others without selfish intentions would not worry about rewards.

In short, the Hebrew Bible presents a view of right and wrong that one might refer to as orthodox. The Law and the Prophets in the Hebrew Bible tend to equate good and bad acts with obedience or disobedience to the law and the covenant. Obedience to the law and the covenant leads to reward in this life and disobedience leads to punishment in this life. The wisdom literature differs in that it does not tie obedience and disobedience to covenant or law. Sages just observe the kinds of behavior that result in rewards and the kinds of behavior that result in pain and suffering. In addition, the Book of Job in the wisdom literature challenges the orthodox view. So Jewish views on morality vary and continue to develop over time. In the New Testament, Jesus and Paul have a great deal to say about true goodness.

MORALITY AS RELATIONSHIP: JESUS AND PAUL

The movement that became known as Christianity grew out of the ancient Israelite faith. The ethics associated with the early Jesus movement and Paul's letters did not encourage actions based upon expectations of rewards or punishments. Instead, Jesus and Paul viewed actions in connection with one's relationship with God. However, the notion of reward and punishment was not absent in the New Testament.

Recent scholarship has attempted to describe Jesus and Paul in their larger social setting. Scholars attempt to describe Jesus as a historical figure. The Jesus portrayed in the New Testament is largely the Christ of faith. The writers of the Gospels do not tell us a great deal about Jesus as a historical person. Historical scholars, on the other hand, have focused on the historical Jesus.

Describing the historical Jesus entails drawing upon the social sciences, archaeological evidence, extra-biblical materials as well as the biblical writings. Scholars are attempting to reconstruct what social life is like during Jesus' lifetime.[16] One thing is clear in this research as well as in the Gospels. Jesus values relationships over rules and traditions. Orthodox Jews in Jesus' day would follow the laws and traditions. These laws and traditions define some people and things as clean and others as unclean. They fear that breaking the laws would lead to punishment. Keeping the law is a way to enjoy God's protection. Following laws and traditions lead to fullness of life.

Jesus, however, saw that the emphasis on laws and traditions had become more important than people. God had provided these laws and traditions for the benefit of the people who needed a guide for life. Judging by the criticisms leveled at Jesus, many scholars concluded that Jesus disagreed with these religious leaders over the nature of laws and traditions. Jesus associated with people considered unclean or impure by certain Jewish officials. The religious leaders accused Jesus of eating with tax collectors and sinners, being a glutton and a drunkard, and being a friend of tax collectors and sinners (cf., Matthew 11:19 and Luke 7:33). To associate with such people broke certain political and social conventions in Jewish society.

Jesus rejected rules and traditions as a means for judging the behavior of others. Instead, he taught his followers to relate to others based on compassion. According to Marcus Borg's translation of Luke 6:36, Jesus told his followers to "be compassionate as God is compassionate" (Borg 1994, 46-68). Therefore, a moral act was one motivated by compassion.

Paul advocates a similar idea. He contends that love should be the motivating factor for what one does. Paul uses the Greek word *agape*[17] when discussing how one person ought to relate to another. The use of this word to denote how one should relate to another person expresses Jesus' message of compassion in a more abstract Greek fashion.

While Jesus' audience consists primarily of peasants who live in the rural areas of Palestine, Paul's audience is primarily urban city dwellers who do not relate to rural life. In rural Palestine, compassion communicates a similar kind of idea as love does for Paul's congregations. The difference is that compassion denotes more of a response based on feeling. Paul's congregations coming from a Greek environment relates to the more abstract notion of love expressed in the Greek word *agape* (Borg 1994, 46-68).[18]

As a result, Christian ethics ought to concern behavior that promotes the welfare of others. This emphasis is more directly related to human motives. One is to act out of love or compassion not from expectation of reward or fear of punishment. Compassion requires one to feel what the other person feels. Jesus in particular calls his followers to care for those individuals whom society intentionally forgets about, avoids, or shuns.

This avoiding or shunning has occurred in every epoch of human history. There have always been those individuals or group of individuals that polite society either ignores as unimportant. The words of Jesus and Paul do not promote this attitude. It is true that Christians often do not live up to this ideal. Many Christians past and present see acting morally as a way of avoiding punishment or gaining advantage in this world or the next.

It is true that the New Testament does have texts that point to a connection between doing good and finding reward. Matthew 6, for example, tells one to forego recognition in this life for reward in the next one. In this passage, one should not do good deeds in public for the praise of others. Still, rewards in heaven await this person. However, the best person would be one who does for others without concern for reward. Those who act from compassion do the will of God.

In conclusion, Jewish and Christian thinking about morals have generally taken several different forms. Jewish and Christian notions about morality have had a significant influence on Western thinking. In ancient Israel and in Christian thought, the communal aspect of ethical thinking is important. In ancient Israelite thought, misconduct adversely affects the community and individual. This type of ethic, therefore, places importance on the community. A community depends upon people abiding by rules and helping each other. When we act, we should consider how our actions affect others.

In the initial stages of Christianity, there was a strong community tie as well. Jesus saw the need for change in his society, and he worked toward that goal. Unlike official Judaism that stressed purity, Jesus called his followers to have compassion, and this compassion for others broke down the political, social, and religious boundaries that separated one person from another.

In one sense, Jesus calls for the destruction of community. Jacques Derrida has noted that community in its strict sense actually excludes people. If everyone were part of the community, then, there would be no outsiders and thus no community. So perhaps a better metaphor for moral thought is not community but open hospitality which is also an important ingredient in Jewish thought (Caputo 1997, 109-113).[19] This notion of open fellowship and hospitality is an advance over the metaphor of community. Open fellowship and hospitality is also consistent with the actions and teachings of Jesus and Paul. Jesus and Paul are about openness to those who have been excluded because of cultural or religious reasons.

Jesus and Paul call for a love that binds people together.[20] There is, however, a different motivation involved for Jesus and his Jewish followers. Jesus encourages actions based on one's love for another and not for rewards. Consequences and rewards are not at the heart of faith. God's instructions or laws come to us from love. Parents instruct their children to protect them not to be mean. The same is true with God. These laws or instructions provide for the well-being of the people. Punishment may serve to bring people back into the community. In theory, Jewish thought is not legalistic, although legalism becomes part of Jewish life just as it is part of Christianity. Many Christians act as if everything depends upon their following the rules to the letter. Many people measure their own value and worth on how well they keep the rules of their faith. The same attitude is common in secular society as well. Therefore, legalism is present in Jewish and Christian communities.

EARLY GREEK ETHICS

Whereas the ancient Israelites' focus is on the community, Greek thinking focuses more on the individual. Plato sees the individual as the starting point for society. Individuals play their part in society to make it function properly. Plato recognizes that humans are not self-sufficient and that different individuals have different talents. Therefore, a functional society needs human beings to cooperate. A new element emerges in Greek thought. Morality or virtue is discoverable through human reason and rationality. The emphasis on reason and rationality continues to be important in Western thinking and culture. To trace this line of thought, we begin with Socrates.[21]

Socrates (470-399)

Socrates, sometimes called the father of moral philosophy, was an oral teacher who did not write anything. Secondary sources provided information about his life and thought. Some of these sources were hostile toward his teachings and others friendly. One of his main ideas concerned the value of knowledge. He equated virtue with knowledge and ignorance with vice. His ethic called for self-understanding, which was for him the highest good. The way to attain self-understanding and happiness was through human *intellect and reason*. Therefore, reason was the means to the good life. The intellect led to knowledge and away from ignorance. Achieving this self-awareness resulted from a life of self-examination.

Socrates described his methods for acquiring truth as follows:

> Before the mind is capable of acquiring new truth, false accumulations of tradition, prejudice . . . and ignorance must all be faced and expelled by denial and

confession. . . . After one . . . has purged his nature of inherited prejudice, traditional illusions and blinding presuppositions, preparation has then been made for the positive aspect of the Socratic method (Helsel 1950, 89).

This Socratic method is based on cooperative teaching. It is informal and conversational in nature. He asks his students the following types of questions: What is piety? What is beauty? What is courage? What is justice? Rarely does Socrates provide answers. His approach sometimes upsets his students because they want him to provide the answers. Socrates, therefore, feels it is his duty as a teacher to make students wiser. He does so by "making them discover their own ignorance" (MacIntyre 1966, 19-20).

Ignorance is the source of immorality. It leads to immoral behavior. According to Socrates, a life lived without reflection is a life not worth living. He assumes that correct knowledge and self-understanding lead to a life of satisfaction. In short, correct knowledge equals correct action and virtue. Virtue in turn leads to happiness (reason=virtue=happiness).[22] According to Socrates, "'No one errs willingly.' No one willingly goes wrong, for no one voluntarily chooses other than what would be good for himself" (MacIntyre 1966, 22).

For Socrates, the moral life, therefore, depended upon one having this correct knowledge. He considered this knowledge to be within the individual just waiting for him or her to realize it. Socrates saw himself as a midwife helping his students through their questions, which would give birth to accurate knowledge. In this fashion, virtue could be attained through a teaching process.

The connection he made between virtue and happiness assumed, therefore, that individuals acted morally because doing so led them to their own personal happiness. Happiness, however, was tied to a virtuous life not a life characterized by vice or immorality. Plato and Aristotle agree with Socrates that correct knowledge produced virtue and happiness.

Plato sought to extend this view by advocating a society governed by those who possessed correct knowledge. This view assumed that what was right or moral was also in the individual's own best interests, a questionable assumption. It depended upon how one defined best interests. Was it in ones best interest to look out only for oneself? Alternatively, was it better to sacrifice one's desires for others at times?

Others in Socrates day took a relativistic stance. They claimed there was no "one" correct view. Morals, truth, and knowledge were all relative. What was true for one person or in one location was not necessarily true for everyone and every location. Both Socrates and his disciple Plato struggled against this relativistic view.

Plato (427-347)

Plato was looking for a firm basis on which to establish such ideas as Goodness, Beauty, and Justice. Greek philosophers known as sophists, on the other hand, had contended that notions such as good, bad, just, unjust, beauty, and ugly depended upon human beings for their meanings. Good, for instance, was what a person or a particular state said was good. Moreover, one could not talk about justice without reference to a specific location or place. What was just in one city was not necessarily just in another. To live within a society was to live according to rules or conventions of that particular society. Conventions of any particular society were equal to a society's morals. The sophists distinguished between nature and convention. The natural person was a premoral or nonmoral agent who did not possess any morals or conventions of his or her own. Therefore, the natural person was not bound by all the conventional constraints placed upon him (MacIntyre 1966, 16). So from this perspective, what should the individual do? The conventional person followed the conventions of whatever place he or she happened to be. How would the natural person respond to this question? The natural person was free from convention, and he or she acted in ways consistent with his or her own self-interests. "All men were by nature either wolves or sheep; they either prey or are preyed upon" (MacIntyre 1966, 16). Briefly, there was nothing constant in morals or conventions. What was moral and what was beautiful depended upon the conventions of different places. They differed from place to place.

To establish truth on an unchanging and universal basis, Plato attempts to fix certain concepts by building them upon eternal Forms or Ideals. An Ideal is the same as perfection. There is a world where things are perfect and unchanging. Christians tend to view heaven in this way. Plato describes his views about this perfect or ideal world in his system of universal ideals.

Plato bases these Ideals on the distinction *between that which is (i.e., Being) and that which comes-to-be (i.e., becoming)*. That which is or the world of Being is not the same as the world we perceive through our senses. We are blinded and cannot see things as they truly are. Therefore, the world of *Being* concerns the eternal world where things are perfect which again is similar to the notion of heaven for Christians. Moreover, since they are perfect, they have no need to change. The world of Being, then, is completely unchanging. It always remains the same. However, we do not live in that world. We live in a world that is always changing. He calls this world the world of *becoming*.

Becoming has to do with our ever changing, imperfect world, the world here on earth. The Greek philosopher, Heraclitus, says that one cannot step into the same river twice. The river changes as water flows into it from other sources. As a result, change in this world is constant. Only in the system of universal Ideals can one find the true basis of order in the areas of morality, politics, and nature. Becoming is the world of change; it is the world that one experiences through the senses of human perception. Opinions, beliefs, and illusions are characteristic of this world. In this world, all things are relative.

The world of Being, by contrast, derives from the world of pure thought. The means by which one can approach this world of Being is through human reason and the knowledge[23] gained by the use of reason. This process allows for rational argument known as the *dialectic*. This method attempts to destroy previous assumptions. Its goal is to move one toward the unchanging and eternal world of Forms or Ideals (MacIntyre 1966, 41-42; Plato 1987, 342-345).

Words as we use them in our daily existence do not have fixed meanings. We do not learn words from a dictionary as a child, but through the experience of language. My use of words like truth, courage, and justice may be similar to how others use and understand them but not necessarily identical. I may apply the word beauty to an object such as a shiny red sports car. Others may not find the car beautiful at all. So how can the philosopher know what is truly beautiful? In the world of becoming, there is no agreement on what is beautiful or just.

Plato, however, thinks that words have an exact meaning. One can only discover this exact meaning through the dialectical process. By means of this process, Plato says that the philosopher can define words in a more exact way so that they are not relative. A word in this sense is an *Idea, which is unchangeable, intelligible, and eternal.* Plato says that words in this ideal sense have a unique and unchanging meaning. Take, for example, the word beauty. Our notions of the word beauty do change because we inhabit the world of becoming, which is constantly in flux. What we consider beautiful today may change or what is beautiful for one person may not be for another. Yet, there must be an Ideal Beauty in the world of Being. If this is true, then we can say that something is beautiful only insofar as it resembles the Ideal Beauty, which is part of the eternal or perfect world of Being.

The same thing holds true for moral concepts. Plato would argue that what is truly moral is not dependent upon the whims of individuals or societies. Human notions of virtue relate to what individuals judge to be trustworthy during their daily life. Plato contends that philosophers must compare and judge worldly notions of good with the Ideal. The true knowledge of what is good, therefore, comes from the realm of Being. As a result, the true or ideal meaning of good or beauty lies beyond the realm of sense experience (Olson 1967, 57-60). One comes closest to the heart of reality by considering the changeless perfection of things or objects. Therefore, when we discover the Ideal we discover the Truth about a thing.

In contrast to this realm of *Being*, Plato describes the visible and material world as a realm of continual *becoming* or change. It is impossible to have stable knowledge because it is always slipping through our fingers. However, Plato does not divorce the realms of *Being and becoming*. This world is like an imperfect image or copy of the eternal world of Being and to some extent, it may participate in that eternal world. It is the job of philosophers to discover the Ideals and help bring earthly notions into conformity with these Ideals. We can "understand what is goodness, what justice is, or what courage is, and so on, by seeing them exhibited in a certain type of state and a certain type of soul" (MacIntyre 1966, 43).

Plato illustrates the value of education and knowledge in his allegory of the cave. If people are confined to a cave where they can only see the shadows of objects cast upon the wall in front of them by a flickering fire that is behind them, then they are content with these distorted images. The shadows on the wall represent the world we live in, which he calls the world of becoming. It is a dim copy or image of the original or "Ideal" world. The world of shadows is a world of dimness, deception, and bondage. One finds the complete truth in the sunlight. Imagine how different these objects look to him or her in the sunlight. By gaining more knowledge, one can move from the world of shadows to the world of sunlight.

To move society toward the light, Plato describes what the Ideal society would be like in his book, *The Republic*. He proposes ways of controlling every aspect of society. Control would entail censoring and sheltering children from the poets while rearing and educating children apart from their parents in state nurseries. He covers the notion of mating the best and brightest human beings with the best producing the best possible offspring and even how to take care of "defective" offspring (Plato 1987, 225-259).[24] In effect, Plato proposes a society ruled by a small elite group of highly intelligent people who knows what is best for everyone. Control by the very best is the key to a perfect society. Can these elites really create a perfect society? What would such control cost us in terms of individual freedom? Are the most intelligent or wise people beyond corruption? Can the elite really know what is best for everyone? Should the state be involved in raising children and manipulating mating practices of humans?[25] Is human nature good? Plato seems to think that it is. He also assumes that people in a tightly regulated and planned society will do the right things.

In *The Republic*, Plato divides society into three classes: Guardians, Auxiliaries, and Artisans. The Guardian class is made up of the wisest individuals. They would be the ones best suited to rule society. Neither the Guardian nor Auxiliary class should own property. Plato believes that owning property could cause these two classes to sacrifice the public welfare for their own private interests. The Guardians are to serve the whole community and not any particular class. The Guardian class would derive its happiness from this type of public service (Plato 1987, 182-187). Plato considers the Guardian class the best suited to lead society. The main virtue for these rulers is wisdom. These Guardians would be the individuals who have shown their superior abilities in the educational process. Society would benefit because of their wise and expert leadership.

The Auxiliary class consists of those obligated to preserve the security of the state. They take on military, police, and administrative duties. For them, courage is a supreme virtue. The Artisan class, on the other hand, comes from the ranks of those who earn their living by economic pursuits. Of the three classes, the Artisan class is the lowest. They are "farmers, manufacturers, traders, rich and poor" (Lee 1987, 42). Unlike the other two classes, the Artisans could own property. Practically speaking, this class has perhaps the most important job; it provides for the physical and economic needs of society. Its virtue is obedience; it is their fate, in Plato's system, to be under the control of others (Lee 1987, 42). Justice in society depends upon everyone playing their part or performing their assigned roles for society.

Yet, how can a society go about finding such gifted individuals? The answer is through the educational system. Members of the Guardian and Auxiliary classes have the opportunity to move upward in society. It is also possible for members of the third class to move upward to a higher class as well. To select these gifted Rulers, Plato devises an elaborate system for the state to educate its citizens.

The first stage of the educational system begins at an early age and lasts until age 18. During these years, children receive instruction in morals and aesthetics. Here, education should help mold the character of children. The next stage lasts approximately two years and consists of physical training and military service. The Guardian class selects the most gifted individual to go on to the next level, which is the study of mathematics. This part of their instruction begins at age 20 and lasts to age 30. After further selection, those preferred persons move to the last stage. These students study philosophy for 5 years. Following this period of education, those elite individuals would have to gain 15 more years of practical experience in lower ranking offices. These individuals then would become Rulers or Guardians, and Plato says that they should divide their time between ruling and philosophy (Plato 1987, 347-355). Plato believes that training and natural ability should determine one's class. Early training may help one move to a higher class. He also says that people are just natural born rulers while others are shoemakers.

Plato would not place his trust in average individuals. Such individuals are "emotional, *irrational*, and capricious; they do not understand what is in their best interests" (Plato 1987, 347-355). The leaders should instruct and educate these people to accept the rule of their legitimate leaders. Plato even justifies the use of "noble lies" to this end. This lie functions to ensure that people remain in their place (MacIntyre 1966, 44). Some have accused Plato of creating a hereditary class with the Guardians. Yet, he envisions a system whereby members of the lower classes can move upward and members of the upper classes can move all the way down to the third class. It was the responsibility of the Guardians to either promote or demote a child based on the child's performance and abilities (Lee 1987, 43-44; Plato 1987, 246-252).

Plato believes that men and women should have an equal opportunity in this process even though he assumes that on average, men will perform better than women (Plato 1987, 45 and 225).[26] Plato fully expects that women as well as men will makeup the upper class. According to Plato,

> 'if we are going to use men and women for the same purposes, we must teach them the same things. . . . We educated the men both physically and mentally.'
> . . . 'We shall have to train the women also, then, in both kinds of skills, and train them for war as well, and treat them in the same way as the men' (Plato 1987, 229).

He redefines family structures in light of this equal opportunity for women. Plato does not assume equality. Some individuals always surpass others at a given task. However, he does not assume that men are naturally superior to women. He even advocates the creation of state nurseries. If the state can take care of the children, then women can compete with men on a more equal footing. In the *Republic*, children would not know their biological mothers and fathers (Plato 1987, 236-243).

Associated with morality or virtue is Plato's notion of the *soul*. He divides the soul into three parts. One part is responsible for *reason* and *rationality* while the other part is responsible for the *physical appetites*. These two parts often clash with one another. There is also the spirited part of the soul. This part of the soul concerns itself with *honorable conduct* and with *anger* and *indignation*. One's place in society or one's class depends upon which part of the soul is dominant (MacIntyre 1966, 39). For instance, if reason is dominant, then one should become a philosopher and rule others.

Additionally, he identifies four cardinal virtues: wisdom, courage, discipline, and justice. Wisdom is the virtue of the Guardians and courage is the virtue of the Auxiliary class. Discipline is a virtue for all society. Justice does not belong to a particular class nor does it apply to a "particular relationship between the classes, but to the society's functioning as a whole" (MacIntyre 1966, 39). If justice prevails in the sense that everyone performs their assigned tasks, then society functions properly and justice prevails. For there to be *justice in one's soul*, all three parts of the soul would have to function properly (MacIntyre 1966, 36-40). For this to occur, the appetite and the spirited will must be in correct subordination to reason (Plato 1987, 218-222). Plato views the soul as being imprisoned in a body. After death, the body becomes a corpse, but the soul does not cease to exist (Olson 1967, 62-64).[27]

Finally, Plato concludes that morality involves allowing different elements within an individual (i.e., sensual desires, intellectual pursuits, or desire for success) to have their proper satisfaction. One should strive to prevent any one of these elements from dominating his or her life at the expense of the others. According to Plato, "physical desire, ambition, and intellect must all have their due and proper fulfillment, and find their proper place in the good life" (Lee 1987, 35).

Aristotle (384-322)

Aristotle, the teacher of Alexander the Great, develops an ethic that is more realistic than Plato's ethic. *Good* for Aristotle is *teleological* in nature. Teleological indicates that our actions and intentions should reach toward an end or goal. Moreover, good, for Aristotle, is functional. Good means that persons or objects perform their designed purpose well. A bridge is good if it allows people to pass without falling or food is good if it sustains life and health. *Human beings are good when they act rationally.* Aristotle says that the function of a human being is to bring the activity of his or her soul into conformity with reason.

By function of a human being, Aristotle means a kind of life. For instance, a person may be a musician. Being a musician defines the kind of life the individual lives. Activity of the soul refers to the course of actions associated with being a musician. When a person fulfills his or her proper function in life, he or she is living a virtuous life that produces happiness. This type of life is what Aristotle calls the "complete life" (Aristotle 1993, 38).

The complete life leads to happiness. For Aristotle, the end or purpose of human endeavor should lead to happiness and the good life. That is not to say that everyone agrees on what constitutes happiness. Happiness depends upon the individual and certain external conditions. Yet, happiness is an end in itself. According to Aristotle,

> The highest good is clearly something that is final. Hence, if there is only one final end, this will be the object of which we are in search. . . . We call absolutely final that which is always desired for itself and never as a means to something else. Now happiness more than anything else answers to this description. For happiness we always desire for its own sake and never as a means to something else, whereas honor, pleasure, intelligence, and every virtue we desire partly for their own sakes . . . but partly also as a means to happiness, because we suppose that they will be instruments of happiness (Aristotle 1993, 38).

Nevertheless, how can one achieve happiness? Aristotle says one can be happy by living a complete life in conformity with virtue. Virtue, for Aristotle, comes out of our daily living. He says that we become either just or unjust in our daily dealings with other people. For instance, it is "by our actions in the face of danger and by our training ourselves to fear or to courage that we become either cowardly or courageous" (Aristotle 1993, 40). According to Aristotle, therefore, human beings learn virtue through good habits and practice. Therefore, we might say that just as a builder learns how to build a building, the virtuous person has to learn how to live a virtuous life.

He concludes that virtue aims at the mean or a balance. Regarding health, Aristotle observes that too much or too little exercise poses a threat to human well-being and health. In the same way, eating and drinking to excess or deprivation of food and drink can be harmful. The same is true of what he calls moral virtues. Too much or too little fear can lead to undesirable results. Courage, on the other hand, means having the right amount of fear. Good health would require consuming the right amount of good food and getting the proper amount of exercise. Excesses and deficits are vices. Moral actions depend upon avoiding excess and deficiency. One can

> go too far, or not far enough in fear, pride, desire, anger, pity, and pleasure and pain generally, and the excess and deficiency are alike wrong; but to feel these emotions at the right times, for the right objects, towards the right persons, for the right motives, and in the right manner is the mean or the best good, which signifies virtue (Aristotle 1993, 40).

The thing that distinguishes rational conduct is the avoidance of extremes and the maintenance of balance. The balance between the excesses of life is the virtue of enough, what he calls the *rational or golden mean*. One can be happy, therefore, by living a virtuous life. His insights offer us practical advice about how to structure our life.

The Epicurean School (342-270 B.C.E)

Epicureanism is a Greek school of philosophy that instructs one in how to live a moral life. People often associate the Greek philosopher Epicurus with hedonism. Hedonism has to do with pleasure, and it often carries with it a negative connotation. Hedonism defines desirable in terms of what is pleasurable for the person doing the action. It says that *only* pleasure is good. An act is good if it brings one's pleasure.

Actually, Epicurean thought differs from this overly simplified description. Epicurean philosophy teaches that pleasure is the highest good. However, they do not define pleasure as engaging in any behavior that brings immediate gratification. They define pleasure in a negative manner. Pleasure, for the Epicureans, means the absence of any mental disturbance. The *good life* is the life that maximizes pleasure by minimizing the pain attached to unnecessary desire and anxiety. Paradoxically, one can achieve the greatest pleasure by living a life of restraint. Self-control is the defining characteristic of this sort of life. This version, therefore, is not hedonistic in the way it is so often understood.

Moreover, Epicurus and his followers regard superstition as bad because it produces fear and anxiety. Explanations for plagues, natural disasters, thunder and lightning have natural and not theological explanations. He does not deny that gods exist, but only that they do not concern themselves with human affairs. For Epicureans, death only means an end to human existence; it is not evil. With death, a person's awareness of pleasure and pain disappears. Epicurus values philosophy because it dispels the fear about such things as death. In short, the Epicureans sought pleasure and tried to avoid pain or anxiety.

Epicurus says, "From pleasure we begin every act of choice and avoidance, and to pleasure we turn again, using the feeling as the standard by which we judge every good" (Epicurus 1975, 163). Consequently, we naturally do what brings pleasure, and we avoid doing what causes anxiety. This feeling of pleasure also serves as a standard by which we can judge acts. Human beings do not choose every pleasure. Humans may need to avoid pleasure sometimes if greater discomfort results from it. Epicurus, however, was not talking about sensual pleasure, but the freedom from bodily pain and a troubled mind (Epicurus 1975, 163).[28]

Relativism

I now return to the relativistic philosophy of the sophists. Relativism indicates that different cultures have different morals or conventions, and they would contend that there is no absolute right or wrong. The notion of right and wrong depends upon what society or the individual believes to be right or wrong. Protagoras (481-411 B. C.), puts it this way: "Man is the measure of all things." One could see in this statement a radical relativism that people determine for themselves what is right or wrong. Many view relativism, however, on a more communal basis in that location determines right or wrong. What is true in the ancient Greek city of Corinth may not be true in the Greek city of Athens. Heraclitus' view on the continuously changing nature of things adds support to a relativistic perspective. His view is incorporated in Plato's notion of becoming. In the social sciences, this view has become known as cultural relativism. It observes that cultures differ from each other, and it discourages any value judgments. Anthropologists seek to observe and describe cultures rather than trying to change or reform them. The Greek tradition has also led to an ethical form of relativism. Ethical relativism defines ethical obligation as following the rules and norms of the society where one is living or visiting.

Relativism does judge, however, since it sets tolerance up as a supreme virtue. Ethical relativism is another modern version of relativism. It is sometimes called normative relativism. This approach looks at relativism from the group's perspective. One has a moral obligation to obey the rules or morals of his or her own group. There is another version that I only mention here. We could call it individual relativism. This view advocates that right or wrong depends on the individual. If an *individual* believes something to be right, then it is right. Our discussion of relativism in chapter seven, however, is about groups and not individuals.

Implications of Jewish and Greek Thought for Today

Greek philosophical ethics as represented by Socrates, Plato, Aristotle, Epicurus, and Protagoras assume that there is a link between living the moral life and faring well. Why should I be moral? Why should I live justly? The answer would be that to do so leads to the good or happy life (MacIntyre 1966, 84-109).[29] Through reason and rationality, individuals can come to know what they should do, which, in turn, leads them to act accordingly. This emphasis has had a significant impact on modern thought. Epicureanism and relativism also continue into modern and postmodern thought. Egoism reflects the Epicurean emphasis on individual happiness and pleasure. Relativism continues to be part of current thought noting the impossibility of absolute moral judgments.

This chapter has also raised an issue that is especially relevant to our current situation. The importance of community and individuality is still a concern. There is a sense in which morality needs to contain a communal and individual element. There is a need for the communal emphasis found particularly in Jewish thought. The individual emphasis is a needed corrective to a one-sided communal view of the moral life. Individual freedom needs to be safeguarded against the kind of state imagined by Plato. Losing oneself in the community may lead to the loss of individuality and free thought. Losing the community, leads to isolation and loss of belonging.

Is there another option for the existence of moral judgments and decisions? Hospitality is an option. It keeps the individual open to the Other.[30] It prevents a narcissistic existence, and at the same time, it prevents the formation of communities that are exclusive. From this perspective, the individual can retain his or her individuality but resist isolation and the loss of belonging. The community can exist as a collective of individuals committed to openness toward the Other without forcing the Other into the community. Can a community that practices open hospitality remain a community? I will say more about this in the final chapter.

Human beings today are more dependent on others than ever before, and yet, we seem to feel independent. We are becoming more isolated. This isolation is made possible in large measure by the advance in technology. Now we have online communities where the individual can remain somewhat anonymous and disconnected. In the educational world, distance education allows one to be part of a college community and retain their isolation. They may never see the other members of the class, talk to them, or ever see their professor face-to-face. It is impersonal, and there is a gulf technology cannot cross. How might this shifting pattern away from social face-to-face interaction change the world we live in? This distance may safeguard the individual. Yet is it a growing threat to real life face-to-face interaction? Yet, it really does not safeguard the individual. Due to the advance in technology, our life's story is there for everyone with a few clicks on a website and perhaps a little money. Privacy is largely absent today, and it appears that many people have given up expectation of privacy in turn for security, which is an illusion. No amount of government intervention can really maintain complete order and security in society.

Even though we may seem to be more independent, we are in fact still very dependent on each other. No one is an island so the old saying goes, and it is still true. As a result, we do need each other. It seems reasonable to suggest that our moral values need to retain their openness to others. That we need to remain open to the world does not mean that human beings should simply accept the status quo or the views present in mainstream culture. We must not lose our individuality. The best of individuality is the ability to question and reflect; the ability to decide after due consideration to act in one way or another. We must sometimes swim against the stream if we are going to stick to our beliefs and principles. Compromise is often possible, but we may sometimes find ourselves in places where compromise is not warranted.

A strong society can be tolerant and make room for those with diverse opinions. Tolerance, for me, does not mean just accepting everything uncritically. Tolerance holds people together in spite of their disagreements; it can allow us to disagree and still respect each other. The end of tolerance does not have to lead to intolerance or violence, however. There may come a time when people go their separate ways because the differences are too great. Still, I am not saying that violence is always wrong. Violence against the Nazis is a good example of where violence is justified to prevent the annihilation of the Jews. Strong individuals can be tolerant and open-minded without sacrificing their principles and integrity.

NOTES

1. The typical way of referring to Jewish people before the Babylonian Exile in 586 BCE was to call them Israelites or Hebrews.

2. In a more modern society, people may see the problem in secular terms. Having concluded that criminal behavior comes about because of an abusive home life, they might seek nonreligious remedies such as cracking down on family abuse hoping to get rid of such behavior. That is not to say that people in today's society do not in fact share a premodern view and see the problem as a religious one.

3. See Genesis 1:1-3, 6-13, Psalms 74:12-17, 93:3-4, 104:1-9. In addition, we can find a trace of this struggle in Exodus 15. Exodus 15 has some connections with an old Canaanite myth. For a detailed discussion of this connection, see Frank Moore Cross 1973, 112-144.

4. Regarding Egyptian society, see James L. Crenshaw 2010, 251-264. The "omen texts" in Babylonian literature function in similar ways.

5. The same caution would also apply to ancient Egypt to some degree. In the case of ancient Israel, the upper class does not necessarily equate with wealth. The writers may have had high status or standing in society, but not necessarily great wealth.

6. All biblical texts or apocryphal ones come from the New Revised Standard Translation abbreviated as NRSV.

7. King of kings is a reference to God, and the scoundrel refers to the Jewish High Priest Menelaus. He tried to advance his own standing and had no regard for the welfare of his people.

8. For clarification purposes, the book of Maccabees is not in the Hebrew Bible. It is included in a groups of writings referred to as Apocryphal Deuterocanonical Books.

9. See Hermann Gunkel 1984, 44-47; and Gerhard von Rad 1972, 50.

10. See James B. Pritchard, ed., 1958, 31-39; and Walter Beyerlin, ed., 1978, 80-84.

11. The dividing of the waters is also present in the priestly account of creation in Genesis 1:6-10.

12. The Deuteronomistic History refers to a group of biblical Books that share and continue the thought introduced in the Book of Deuteronomy. It includes the following biblical books: Joshua, Judges, 1 and 2 Samuel, and 1 and 2 Kings.

13. Yahweh is the Hebrew name for ancient Israel's God, which is usually rendered LORD in English translations.

14. The reader may have observed that the discussion of the prophets made no mention of telling the future. This is the one aspect of Hebrew prophesy that is sorely misunderstood in many modern communities. The Hebrew prophets were not fortune tellers. They told what would happen in the near future, and typically, it was contingent upon how the people responded to the message. It was forth-telling and not foretelling. The word of the prophets never envisions events happening hundreds of years in the future but in the near future—most always within the lifetime of the prophet.

15. Egyptians believed in life after death. Originally, the pharaoh was the only one who enjoyed the next life. With the diminishing of the pharaoh's authority, the belief developed that not only the pharaohs, but others could enjoy the life to come. For this enjoyment to be possible, the Egyptians believed that they had to preserve the body through mummification. The *ba* or soul left the body at death but returned. When the soul or *ba* returned to the body, it continued to have a strong physical appetite or the need for food and drink. The Egyptians actually furnished the tombs with furniture and other supplies. These supplies included "jars of water, wine, grain, dates, cakes, and other foods, such as portions of beef and fowl that had been dehydrated or reduced to ashes" (Noss 5th ed. 1974, 41). As a result, the dead depended upon the living for food, drink, as well as other possessions needed for the next life. The possibility of lacking these things in the next life must have been a source of concern. Nobles sometimes left endowments to care for their needs after their death. Prayers engraved on the tomb had the power of supplying

the needs of the dead, and it was the *duty* of those passing by to say these prayers on the dead person's behalf (Brested 1954, 225-235).

16. One can distinguish the "historical Jesus" from the "Christ of faith." The Christ of faith refers to how the Gospel writers portrayed Jesus in light of the Resurrection. The earliest Gospels were written some forty years after Jesus' death, and they in large part reflect the theology of the Church. They were more concerned with Jesus' divine origin than with his historical earthly existence.

17. The Greek word (agape) literally means love.

18. Wayne Meeks contends that Paul's congregations were not from either the upper or lowest segments of society. Concerning the status of Paul's congregations, consult (Meeks 1983, 51-73).

19. Caputo describes Jacques Derrida's views on community and hospitality. Both words carry within their etymology their opposite. As a result, hospitality is "formed from the Latin *hostis*, which originally meant a 'stranger' and came to take on the meaning of enemy." It also has the notion of master or one who has the power to extend hospitality.

20. There is also an individual emphasis in Christianity that focuses upon personal salvation.

21. I am focusing on the rational element in Greek thought. I would just mention that Friedrich Nietzsche in his book on the *Birth of Tragedy* identified another side of Greek life associated with the passions and the Greek god of wine, Dionysus (Nietzsche 1967b).

22. See the comments of Nietzsche 1982, 72-73; and Nietzsche 1990b, 43. Nietzsche rejects this view.

23. Our English word epistemology derives from this Greek word. In brief, epistemology refers to a branch of philosophy that investigates the nature of knowledge.

24. Desmond Lee, the translator of Plato's *Republic* concludes that Plato approved of infanticide under the following conditions: (1) when the child is defective (2) when the child was born to over-age Guardians, and (3) when the child is in any sense illegitimate (Lee 1987, 246).

25. Plato proposed mating festivals for those who had advanced to the highest level of the educational process (Plato 1987, 236-243).

26. We will discuss this aspect further in the chapter 10.

27. According to Plato, humans consist of a body and a soul. While the body is temporary, the soul is not. It existed prior to one's birth, and it will continue to exist after the death of the body.

28. Epicurus recommends prudence above all else. For the stoics, nature and reason invite the individual to observe the four traditional virtues: prudence, courage, control, and justice.

29. On the other hand, stoicism, a Greek and Roman ethical system of thought, sought virtue for virtue's sake and not for the happiness that it produces.

30. Capitalizing Other is a common practice in postmodern writing. It stresses the importance of the Other as one who is different and in some cases as one who lays a claim on me.

Chapter Five
Foundations for Modern Moral Thinking

Two things fill the mind with ever new and increasing admiration and awe, the oftener and more steadily we reflect on them: the starry heavens above me and the moral law within me (Kant 1956, 166).

Modern thinkers have tried to build their systems of thought on firm foundations. The modern emphasis on reason is heavily dependent on Greek philosophers such as Socrates, Plato, and Aristotle. René working in the seventeenth century tries to lay a firm foundation for all knowledge. He bases such an attempt on the mind and its ability to use reason to discover the Truth. Descartes' method is dualistic. Dualism distinguishes between mind and body, and it this dualism is prevalent in modern thought. Reason is the main tool for determining what is true or moral.

Most modern ethical theories fall into two main categories: consequentialists and nonconsequentialists. Consequentialist ethics solve ethical problems through moral calculations of probable outcomes of an act. The consequences of an act make it good or bad. Nonconsequentialist ethics focus on a person's moral duty without consideration of consequences. In this ethical perspective, one's motive is important. A third approach, moral or ethical relativism, does not fall into either of these categories. Moral relativism has generally not been popular with modern philosophers. It does fuel the thought of some sociologists who want to improve society. One could view moral relativism like the other two types above as an absolutist ethic. It says that one should tolerant differences, and one should follow the rules of the society to which one belongs. These tend to be absolute judgments. Still a relativistic view recognizes that moral values differ over time and from place to place.

CONSEQUENTIALIST ETHICS

A modern consequentialist ethic takes two main forms: ethical egoism and utilitarianism. Ethical egoism encourages acts that result in the individual's own happiness either in the short or long term. Those actions that harm or deny a person's happiness are bad and as one should avoid them. Ethical egoists generally assume that human beings are selfish by nature and naturally seek their own self-interests. They argue that the individual has a moral obligation to act in his or her own best interests. Some people may think from this description that ethical egoists always act selfishly. However, the ethical egoist may understand that consideration for others often increases his or her own happiness. We may even make personal sacrifices for the good of others if the results of the sacrifices bring about our own pleasure. The notion that one should pursue his or her own self-interests is what makes one an egoist in the ethical sense. I will say more about egoism in chapter eight.

Working for the common good is an important aspect of an evolutionary type of ethic proposed by Charles Darwin and Herbert Spencer. The ethic of Darwin and Spencer is essentially utilitarian. Utilitarian ethics call for one to do what brings about the greatest good for the greatest number of people. Darwin and Spencer's ethic is utilitarian in that it focuses on doing what brings about the best results for everyone. Thus, it seeks the common good in contrast to ethical egoism, which consider each person's happiness as an end in itself.

A utilitarian ethic considers the happiness of everyone including the happiness of the individual. My happiness is considered, but it is given no extra weight. My happiness is no more important than the happiness of anyone else. Utilitarians say that an action is good if that action produces more good consequences than bad ones for the people affected. This ethic requires calculation and judgment. Motives are not important for egoism or utilitarianism. I begin the discussion of consequentialist ethics with the work of Thomas Malthus, Darwin and Spencer.

Thomas Malthus (1766-1834) and the Threat of Overpopulation

Thomas Malthus' views on population, published in his *Essays on Population*, influence the views of Darwin on the survival of the fittest (Wallbank, Taylor, and Bailkey 1976, 27). Malthus is an ordained Anglican minister and professor of history and political economy at the East India College in England. Malthus recognizes and analyzes the threat of overpopulation. The consequences of overpopulation would pose a serious threat to human survival. Specifically, Malthus argues that the land's capability to produce enough food cannot keep pace with the geometrical increase in the population (Hinde 2003, 85). The result of this increase in population would be human misery and human suffering, at least for some people. Malthus is a supporter of *laissez-faire* (i.e., government should not interfere in business). He and a number of his contemporaries reject the utopian views of his day. They really do not believe that it is possible to correct the social ills of society.

Efforts to help ease human suffering were not welcomed by Malthus. The poor laws of his day in England were meant to provide aid for those out of work or unable to work. Consequently, those out of work or those unable to work could apply for relief. In the eighteenth century, as financial resources decreased, a change was made. Now the amount of relief one received depended upon family size. Malthus was particularly opposed to this change. Such government intervention encouraged population growth instead of reduction, and it would additionally lead to laziness (Hinde 2003, 84).   *Delay or to prevent*

Malthus identifies certain restraints that could help impede population growth in the long term. Hardships of raising a family and one's inability to provide for them could lead to a higher death rate. Increases in population lead to malnutrition and starvation, which brings about diseases and a higher death rate. In his second essay on population, Malthus calls for moral restraint. He says that those who are unable to provide a "decent standard of living" for potential children should freely decide to delay getting married and having a family (Hinde 2003, 84-85, 112). Another possible way to help the situation would be to limit the number of children in one's family through sexual restraint.

Nevertheless, the lack of self-restraint would lead to worsening conditions for society. Nature is also a factor. Natural disasters, wars, and famines are ways in which nature works to restrain population growth. In this way, the natural law reduces the overall population. This process of thinning out the population is necessary. Malthus, however, is not optimistic. All living things including human beings would eventually become extinct (Loubère 1994, 190).

The issue of population control has become an important issue today. Along the lines of Malthus, we could ask several questions: Should national or local government encourage birth control? Is there really a population problem in this country and around the world? Will there be enough food, clean water, and other essential goods to sustain humanity in the future? Is it a problem of distribution or shortage? Should we in the United States help fellow citizens before turning our attention to other less fortunate countries? Is there really a need to control populations, or can technology solve the problem?

These and other questions are important for anyone interested in the issue of overpopulation. One of the key issues is moral responsibility. Are we morally responsible for our neighbors at home and abroad? What are the consequences of having a large family on society as a whole? World population has grown from one billion people at the beginning of the nineteenth century to 6.25 billion only a mere two hundred years later. The population is growing about seventy five million people every year. By 2050, the population could be nine billion people. Where will the resources come from to provide for this growth? (Pierce, Jessica 2005 44) Growth requires more of everything including energy. Science may solve some of the problems, but it may take government intervention at some point.

Since families and individuals in this country consume much more of the earth's resources than people in many other countries, some people might conclude that large families in this country are too much of a strain on the world's resources. Should the government encourage or even force smaller families in an effort to conserve the world's remaining resources?

This whole issue is complex. It becomes even more complex when one considers certain religious beliefs. Teaching or encouraging families to use birth control may lead to a storm of protests. How can one be sensitive to other people's religious sensibilities and still advocate limiting the number of children per family? For some, the notion of limiting the population is immoral. In the Catholic faith, the Church does not permit birth control. The issue that Malthus raises continues to be an important concern. It is a moral issue and one that we cannot ignore. Failure to deal with this issue could indeed threaten human survival. From a utilitarian perspective, one would need to pursue policies that would ensure human survival.

The Evolutionary Ethical Perspectives of Charles Darwin (1809-1882)

The rise of utilitarian ethics coincides with the evolutionary views of Darwin. In *The Origin of Species*, first published in 1859, Darwin begins setting out his views on evolution.[1] These views become controversial later in 1871 when he publishes the *Descent of Man and Selection in Relation to Sex*. The book develops the theory of human evolution (Ruse 2004, 29). In his view, one should do those things that lead to survival.

Darwin and Spencer saw evolution in terms of progress. For Darwin, God worked through natural laws and evolution was the way in which the human race improved over time. Darwin was a deist, and he believed that God "works through unbroken law." For Darwin, God arranged the world in a particular fashion so that it would evolve in an "upward progression." For him, the progress of culture and the progress of biology were interrelated. This progressiveness was part of every aspect of creation leading to a "progressive increase of the wisdom and happiness of its inhabitants" (Ruse 2004, 28).

Darwin's views also take various political forms as well. The Nazis, Lenin-Marxists, and capitalists all appeal to Darwin's evolutionary hypothesis. The Nazis use Darwin to defend the position that they are the perfect race. Lenin-Marxists reinterpret Darwin to support the view that communism is the perfect form of government. Capitalists use Darwin's theories to sustain their belief that the marketplace is where the strong weed out the weak. These capitalists do not believe that we should have social programs to take care of people (Wallbank, Taylor, and Bailkey 1976, 302-304). All three tendencies depict a world where human civilization is on the road leading to continual progress culminating in an ideal society.

An evolutionary view of ethics might therefore encourage certain actions on the basis that they lead to a more reliable survival of the human race. Darwin and Spencer propose a utilitarian ethic based on Darwin's evolutionary views. Unlike most utilitarians, Darwin's main concern is not happiness of the individual but human survival. In this scheme, the individual is much less important than the group. For Darwin, the highest good of a society involves creating the type of society where the majority of people flourish. Flourishing means they would be in good health and doing well under whatever conditions are present in that society. Human survival and flourishing as a group is essential. Such a strategy allows for the perpetuation of the human race.

Herbert Spencer (1820-1903)

Darwin's friend, Herbert Spencer, worked to show how Darwin's evolutionary theory related to the field of ethics. He associated morality with societal evolution. Societal evolution for him meant progress. Spencer thought that there were degrees of evolution and that societies generally progressed up the ladder as they obtained higher degrees of morality. Societies evolved from groups joined by kinship and common custom to those governed by the military. The final stage moved toward industrial societies where cooperation replaced violence.

He also believed that behavior progressed more and more toward the goal of preserving life. Consider his statements concerning the difference between military and industrial societies.

> In a society organized for militant action, the individuality of each member has to be subordinated in life, liberty, and property, that he is largely, or completely, *owned* by the state; but in a society industrially organized, no such subordination of the individual is called for. There remain no occasions on which he is required to risk his life while destroying the lives of others; he is not forced to leave his occupation and submit to a commanding officer; and it ceases to be needful that he should surrender for public purposes whatever property is demanded of him.
>
> Under the industrial *regime* the citizen's individuality, instead of being sacrificed by the society, has to be defended by society. Defense of individuality becomes the society's essential duty. That after external protection is no longer called for, internal protection must become the cardinal function of the state. . . .
>
> For it is clear, that other things being equal, a society in which life, liberty, and property, are secure, and all interests justly regarded, must prosper more than one in which they are not (Spencer 1899, 607-608).

Therefore, industrial societies are more highly evolved than militant ones. The militant aspect of society eventually gives way to a cooperative society. Cooperation is important because societies also become more diverse as they grow, a process he refers to as differentiation. Diverse elements or people in a society must cooperate and work together for the good of the whole. The main point is that a society based on cooperation rather than militancy leads to a more reliable survival and a happier group of people. Cooperation has consequences that work out for the common good of the larger society.

This view led to a growing optimism. Many came to believe that societies were continually progressing toward some ideal society. Spencer maintained that nature operated in such a way that the greatest number of people benefited. In fact, Darwin took the phrase "survival of the fittest" from Spencer. According to Spencer, ethics should commend those actions that produce the greatest amount of good for society. While the struggle for survival continued, human actions generally became less militant and more industrial through time.

Impact of Evolutionary View

Early in the twentieth century, this evolutionary worldview pervaded both education and religion. The belief was that human beings were continually getting better and better. Human perfection along with scientific progress would transform the world into an ideal place to live. In this scheme, human beings were not evil, but they were improving over time. The modernist or liberal perspective in Christian theology tended to view human potential positively.

Key historical events such as World War I and World War II largely destroyed this optimistic view of human nature. In Christian theology, some liberals modified their views on human nature moving closer to the older views on human nature. Some of these theologians began to take the darker side of human nature much more seriously.

Today, in religion at least, theologians are much more cautious in assessing human nature. In scientific circles, Stephen Jay Gould has written a good bit on this topic. He has vigorously opposed the equation of evolution with progress toward certain humanistic ideals or goals (Ruse, Michael 2004).

A line from the movie *Contact* arrives at the heart of the human situation. The movie *Contact* is based on a book by Carl Sagan by the same title. The movie and the line sums up the reality of the past and present with regard to human nature. In this move, Jody Foster plays the part of Ellie Arroway who as a young girl lost her father. She grows up to become a scientist and is selected to take a trip through a wormhole and make humanity's first contact with an alien race. This race has already been listening and watching human broadcasts since 1936 when the Olympic Games were held in Berlin, Germany. In this broadcast, Adolf Hitler delivers the opening address. The aliens take this broadcast and return it to earth with additional information about how to create a machine that allows for travel to their home. Upon her trip and contact with an alien being who oddly appears to her in the image of her dead father, the alien sums up humanity very aptly in the following line: "You're capable of such beautiful dreams and such horrible nightmares." Thus, we are, and we are unlikely to ever change. *Disapproval*

Our term "primitive" is often a pejorative way of distinguishing ourselves from cultures from the distant past. Due to our technology, philosophy, medicine, and a number of other things, many people see themselves as superior to their own ancestors. In truth, many of us still hold to a type of evolutionary perspective where later means better. Another good illustration of human nature comes from my brief description of Dan Brown's novel *Angel and Demons* in chapter three. As I point out there, the priest-scientist does not realize that the power that could save us could also be used to destroy us. There are those capable of doing great good and great evil and most if not all of us are capable of doing some good and bad.

There is another side to this view of progress; humans are actually becoming more evil. This view is a popular in some circles. There is a tendency to view human beings today as less civilized than those from the relatively recent past when true virtues existed. "The good ole days," to hear some tell it, is a time when good prevails, a time when one does not lock his or her doors at night or fear of letting children play outside.

One possible reason for such views was that news and information were more limited then. Perhaps there was such a mythical time when people did not lock their doors at night. They did not worry about being mugged or assaulted. Nevertheless, those same "good ole days" were not so good for other people who lived in fear and danger.

One example from the book *The Rising Tide* by John M. Barry certainly should prevent us from any nostalgia for times past, and I think there is value in keeping these kinds of stories alive. They are horrible, but they also keep us aware of what humanity is capable of doing and what so-called "good people" can do to those who are outside their group or community. The book, *The Rising Tide* tells about the Great Mississippi Flood. Yet the book tells a larger story of life for blacks in the Mississippi Delta and the surrounding areas. Barry recounts the story of a French journalist Ho Chi Minh who

> collected clippings that included headlines such as, from the New Orleans States. 'Today a Negro will Be Burned by 3,000 Citizens,' and from the Jackson (Mississippi) Daily News, 'Negro J.H. to be Burnt by the Crowd at Ellistown This Afternoon at 5 P.M.' The Vicksburg Evening-Post reported the lynching of a black husband and wife accused of murdering a white man: The blacks were forced to hold out their hands while one finger at a time was chopped off. The fingers were distributed as souvenirs. The ears of the murders [sic] were cut off. . . . (Barry, 1997)

I could continue this gruesome account by Barry, which does not get any better, but my point is that we are not getting better or worse. Some might say that people today would not act like the white people in Barry's account. Yet what has changed? Given the right circumstances or situation, humans are still capable of such actions.

An earlier chapter discusses the power of morals to force or bring about conformity. Social situations add another dimension to the power of morals. Certain social situations can occur that change us or force us to do things we would not do under normal circumstances. The experiment by Stanley Milgram shows us that most people in his experiment would give potentially lethal electric shocks to strangers if an authority figure tells them to do so.[2] In my view, human beings past and present are capable of the most unbelievable acts of kindness and the most horrific conduct. Additionally, social situations have the power to bring out the best and worst in human nature.

Even though we have made significant strides in science and technology, can we claim to be better than those people living many years ago? Each age might think of itself as better or as worse than the age before. Technical advancements and change in society do not mean that we are better or worse than the civilizations of the past.

Utilitarian Ethics of Jeremy Bentham (1748-1832), James Mill (1773-1836), and John Staurt Mill (1806-1873)

The twin concepts of utility and happiness establish the basis for utilitarianism. Utility can have several meanings. It can mean that something is useful, gives pleasure, or that it serves a particular interest. The utilitarian approach to ethics measures human institutions according to the amount of pleasure or happiness they produce. This view is particularly associated with Jeremy Bentham. Bentham believes that government should secure as much *individual freedom* as possible. Freedom is an important aspect of happiness for Bentham, James Mill, and his son John Staurt Mill. People should be free to conduct their own affairs. James Mill believes that the bourgeois merchants and factory owners should have the greatest amount of freedom to conduct their business. In the end, he believes that the continuing self-interest of the manufacturers would agree with the self-interests of the workers (Wallbank, Taylor, and Bailkey 1976, 136).

His son, John Staurt Mill, questioned this conclusion. In considering the distribution of wealth, John Staurt Mill agreed that society should give producers "maximum freedom" according to the natural law. However, he qualified this statement.

> Distribution of wealth depends on the laws and customs of society, and these can be changed by the will of men. The idea that all competition is good needed examination; competition in production increased the volume of goods, to the general advantage of society, but the division [i.e., distribution] of products favored the strong against the weak, and civilized society might revert to the jungle (Wallbank, Taylor, and Bailkey 1976, 136).

Therefore, John Staurt Mill acknowledged that societies might want to put some restrictions upon free enterprise. Such restrictions were necessary to promote the overall good and prevent the slide back to the jungle.

John Staurt Mill defines utilitarianism in terms of the greatest happiness principle, which

> holds that actions are right in proportion as they tend to promote happiness; wrong as they tend to produce the reverse of happiness. By happiness is intended pleasure and the absence of pain; by unhappiness, [he means] pain and the privation of pleasure. . . . The theory of life on which this theory of morality is grounded . . . [asserts that] pleasure and freedom from pain are the only things desirable as ends, and that all things desirable (which are as numerous in the utilitarian as in any other scheme) are desirable either for the pleasure inherent in themselves or as means to the promotion of pleasure and the prevention of pain (Mill 1957, 10).

The goal of life is happiness. Therefore, we should direct our actions toward that goal; the legitimate goal is to produce the greatest happiness for the greatest numbers. Unlike Bentham, however, John Staurt Mill does distinguish between different types of pleasure. He maintains that not all pleasures are equal in quality. For Mill, one has to distinguish between pleasures by means of the following test: "Of the two pleasures, if there be one to which all or almost all who have experienced both give a decided preference . . . that is the more desirable pleasure" (John Staurt Mill 1957, 12).

The object for the utilitarian is for one to act in a way that produces the greatest possible balance of good over bad for everyone affected by his or her action (Mill 1957, 16). By good, utilitarians understand happiness or pleasure. For example, we may consider telling the truth to be the right course of action in one situation because it produces more happiness than the alternative. The opposite, however, is also possible. Since the judgment concerning right and wrong depends upon the consequences of an act, we can truthfully say that withholding important information or lying may sometimes produce more happiness than would come from telling the truth. If a large asteroid is headed for us and we could do nothing to stop it, would telling the truth be the responsible thing to do? Telling might lead to a complete breakdown of society. In such a case, the utilitarian would have to determine if the positive consequences of telling the truth would outweigh the negatives ones.

As an ethical theory, utilitarianism has certain advantages and disadvantages over other ethical systems. One could think of many different kinds of situations where one party decides how to act based on some sort of weighing the strengths and weaknesses of an action. To illustrate the advantages of the utilitarian approach, we could examine the issue of whether gambling should or should not be legalized. What are the advantages and disadvantages? A utilitarian approach would require one to look at all relevant data and evaluate whether the consequences of legalized gambling would be to the benefit of more people than it might harm. We should note both the positive and negative aspects of gambling.

Once we gather all the germane data, the decision on whether we should legalize it depends upon its impact on the population affected by the decision. If gambling turns out to produce more good than bad for the greatest number of people affected by it then we may consider it morally justifiable. On the other hand, if our data shows that the results would ultimately benefit only a select group then it is wrong. The advantage to such an approach is that it causes us to look at both sides of an issue. This approach would be useful for looking at most ethical issues. Yet while this might be a good practice for us in making ethical decisions, one may reject it as a way of making a final decision.

There are a number of disadvantages of a utilitarian perspective. In extreme and rare cases, a utilitarian ethic may cause one to help the majority of people in a community by sacrificing the needs of the minority. Imagine a situation in a small town where a murder has been committed. A white woman is killed on a back street with no witnesses. There has been ongoing racial tension in this town, and this situation promises to fuel the flames of hatred and possibly prompt acts of violence. Imagine further a sheriff who wants to avoid this possible bloodshed. He finds a vagrant who has the opportunity and means to commit the murder even though the sheriff has no hard evidence that the vagrant actually committed the crime. The vagrant has no alibi, and he has a violent criminal past as well. Would it be acceptable to charge this person with the crime if it would ease tension and prevent the possible outbreak of deadly violence? Is this a case where the utilitarian might justify sacrificing the rights of the one for the many?

Additionally, how could one justify a policy to protect minority rights based on a strict utilitarian ethic? A utilitarian ethic would always obligate us to do what is in the interests of the majority even if it has to sacrifice the needs of the few.

Moreover, how can one determine or quantify the amount of pleasure or pain an act will produce? What may represent two units of happiness for one individual (e.g., playing loud music) may represent two units of pain for another. Since happiness is not the same for everyone, calculations of pleasure and pain would be ineffective in many cases.

Not only is it impossible to quantify the amount of pleasure or pain an act produces, it is also impossible to predict or foresee all the possible consequences of an act. Bentham uses the term "hedonic calculus" to evaluate pleasure and pain. This calculus assigns units of pleasure and pain to any act. One should do the act resulting in the greatest happiness for the greatest number of people. To determine which act to perform, one must give numerical values to each act. However, even if we could make such designations, how can one know ahead of time what the consequences of an act will be? Often acts have unintended or unforeseeable results. The utilitarian would even be at more of a disadvantage if he or she tries to determine the long-term consequences of an act.

Therefore, an ethic that depends upon such tenuous utilitarian calculations is imperfect at best. Utilitarianism has a practical advantage of examining all sides of an issue before acting. Yet, as a sole base of morality, utilitarianism is lacking. It assumes that an act should be for the good of a majority, but is this fair? Do we have an obligation to set aside our own interests or the interests of a small group in favor of the larger group? Can we boil morality down to calculations?

In sum, we have seen how the work of Malthus influences the evolutionary views of Darwin. The struggle for survival appears to be a basic element or ingredient in life. For Darwin, one can evaluate human conduct in terms of this survival value. Darwin's ethic is utilitarian in the sense that it advocates the greatest good for the greatest number of people. Greatest good has to do with survival of the greatest number of people. That is not exactly the same thing as utilitarians who advocate the greatest happiness for the great number. According to Darwin, the greatest good has to do with the survival of the fittest. Strictly, therefore, it does not equate good with the greatest happiness. Evolutionary ethics and utilitarian ethics are social in nature because they consider the good not just of the individual, but also the larger society.

Karl Marx (1818-1883)

Marx's view on morality is also consequentialist in nature, but it is different from the ones just discussed. Marx judges an action based on whether it leads toward an egalitarian and just society. His views on justice and equality have been influential. Liberation theology to varying degrees has drawn on these views. Marx is an idealist in the sense that he thinks that a classless society would emerge from the demise of capitalism.

Marx's analysis leads him to the understanding that capitalism would destroy itself. For him, this change would come about through the natural process of evolution. Evolution is a powerful force that shall ultimately prevail. Philosopher Georg W. F. Hegel influences Marx's views in this regard. Hegel's dialectic describes history as moving to higher and higher levels because of the resolution or synthesis of conflicting or contradictory ideas. Therefore, the resolution or synthesis of conflicting ideas would lead one closer to the Absolute. Marx replaces Hegel's notion of the Absolute with the economy.

For Marx, class struggle becomes the main source of historical progress (Sarup 1993, 91-92). In the process of class struggle, eventually the working class would become aware of how the owners of the means of production use and exploit them for their own benefit. This situation leads to a future revolution in which a higher form of "human society" would arise. In this ideal society, the class society would pass away.

Many people have rejected Marx's notions as utopian ideas that can never work in real life. Marx's view that people would be content when this new ideal society emerges is naïve. It shares an overly optimistic view of human nature. However, his analysis of class conflict and class struggle continues to be important for modern social scientists, for those still working in a Marxist tradition, and certain theological and ethical thinkers. His desire for a just and equitable society is still alive.

Marxism and Morality

Marx's thought is closely connected with a particular moral view. This moral view strongly deplores any exploitation. As Steven Lukes points out, Marx's thought is not exactly consistent when it comes to morality. Lukes describes this inconsistency as a paradox. Paradox is a statement that is seemingly "self-contradictory and absurd, though possibly well founded and essentially true."[3]

The paradox consists of two seemingly contradictory positions. On the one hand, Marx says that religion, which includes morality, is the opiate of the people. In other words, the exploiters use religion and morality as a tool or means of control. Religion dulls the senses and promotes a view of life that is otherworldly. Its message is for the *proletariat* or oppressed or working class to endure the suffering in this life in hopes that the next life will be better. The *bourgeoisie*, therefore, uses religion and morality to keep the *proletariat* from revolting. Marx sees it as his duty to wake up the *proletariat* (Lukes 1985, 3).

On the other hand, Marx's views and judgments were rather moralistic in tone. If morality is about justice and fairness, then his views were moralistic. He feels compelled to shine a light on capitalistic exploitation of the working class in England. Marx and Friedrich Engels forcefully criticize the horrible working conditions during the industrial revolution. They condemn the exploitation of women and children. Condemnation of the oppressors continues to be part of all work done in the Marxist tradition. Lukes points out that in any Marxist writing no matter how scientific or academic one

> will find condemnation, exhortation, and the vision of a better world. . . .
> Notice that the paradox, the seeming contradiction, lies at the level of general belief. On the one hand, morality, as such, is explained, unmasked, and condemned as an anachronism [i.e., a chronologically misplaced event -- we no longer need it]; on the other, it is believed in and appealed to, and indeed urged upon others as relevant to political campaigns and struggles. . . . In short, what is striking about Marxism is its apparent commitment to both the rejection and the adoption of moral criticism and exhortation (Lukes 1985, 3-4).

Lukes concludes that Marxism is a consequentialist moral theory. It is completely engrossed with the notion of human freedom, which can only occur fully in a classless society. The goal for Marxism is perfection, and one can judge all actions by whether they lead us toward a higher form of society. Actions should strive to produce a society where human beings can realize their full potential without enslaving or oppressing others. It is a society where one benefits from his or her own labor instead of benefiting his or her oppressors. One is to act with an eye to the future and not an otherworldly future. The future that counts is a future in this world. One needs to make changes so people can have a fulfilling life in the present. Religion often focuses on the otherworld, which keeps one from taking meaningful steps to eliminate oppression in this world. It is within human history that the higher form of society must arise (Lukes 1985, 142-147). His consequentialist view, however, is different from utilitarianism. For Marx, an act in theory may lead to the happiness of the majority of people and be wrong. What makes an act good is that its consequences lead us toward a classless society.

We can see Marx's influence today in certain ethical and theological systems. Some theologians and ethicists have drawn on the Marxist tradition to create an ethical perspective, which sides with the oppressed. *Liberation theology* is the religious manifestation of this perspective. One of the fundamental tenets of this position is the belief that God is on the side of the oppressed. Therefore, we have an ethical obligation to work for changes in societies that would demolish oppressive societal structures. The feminist and civil rights movements share with the Marxist tradition a desire to eliminate oppressive social structures.

Not all liberation theologians or ethicists identify with the Marxist tradition. Some may simply employ Marxist categories of oppressor and oppressed. Marx's work has influenced them to some extent. Many Christian ethicists and theologians may espouse an ethic that opposes oppression without necessarily associating themselves with Marx. Many elements in the biblical tradition support the view that God sides with the oppressed. The words of the prophet Amos or the Exodus from Egypt provide just two examples.

Morality and Economic Systems

The discussion of Marxism raises the issue of morality in relation to economic systems. Some people feel that capitalism is the only moral economic system. In theory, everyone can compete and be successful if they work hard enough (i.e., the American Dream or myth). Darwin's evolutionary views have much in common with a pure capitalistic philosophy. In a purely capitalistic system where there are no governmental controls, survival of the fittest might become a reality. Consequently, there is a close fit between capitalism as expressed by Adam Smith and others with Darwin's views on human evolution.

Capitalism has a commitment to the principle of *laissez-faire*, which calls for the government to mind its own affairs and leave business alone. To put it in terms of the contemporary debate, it is a resistance to government intervention or regulation. Deregulation is the view that things operate best when government is involved the least. In the words of Lord Macaulay,

> Our rulers will best promote the improvement of the nation by strictly confining themselves to their own legitimate duties, by leaving capital to find its most lucrative course, commodities their fair price, industry and intelligence their natural reward, idleness and folly their natural punishment, by maintaining peace, by *defending property* [italics mine], by diminishing the price of law, and by observing strict economy in every department of the state. Let government do this: the people will assuredly do the rest (Wallbank, Taylor, and Bailkey 1976, 135).

The idea is that when governments leave businesses alone to find their own way, the strong weed out the weak and make for a stronger marketplace. In short, there is more competition, which results in better products at a lower price.

Others might point to Marxism and socialism as being moral because of their concern and commitment to the oppressed and their strong opposition to the oppressor. Many in the West are reluctant to use Marxist viewpoints as a tool to evaluate or analyze capitalism. Yet, Adam Smith, a strong proponent of capitalism, has doubts about its morality. Smith notes that the

> common wages of labor depend everywhere upon the contrast usually made between two parties, whose interests are by no means the same. The workmen desire to get as much as possible, the master to give as little as possible. . . . It is not, however, difficult to foresee which of the two parties must, upon ordinary occasions, have the advantage in the dispute. . . . In all such disputes, the masters can hold out much longer. Many workmen could not subsist a week, few could subsist a month, and scarce any a year without employment. In the long run the workman may be as necessary to his master as his master is to him, but the necessity is not so much immediate (Heilbroner 1993, 131).[4]

Smith concludes that society is better off with capitalism, and that we can maintain order better if society recognizes differences of rank based on birth and fortune (Heilbroner, 133). In short, this system may have some flaws, but it is the best one.

Many believe that the shortcomings of capitalism are outweighed by its overall benefits. Capitalism provides a motive and incentive for people to be productive. It does not rely on the unselfish goodness of human nature. It is more in line with human nature. The capitalistic system encourages individuals to look out after their own interests to survive.

It is true that businesses do sacrifice their own advantage at times for the good of the public. Sometimes the motives may be relatively unselfish. Yet these actions often depend on the assumption that responsible behavior of either the individual or business pays off in tangible rewards of some sort. Businesses typically advertise their good deeds in hopes of tangible payoffs. It seems natural that people plan their actions based on a profit motive. We may inquire of any action as to its probable costs, and the likelihood that the action will produce a profit. From this perspective, we understand human nature as being rational and seeking its own good. On the other hand, capitalism seems more in line with an egoistic perspective. Even though, Bentham and James Mill would argue that what is good for business is good for the larger population.

I assume that most people do not support pure capitalism or capitalism without any government regulation. Most people believe that it is necessary to impose some restraints on capitalism to protect society from the greed of those who are only concerned with the bottom line. An example of what can happen when the concern for short-term profits outweighs the concern for responsible action takes place in the Gulf of Mexico. On April 20, 2010, the oil rig, the Deep Water Horizon leased by British Petroleum explodes and kills eleven workers. The explosion causes great harm to people and wildlife in and around the Gulf Coast. Such events further erode people's faith in big business to act responsibly. Many people do not trust companies or businesses to have the best interests of others in mind when they contemplate how to conduct their business affairs.

Others, however, consider Marxist economics moral because of its attention to the plight of the exploited. Marx dreams of a world where everyone receives fair treatment. In retrospect, it is hard to imagine that he really believes in a future where people would be content to live as equals. Marx seems to have faith in the goodness of what human beings could become in a new era. From observing capitalism and forms of socialism, one can conclude that economic systems are neither necessarily moral nor immoral. The ideals of socialism are noble, but the reality is something else. Capitalism, on the other hand, does not have to end in greed and short sightedness. Yet, some people might argue that self-interest is what provides one with a competitive advantage. Good people who have earned a great deal of money can do good things with some of that money. From a moral perspective, neither capitalism nor socialism can produce a totally just or moral society. One might argue that economic systems are morally neutral in themselves.

In this country, there is a political struggle between those who want to keep government from interfering with private enterprise and those who want government intervention or more government regulation. This represents two different sets of values. Those who see government as a positive instrument to control and regulate businesses may appeal to the notions of fairness, justice, and equality of all people. The main concern for these people may be for members of society who have not had a fair chance in life. They may want to institute many different social programs to ensure equality. They may also want to protect the public from capitalists who only want to make as much as they can any way they can. Others may value hard work and success, and they may see social programs as being unfair; one should work for what one gets. The poor may be seen as lazy people who are unwilling to do what it takes to be successful

A Buddhist view of economics provides an alternative economic attitude. Buddhists view work as an activity that enhances the life of the worker. It should be rewarding and a negative experience. Some Christians may view work as a curse brought about by original sin.

On a Buddhist account, work should not be seen as a means for obtaining wealth, but satisfaction. Whereas Western thinking seeks to minimize or even eliminate human labor, Buddhism like Marxism values labor. In Buddhism, people work not to gain happiness by possessing material things but to gain satisfaction with the minimum of materialistic possessions. Their view of life also causes them to view the environment differently. They do not view the natural environment as resources to be exploited. They distinguish between renewable and nonrenewable materials. To depend upon nonrenewable resources is immoral parasitic behavior (Schumacher 1993, 461-466). This attitude seems to present a more comprehensive view of life. Too often, we in the West separate economic, religious, and moral realms to justify questionable behavior that may adversely affect others and the environment under a slogan of *laissez-faire*. Perhaps, we could learn a great deal from the Buddhists perspective.

Returning to Marx, we can see that he offers us a master narrative or grand theory about the movement of history, which ends in a society characterized by fairness and lack of oppression. His views offer us a glimpse of an ideal society where equality is possible. It is a society where there is an elimination of wealthy elites using workers for their own personal and selfish gains. It is a grand vision of an ideal society that today seems always beyond reach. Marx's views continue to inspire and uncover unjust and oppressive structures in society even if they no longer provide an ultimate solution to societal problems.

NONCONSEQUENTIALIST ETHICS

Nonconsequentialist ethical theory, sometimes called deontological ethics, attempts to determine right and wrong based upon the *motive* of the actor. An act is only good if one does it out of a sense of duty. Immanuel Kant is a leading representative of this school of ethics. His ethic is an *absolutist ethic* in the sense that there is only one right act. For instance, stealing is never right. The consequences of an act have nothing to do with its rightness or wrongness. This ethic, then, is nonconsequentialist. Deontological approaches to ethics often rely upon intuition and rules for knowing right and wrong.

A deontological or nonconsequentialist ethic must consider the *actor's motive* before it can determine the value or worth of his or her act. Imagine the following scenario. Karl is at the scene of a car accident where he finds an elderly woman partially thrown from a car that could roll down a hill at any moment. Her legs are trapped inside the car. There are no medical personnel there, and she is calling for help. She pleads with Karl to help her get out of the car because she is experiencing intense pain and is afraid the car is going to flip over. He decides that he could help free her from the vehicle, but in doing so, Karl breaks a rib. As it turns out, she could have remained in the car safely until the paramedics arrived on the scene. In retrospect, his act produces bad consequences. His motive, however, is to do his duty which requires him to help the woman by responding to her needs.

So, is such an act good or bad? For nonconsequentialist theories, the consequences of one's acts are irrelevant. In our example, one can judge the act good because Karl's motive is good; he is doing his duty. His duty is to ease her suffering and get her out of danger. He considers it his duty to do so. The results of our actions are not always under our control. We are only responsible to do our duty. If our motives derive from this reason, then the act is moral.

Suppose that Karl comes to the accident scene and decides not to risk moving the woman out of fear of possible legal repercussions for himself. Therefore, he calls the proper authorities and reports the accident. He then waits for the paramedics to arrive before he leaves the scene. In this scenario, the paramedics arrive and rescue the woman, and she sustains no additional injuries. From a nonconsequentialist ethic, one could judge Karl's actions as morally questionable even if the consequences of his actions are good. His primary motive is to avoid getting involved and facing possible legal problems. Is such a motive consistent with his duty?

Kant's moral reasoning about judicial punishment provides another example of nonconsequentialist ethics. Kant maintains that

> judicial punishment can never be administered merely as a means for promoting another good either with regard to the criminal himself or to civil society, but must in all cases be imposed only because the individual on whom it is inflicted *has committed a crime* (Kant 1952, 446).

Therefore, we should not support capital punishment because it deters people from taking innocent life. While a utilitarian might defend capital punishment for its deterrence value, the nonconsequentialist would not defend it on that basis. For Kant, it is simply the duty of society to punish wrongdoing.

One of the problems with such nonconsequentialist's views is that following rules and doing one's duty does not always provide a clear answer to our moral quandary. Certain situations do not lend themselves to easy answers. Many times, we may feel no assurance that we did the right thing or that we did enough. We may never eliminate the ambiguity involved in the process of making moral decisions. We may find that two or more duties can come into conflict with each other on occasion. One's duty to his or her family can conflict with his or her duty to an employer.

There are two forms of nonconsequentialist ethics. The first one stems from a religious point of view. The second one comes from the philosophical perspective. It entails a more in-depth discussion of Kant's views on the subject of ethics. Before discussing Kant, a few words about a religious nonconsequentialist ethic are in order.

Religious Nonconsequentialist Ethic

The religious nonconsequentialist ethic is sometimes called the divine command theory. From this perspective, an act is wrong if God forbids it and right if God commands it. It is right to obey and wrong to disobey. Some Christians contend that God gives us an absolute moral code, which one finds in the Bible. However, other religions have their own scriptures. Muslims may look to the Quran for these absolutes. As a result, such positions have limited appeal. They have power only over those who take a very fundamentalist view of sacred texts. Even those people who read the same scripture often carry away different interpretations of it. Divine revelation may come down to human beings, but individuals in all their imperfections have to interpret the revelation. Even if the revelation is divine, the receiver is not. Additionally, we live many hundred years after these revelations. Therefore, we have to reinterpret those original interpretations. The interpretations today are many and conflicting. For those who seek clear and simple answers by appealing to Scripture, it is not simply a matter of choosing the right religion but the right denomination or sub-group within the right religion that happens to have all the correct interpretations.

This approach, then, depends upon one's interpretation of the Bible, and these interpretations are not the same for everyone. From a larger perspective, a Muslim and Christian would not necessarily agree upon what God commands or forbids since they do not share the same Scripture. We might also wonder if something is wrong just because God forbids it or right because God commands it. Alternatively, does God forbid an action because it is wrong? If this is the case, then right and wrong governs what God commands and forbids. On this view, even God is subject to the moral law. This view is more consistent with Kant's ethical philosophy.

Moral Philosophy of Immanuel Kant (1724-1804)

Kant always remains close to his home. He spends his entire life in Königsberg in East Prussia. He is also educated in Königsberg and teaches logic and metaphysics at the University in Königsberg. He writes on many different topics including moral philosophy. To understand his moral philosophy, I begin with a discussion of his critique of pure and practical reason.

Critique of Pure Reason

In this work, Kant argues that pure reason can lead us only so far. It cannot provide guidance in the arena of ethics. It cannot tell us what our moral or ethical duties are. In this work, Kant distinguishes between ultimate realities (i.e., *nomena* or the things in themselves) and things as they appear to us through the senses (*phenomena*). Phenomena, therefore, refer to how things or objects appear to us in human experience. Kant keeps these two things separate.

Science and human experience do not address themselves to ultimate realities (i.e., *nomena or the thing in itself*). They only address the way things appear to us (*phenomena*) through the senses. External objects excite the human senses. The mind takes these sensations and through a rational process makes sense of them. To make sense of things, the mind has to take in sensory information and arrange it in a meaningful way.

In this way, it is possible to gain a level of universally valid knowledge of nature. For instance, scientists study nature and discern patterns in it allowing them to formulate and test theories and hypotheses. In this realm, however, the mind is not without limits. It has to interpret the data. There is no way to know or penetrate into the thing itself. Knowledge based on pure reason, therefore, is conditional and not completely certain.

Knowledge is conditional in the realm of pure reason. One can describe the laws of nature in terms of cause and effect. Thunder, for instance, is the result of a lightening bolt that rapidly heats and expands the air around it causing a shock wave, which we then hear as thunder. One can also develop conditional imperatives. These imperatives are based on reasoning about causal relationships. Kant calls these laws of nature *hypothetical imperatives*.

With regard to hypothetical imperatives, "an action is good for some purpose, either possible or actual" (Kant 1964, 82). For instance, the hypothetical imperative says that if one wants A, then he or she must do B. These hypothetical imperatives either instruct one that he or she should do something either to get a certain result (i.e., the hypothetical imperative of skill) or that one should do something to gain happiness (i.e., the hypothetical imperative of prudence). In the first instance, we could say that one ought to obtain a good education if he or she wishes to get a job. In the latter instance, we might advise a person that if he or she wants to be happy, he or she ought to find a certain kind of job that coincides with his or her own interests thus producing personal happiness (Kant 1964, 82-84).[5]

The key here is that the moral philosopher cannot gain access to the world of morality and duty from pure theoretical reason alone. It is not sufficient as a basis for morality. A person cannot infer the moral law from the world of nature by "adding empirical facts and more empirical facts to infinitely expandable store of factual information" (Beck 1956, xiv). What one requires for moral laws is a different type of knowledge. We need knowledge that is not conditional or hypothetical but unconditional and absolute. Pure reason cannot produce unconditional and absolute knowledge. Kant thinks that a pure ethic (i.e., the *a priori*[6] part of ethics) is independent of nature since nature is completely impersonal and nonmoral. Nature is governed by casual necessities. Humans are free (Beck 1956, xviii). In other words, causal necessities do not govern human behavior as it does lower forms of animal life or nonbiological life. So if morality is not found in pure reason, where is it found? Kant says that we have to look for a moral law outside the natural world.

Kant took it for granted that human beings possessed a moral awareness, which made it possible for them to act freely. Humans were not governed by their social environment. Even though Kant lived in a time of rapid social change, he taught at a university and remained isolated to a degree. He recognized that different societies had different moral schemes, and that one could examine these moral schemes within the realm of nature. Still, he insisted that pure morality stood outside these systems, and that rational beings stood in judgment over the different systems of morality derived from the world of pure reason.

Kant assumed that all rational beings agreed on morality if they used their rational ability correctly. In the end, Kant's assumption depended upon belief or faith, not on empirical data (Beck 1956, xv-xvii). A discussion of Kant's moral views, therefore, moved away from pure reason and into the realm of "pure practical reason." In his book, *Critique of Practical Reason*, he argued that practical reason alone provided what pure reason could not, the sole basis for moral conduct.

Critique of Practical Reason

In *Critique of Practical Reason* (1788), Kant lays out the definitive statement of his ethical theories. He attempts to set out an absolute ethic by pursuing moral principles that do not rest on the consequences of an action. He contends that we can come to know moral principles through *practical reason alone*. One should notice the importance of reason or rationality for Kant. Kant's major ethical doctrine derives from the notion of practical reason. Practical reason, for him, is the sole foundation for moral action.

Since we are rational beings and since moral laws are discoverable by means of practical reason, we find ourselves subject to various *moral duties or obligations*. What is a little strange is that for Kant the moral law is both beyond the individual but also within him or her. It is universal, but the person can discover it through reason so it is within us as well, which sets humans apart from other animals. It is part of what Kant calls *a priori* knowledge. This type of knowledge is independent of human experience (i.e., it does not come through our socialization), and it resides within each person (i.e., it is innate). In this way, the moral person is autonomous.

Autonomy comes from two Greek words: *autos* and *nómos*. *Autos* means self and *nómos* means law. Autonomy means the law of the self. For Kant, the autonomous individual is one who essentially determines for himself or herself what is moral by means of practical reason. Moreover, the autonomous individual has a moral duty, which he or she can discover through practical reason. In doing so, the autonomous individual is not following some external law, but acting upon a moral law within as well as without (i.e., the moral law). In effect, the autonomous individual who employs practical reason obeys commands that come from that individual. This situation is the same as obeying the moral law within. Therefore, practical reason is the tool for clarifying and defining our moral duty. This sort of knowledge allows moral reasoning to occur independently of any factual knowledge drawn from scientific or empirical data grounded in certain cause and effect relationships.

A priori knowledge makes it possible, therefore, for human beings to know or discover basic moral principles through practical reason alone. The basis of such knowledge is *necessity* and *universality*. For example, Kant acknowledges that the universal moral law requires pure motives and perfection from all rational beings. Since pure motives and perfection are not completely possible in the present life, there must be another life where such fulfillment is possible. So whereas pure reason cannot posit an afterlife or the existence of God, practical reason can by positing the *necessity* of such a belief of a life beyond.

It is possible, therefore, for human beings to have an *absolute type of knowledge*. As animals, human beings respond to impulses and desires in search of happiness. This natural aspect of human nature is not part of the moral philosophy that is based on *a priori* knowledge.[7] As a rational being, however, we find ourselves subject to the moral law since all rational beings possess a moral sense. As a result, we have an absolute and unconditional moral obligation (i.e., duty) to obey the moral law. He called this absolute and unconditional obligation the categorical imperative.

The categorical imperative says, "So act that the maxim [rule] of your will could always hold at the same time as a principle establishing universal law" (Kant 1956, 30-33).[8] This categorical imperative does not explain or describe; it exhorts and prescribes, and its judgments are verdicts. If I perform one act to get a certain result (hypothetical imperative), I might ask why I should want those results. Why should I want to go to college? Why do I want this particular job? For morals, however, Kant says that we need judgments of inherent worth. In this situation, *one ought to perform these actions just because they are right, and therefore it is one's duty to do them.* Therefore, the categorical imperative is unconditional, absolute, and binding on every rational creature. Because we are rational beings and because we all have a sort of moral sense, we find ourselves subject to a moral obligation, to a command. We have a duty, therefore, to obey this command.

In short, we can identify three simple steps required for the categorical imperative. First, we must formulate a rule. Second, the rule must be universal, which means there is no exception to the rule. Third, we must evaluate this rule to see if it can stand as a universal rule.

Kant gives several examples of how this categorical imperative works. In one of these examples, he addresses the issue of making a promise. He poses a situation where a certain individual asks to borrow money knowing that he or she cannot repay it. Yet, this person knows that no one will lend him or her money unless

> he gives a firm promise to pay it back within a fixed time. He is inclined to make such a promise; but he has still enough conscience to ask "Is it not unlawful and contrary to duty to get out of difficulties in this way?" Supposing, however, he did resolve to do so, the maxim of his action would thus run: "Whenever I believe myself short of money, I will borrow money and promise to pay it back, though I know that this will never be done." Now this principle of self-love or personal advantage is perhaps quite compatible with my own entire future welfare; only there remains the question "Is it right?" I therefore transform the demand of self-love into a universal law and frame my question thus: "How would things stand if my maxim became a universal law? I then see straight away that this maxim can never rank as a universal law of nature and be self-consistent, but must necessarily contradict itself. For the universality of a law that everyone believing himself to be in need can make any promise he pleases with the intention not to keep it would make promising, the very purpose of promising, itself impossible, since no one would believe he was being promised anything, but would laugh at utterances of this kind as empty shams" (Kant 1964, 89-90).

This quotation highlights two aspects of Kant's moral theory. First, he distinguishes between making a moral decision based on consequences and making decisions based on duty. We should act out of or for the sake of duty. I can rationally determine that I have a moral duty to help a person so I decide to act upon that duty. Therefore, I should act out of duty and not in *conformity with* duty. What is the difference?

Acting out of duty is acting after determining I have a duty to act. The other is imitation. Kant does not believe that true moral actions come because of one person following the example of another even if that person is Jesus. It is not enough just to imitate the example of Jesus. There should be self-determination of what my duty demands of me. Imitating another person's example of what is moral is not enough (Derrida 1995 8-11, 23, 140-141).[9] The autonomous self, however, has the moral law within. One has a moral duty to act from this moral law. The individual can determine his or her duty, command an action, and obey that command. This individual both commands and obeys his or her own command and in the process is acting "out of" duty.

Kant maintains that one should make decisions out of a sense of duty without consideration of the consequences of an act. Returning to his example of breaking a promise, the consequences may in fact be "quite compatible with my own entire future welfare." Yet the question of morality does not concern itself with consequences. Whether they are beneficial or not has no bearing on the issue of right or wrong. For Kant, a rational individual would conclude that if it is wrong for me to break a promise then it is wrong for anyone to do so. Kant would argue that rational creatures would agree that it is wrong for anyone to break a promise under any circumstances.

This basic moral principle, the categorical imperative, calls for one to act in a way that he or she could will his or her action to be a universal law. In other words, we would expect everyone to abide by the same rules that we find to be morally binding. For instance, if we think it is moral for us to cheat others out of money, we would have to think it is moral for them to cheat us. Universalizing the rule that it is morally acceptable to promise anything when in need with no intent of keeping the promise is inconsistent. Not many people would find this an acceptable moral rule. In essence, a person would be willing or desiring two contradictory things. We want to be able to make promises, and we desire that others keep their promises. At the same time, however, we would want people to be free to break their promises when it is desirable for them to do so (Frankena 1973, 31). The issue is not about the consequences of breaking promises, but that breaking a promise could not work as a universal law.

However, certain situations may call Kant's categorical imperative into question. Consider the following example. A young woman has a bad accident, which paralyzes her from the waist down. She is athletic and enjoys all sorts of sports. She has undergone psychological and religious counseling. After a year of agonizing, she decides that she wishes to end her life. This decision has not been a hasty one, and she has set out her reasons for making the decision. She is of clear and sound mind. If someone asks her if she could will her act for anyone in a similar situation, she replies yes without hesitation. This situation just points out that Kant's assumption that all rational beings will agree is questionable. One might even contend that there are times and situations when stealing and breaking promises are necessary. His categorical imperative is not an absolute in the sense that every rational person will agree on a course of action. There are exceptions to every rule.

Not even the Judeo-Christian Scripture is as absolute about morals. There is a story in the Bible where a harlot receives praise for acting dishonestly (e.g., Hebrews 11:31). In the biblical story about a harlot named Rahab (Joshua 2:1-7; 14; 18), Joshua sends spies to see if the ancient Israelites can take the so-called "promised land." They come to the city of Jericho where Rahab the harlot shows them hospitality and hides them from the king. While there, the king hears that two spies are at Rahab's house. Upon hearing this, he sends his men to her house to capture the spies. When the king's men ask Rahab where the spies are, her reply is that the men have already left. In truth, she is hiding them. In compensation for her assistance, the ancient Israelites do not harm Rahab or her family when they destroyed the city of Jericho. Moreover, in the New Testament, the book of Hebrews lists Rahab as one of the heroes of faith. Was she wrong to lie?

To reiterate, Kant believes that practical reason alone can supply the *moral law*. This moral law is absolute and universal (i.e., binding on all rational beings). There are no exceptions. So, on what basis should we act if our acts are to have moral worth? This question brings us to Kant's discussion of the good will.

The Good Will and Moral Worth

Regarding the good will, Kant says, "It is impossible to conceive anything at all in the world, or even out of it, which can be taken as good, without qualification, except a *good will*" (Kant 1964, 61-69). By good will, Kant means the human capacity to act freely from principle. Everything else except for the good will can serve as an instrument for good and bad. For instance, one can employ power, wealth, happiness, or wisdom for either good or bad purposes. The good will makes itself known by acting out of a sense of duty, and it is from this sense of duty that *moral worth* emerges. Reason or rationality must be involved in determining what we do. I determine A is my duty. My conclusion derives from an act of reasoning about what the moral law within me demands.

For Kant, an act only has *moral worth* when one does it out of a sense of duty, *because the moral law requires it*. Motive or intention is the most important thing for Kant. Actions motivated by compassion, sympathy, or some other emotion have no moral worth. One may act out of duty and at the same time be sympathetic or compassionate toward the other, but duty has to be the motivating reason for action if the act is to have moral worth (Kant 1964, 65-67).

One's motives, therefore, are an important aspect of Kant's ethic. Kant, therefore, emphasizes what one ought to do. This perspective is primary in Kant's ethic. On his account, one could do a good thing such as give aid to poor people. If, however, one gives to the poor out of sympathy for their plight, then this act would have no moral worth because it derives from the wrong motive. Such an act may have good consequences, but unless one does it out of duty, it has no moral worth.

Humanity as an End, and Never as a Means Only

Kant's principle of the treating others and oneself as an ends is an important aspect of his ethics. He says, "Act in such a way that you always treat humanity, whether in your own person or in the person of any other, never simply as a means, but always at the same time as an end" (Kant 1964, 96). Kant goes on to say this principle has two aspects. First, one should treat oneself as an end and not as a means to an end. Second, one must treat others as an end and not as a means to something else. Therefore, a person has a moral duty to himself or herself as well as to others. The duty is to treat ourselves and others as an end and not as a means to something else.

Regarding the treating of oneself as an end and not as a means to an end, he uses the example of suicide. Kant considers suicide from the angle of his categorical imperative as well as from the perspective of the ends.[10] Only the latter aspect concerns us in this context. Kant regards suicide as an act where one is treating one's self as a means to something else. One is trying to escape suffering or some intolerable condition. Since a person is not a thing, he or she should not use himself or herself as a means of escaping some undesirable situation. Such an escape would amount to using one's own body as a means of rewarding our own proclivities. Morality for Kant is not about obtaining our own happiness. We should "seek our own perfection" (Paton 1964, 34). Kant does not elaborate further on this point. He leaves it to the study of morals to define this principle further in relation to such problems as the amputation of a limb to save one's life (Kant 1964, 96-97).

On the other hand, some individuals may believe that in certain situations they are not treating themselves as means to an end by the act of taking their own life. Their conclusion does not necessarily mean they are irrational. It may be that they just begin the reasoning process with a different set of values and presuppositions.

The second aspect of this principle of not using one as a means to an end relates to how we treat others. One should treat other persons or rational agents as an end and not as a means to an end. What is the difference? Consider again the act of making a promise. To ask for money and promise to repay it without any intention of doing so is to use another person for one's own selfish gain. Using one as a means to an end in this context just indicates that one did not consider the other person. He or she was just a means of gaining money. The other person was an object or thing one uses. In breaking a promise, Kant says that the "person whom I seek to use for my own purposes by such a promise cannot possibly agree with my way of behaving to him" (Kant 1964, 97). In short, Kant is saying we have a moral obligation to treat other *rational beings* as we expect others to treat us.

This principle addresses many different circumstances from everyday social interactions to more extreme situations. Most people spend much of their day interacting with others. Many situations occur when one individual can use another for personal gain. Companies or individuals may sell products that they know to be dangerous or unsafe just to make a profit. An individual may attempt to hide the flaws of a car to sell the car at a price in excess of what the car is worth. On a criminal level, many individuals treat other individuals as objects to be exploited. Some individuals kill another person for the money they possess. Date rape consists of one party ignoring the wishes of another to gain pleasure at another person's expense. Abuse of children and spouses is treating a person as an object and not an end. Treating people as a means to an end is simply using another person for our own purposes without consideration of the other person's dignity, needs, or feelings.

It is true that all of us to some extent use other people. A married couple may use each other to satisfy certain desires or needs. In some cases, two friends may depend on each other for any number of reasons. Kant, however, is referring to situations where one person uses another without regard for the other's welfare. It is a situation where there is no concern for the feelings of the other party. In such instances, the individual who is using another person would likely feel abused if the other person treated them in the same way. Using people for selfish gain takes place in all areas of life. His views are similar to the Golden Rule. This principle is a helpful tool that can serve as a guide for human action toward others. Yet, we may not all agree upon what it means to use ourselves or other persons as means or what is actually involved in treating ourselves or others as an end.

Kant's View of Autonomy

Before concluding our discussion of Kant's moral theory, we need to say a little more about autonomy. We have touched on this already. Autonomy simply means that one governs his or her own actions. According to Kant, *all rational beings* can regard themselves as author or maker of the moral law (Kant 1964, 98-99). The individual should not follow external or outside laws, which would be *heteronomy*. *Heteronomy* also comes from two Greek words meaning the law of the other. The key to Kant's view of autonomy is that we are rational beings, and as such, we only make laws that are universal and unconditional in nature. The moral law that is within the rational individual is, therefore, absolute and universal. The moral law is assessable through reason. In short, the command is categorical. Still, the autonomous self is free, since he or she makes the moral law and freely decides to follow or not follow it (Kant 1964, 97-98).

Critical Concerns

Some may say that Kant's theory has the value of giving us a clear sense of right and wrong. His view of treating others as an end is in my view helpful. Yet there are at least three problems with his theory. First, we might question his view of moral worth. According to Kant, only an action motivated by a sense of duty has moral worth. If an individual performs a good act for any motive other than doing his or her duty, the act has no moral worth. If one acts out of sympathy, it may produce good results, but Kant does not believe the act has any moral merit. If I see famine victims in some third world country, and I reason that I have a duty to help, my act, according to Kant, has a moral quality because its primary motivation derives from a sense of duty. However, one could legitimately contend that an individual who possesses a "strong sense of human sympathy is superior to someone who acts solely out of an abstract sense of duty" (Shaw 1993, 26).[11]

A second criticism concerns the categorical imperative. Is it an adequate test of right? Kant says that a rule should function *without exception*. Yet, why is this so?

> Suppose, for example, we decided that stealing is sometimes right, perhaps in the case of a person who is starving and our maxim becomes "Never steal except when starving." This rule seems just as universalizable as "never steal." The phrase "except ..." can be viewed not as justifying a violation of the rule but as building a qualification into it. Critics in effect are asking why a qualified rule is not just as good as an unqualified one (Shaw 1993, 26-27).

Going further, I would question the wisdom of universal rules altogether. Rules are simply not sufficient. They may give comfort by telling us that we have done our duty or that we have done what the rule requires, but that may often fail to quell the feeling that we should have done more or that we went too far in intruding on the other. In short, some would question the desirability of basing ethics on rules. Moreover, there are justifiable doubts about assuming we can develop rules or standards that are universal in nature.

A third difficulty involves his assumption that all rational beings can agree on what is right and wrong. This assumption is untenable. Consider the issue of suicide. One could be suffering great pain and wish to commit suicide. Furthermore, this individual may be willing to universalize his or her decision to say that when anyone is suffering as I am suffering, then they should take their own life. This decision seems rational. Yet, Kant would say that suicide is always wrong. Kant's argument on suicide derives its force as much from religious presuppositions as it does from reason.[12] Does rationality ensure agreement on moral issues?

CULTURAL AND ETHICAL RELATIVISM

Relativism is the completely different from Kant's ethical views as well as those of the consequentialist perspectives. In modern thought, a relativistic view has played a significant role in the social sciences. In chapter seven, I discuss the work of Durkheim who held a relativistic view on morality. In essence, modern cultural relativism notes how values differ from region to region and over time. One only has to compare and observe the changes in the nature of TV shows from the 1960's with present shows to see the difference. Similarly, one can compare the change in family life over time. In looking at the differences, it is clear that morals change, and there is in fact a wide diversity of moral values in today's societies.

Not only is time a factor but also space. Comparing the morals of people who are living far away from one another often reveals they have different values. People living in large urban areas, for example, may have values different from those living in rural areas. In recent presidential elections, one can see a significant difference in voting preferences in different parts of the country, which also reflects differences in values.

Observations about the diversity of these values have led many cultural anthropologists and moral philosophers to advocate tolerance and respect for the values of other cultures. Such anthropologists and philosophers discourage passing judgment on the values of other cultures. This view is at odds with those philosophers who seek universal set of moral principles that are the same over time and in all locations. Such philosophers cannot deny that there are differences over time and space. All the same, they believe there is only one set of moral principles, and these principles allow one to judge the values of different peoples at different times and places. Relativists, on the other hand, reject such universals.

There are two types of relativism: cultural and ethical relativism. Cultural relativism is not really an ethical theory; it simply recognizes diversity and encourages social scientists such as anthropologists not to judge one culture by the standards of another. Cultural anthropologists who hold this view encourage us not to interfere in the normal development of societies. This sort of relativism would fit into the general category known as cultural relativism. According to anthropologist Franz Boas, one can only judge another culture by its own standards and rules, but not by outside standards (Garbarino 1977, 47-50).

Moreover, cultural relativism says that all values are relative to a given society, and it denies universal standards. It does not necessarily have to deny that some values are better than others. For example, Boas and his followers made a value judgment when they "decried the use of words like 'primitive' because they saw such terms as pejorative. Instead of primitive, for example, they suggested 'nonliterate'" (Garbarino 1977, 50). Cultural relativism tolerates differences, and it values diversity. It says that we should be tolerant of other people's beliefs. Tolerance becomes the supreme value. Nevertheless, it does not have tolerance for those who try to interfere in the normal cultural development of a society.

Sumner sets out many of the ideas involved in cultural relativism. He discusses how habits rise to the level of rules. These rules are what Sumner calls *folkways*. Folkways vary from society to society because different societies have different needs (Sumner 1975, 82-88). Folkways (i.e., rules) over time may become *mores*. This transformation occurs when a group further develops them into doctrines of human welfare based on the notions of truth and right. From this perspective, a culture's moral values are right if they satisfy a society's needs. The assessment of moral values from this perspective, therefore, is pragmatic. This position does not accept the view of universal right or wrong. The notion of right and wrong is pragmatic; an act is right if it meets the needs of a given society.

Ethical relativism, on the other hand, not only recognizes that rules and customs differ from culture to culture, but it also maintains that judgments concerning what is right and wrong *depends upon* the society to which one belongs. The individual, therefore, has a *moral obligation* to obey the rules of his or her own society or culture. It also says that one should not judge the moral values of other societies as wrong. Whatever a society deems to be correct is correct for that society, and the members of that society have a *moral obligation* to adhere to these morals. From this point of view, there are no absolutes; morality depends upon what a society says is moral, and what society expects from its members. In ethical relativism, however, one has an ethical or moral obligation to obey the rules of the particular society in which he or she lives.

Strengths of Cultural and Ethical Relativism

There is some real value in *cultural relativism*. This approach certainly encourages tolerance of other cultures. If we began with an attitude of tolerance, we might understand the differences rather than judging them. Most of us need to be more tolerant of other views and perspectives. It also stresses the pragmatic view of moral values. Values should work in a particular society to make life better. As societies change, new values tend to displace older ones in a slow evolutionary process that makes society more adaptive.

Furthermore, it implies that outsiders cannot know what is best for another culture. In some instances, our value system may help increase the quality of life for other people, but not always. Some non-Westerners have judged our value system as empty. To some extent, we have to allow other cultures to find their own way. It is debatable whether one society ever has the right to intervene in the affairs of another society.

Ethical relativism also has a positive element. It promotes the view that one should obey and respect the rules or laws of the society in which one lives. Both cultural and ethical relativists serve to caution us about passing uninformed judgments on others since it does not accept the notion of ethical progress in the sense of evolving to some ultimate right view. It does see the necessity for evolutionary or slow adaptive change. While they may accept natural or evolutionary changes in societies, they would not necessarily have to judge these changes as better or worse in an ultimate or unconditional sense. Some relativists may try to guide slow adaptive change to improve or keep society functioning smoothly.

This last view is positive and negative. Negatively, it discourages one from trying to change society. Positively, however, it cautions us about passing judgment on past moralities. Our moral values are not automatically better than those of ancient people just because we come after them historically. In addition, our views of truth and morality are in a constant state of change. Our view is just one view in an endless succession.

In addition, this view seems to form some absolute or universal principle of non-interference. Ethical relativism undermines any moral criticism of a society's practices as long as their actions conform to their own standards. From the perspective of ethical relativism, one cannot say that slavery in a slave society is wrong as long as that society deems slavery morally permissible. Moreover, who could take such a neutral view toward the Holocaust? While ethical relativism may work in some cases, it is unsatisfactory as absolute principle. Ethical relativism only secures the position of the status quo. Racism or sexual inequality might be permissible if the majority of people in a given society share these views. Ethical relativism does not really offer an individual or minority any basis for fighting against an unjust societal system. Since one should abide by the rules and customs of his or her own society, reform makes little or no sense. If a society accepts a certain practice as valid, then it is valid. Change may occur naturally, but one should not interfere with the normal course of societal development.

I agree with the cultural relativists that we should be tolerant. Being tolerant, however, does not restrain or stop a person from opposing things that he or she considers immoral. Tolerance in a positive sense does not mean that we have to accept passively the other person's values and beliefs. One may even be doing another person or a group a disservice by not taking issue with them on certain issues. Tolerance is an attitude of respect and a willingness to accept those with whom one differs. It does not mean that two parties cannot disagree with each other and discuss those disagreements. It means listening, hearing, and expressing.

Take for instance the following hypothetical situation. Fred is a faithful member of the First Methodist Church in Clarksville, Texas. He often finds himself disagreeing with other church members regarding the interpretation of certain biblical passages. He maintains openness to their views, and he affirms their right to interpret the Bible even though their interpretation disagrees with his own. Fred can tolerate most differences of belief unless they violate certain deeply held principles. Therefore, Fred feels that at some point he must voice his opposition. His love for these people may require him to stand in opposition to their views. Not many people would really adopt the view that we should passively tolerate all actions and beliefs when they violate our own conscience. There are positive means of disagreeing, and there are ways of disagreeing that can have positive results as well.

CONCLUSION

This chapter has discussed consequentialist and nonconsequentialist ethical theories along with relativist ones. Modern ethics of a secular nature attempt to produce ethics that tell one what to do in any given situation. Consequentialist and nonconsequentialist ethics maintain the view that knowledge and ethics must be built upon strong foundations. Both types of theories see their ethical philosophy as providing guidance that is universal and tells us exactly what is required from us. Relativism, particularly ethical relativism, while recognizing the need for tolerance and recognizing diversity, calls for adherence to moral rules of the culture to which a person belongs. It does not recognize universal standards of moral behavior or a universal ethic built on a strong foundation.

In the next chapter, we begin to see cracks in the foundation built on modern thought. We begin with a comparison between modern and postmodern thought. Our main figure in this discussion is philosopher Friedrich Nietzsche who has become increasingly popular. His work has influenced existentialism, and especially postmodern moral thinking.

NOTES

1. It is interesting that another English naturalist, Alfred R. Wallace, after reading Thomas Malthus' *Essays on Population*, came up with evolutionary views very similar to those of Darwin. Darwin says, "I never saw a more striking coincidence" (T. Walter Wallbank, Alastair M. Taylor, and Nels M. Bailkey 1976, 271).

2. For more detail, see chapter two for the discussion of Milgram's experiment.

3. Lukes takes this definition from the *Oxford English Dictionary* (Lukes 1985, 1).

4. Heilbroner is quoting a passage from Smith's book the *Wealth of Nations*.

5. Also, see Alasdair MacIntyre 1966, 195.

6. *A priori* knowledge refers to knowledge that is independent of experience. This type knowledge can be of two kinds. It may apply to the ordering of information taken in by the senses or to innate or intuitive knowledge, which is self-evident and *can be validated by reason.*

7. What Kant is doing is dividing the human person. As animals, we are socialized. We are affected by cause and effect. Our actions fit with the hypothetical imperative. I do A to get a certain result. I obey my teacher to avoid punishment. The moral life, however, is governed by the moral law.

8. Another translation of this imperative is as follows: "So act that the rule on which thou actest would admit of being adopted as a law by all rational beings." This translation of the categorical imperative comes from John Staurt Mill. See John Staurt Mill 1957, 6. Another common translation reads, "So act that you can will the maxim of your conduct to be a universal law."

9. Derrida's discussion of duty is in relation to the notion of responsibility (1-31).

10. Concerning the categorical imperative, see Kant 1964, 89. Also, see Robert B. Brandt's rejection of Kant's reasoning in Brandt's 1993, 94.

11. Also, see Noddings 1984.

12. See Brandt 1993, 93-94.

Chapter Six

Cracking Foundations: A Shift to Non-Foundational Morals

We do not, after all, know who we are. Questio mihi factus sum. A bishop said that. That is not the metaphysical foundation of a new morals but the lack of foundation which inspires trepidation about all of our schemes and compassion for all of us who must in any case take action (Caputo 1987, 259).

Before getting to postmodern thought, we need to distinguish between modern and postmodern moral thinking. By modern moral thinking, I am referring to ethics based on Enlightenment principles stressing *Reason, Truth,* and *Objectivity.* As we can see from the previous chapter, modern moral theories set out to provide rules or guidelines for determining right and wrong. Both consequentialist and nonconsequentialist ethical views depend on rationality.

Much of this thought goes back to the influence of the Greek philosophers. Modern thought seeks the proper foundation upon which to build secure knowledge. Feelings and emotions cannot guide us. Only reason and experience can guide us to a secure foundation for thought. There are rationalists who only stress reason as the way to truth and secure knowledge. Empirical thinkers, on the other hand, stress reason and experience.

Postmodern moral thinking stresses the limitations of human reason and objectivity as a tool for obtaining truth. Deontological or nonconsequentialist ethics as well as consequentialist ethical theories belong to the modern Enlightenment approach. Nietzsche's work, however, paves the way for a postmodern moral thinking. The postmodern perspective is quite different from the modern one. Postmodern thinking calls modern theories of knowledge and ethics into question. It does not accept the argument that humans can discover a timeless and universal truth through reason and experience.

RATIONALISM: RENÉ DESCARTES (1596-1650)

We begin with the work of René Descartes. Descartes is a soldier, mathematician, philosopher, and scientist. He enjoys adventure and is a person who loves his privacy. Descartes' method for establishing truth, known as the *Cartesian method*, is dualistic. The mind, one part of this dualism, is capable of discovering truth. The body, the second part of the dualism, includes one's feelings and emotions, which are not able to lead one to truth. While one can trust the former, he or she cannot trust the later. Descartes decides that he would begin his search for certainty by doubting everything and see where that would take him. Through this process, he comes to believe that the only thing he could know with certainty is that there is a subject, an ego or "I" who can doubt in the first place. For there to be doubt, there must be someone to do the doubting. This revelation leads him to his first principle. This first principle could guide him to absolute certainty, a principle that would make it possible for one to derive additional knowledge. The principle is *cogito, ergo sum* (I think, therefore I am).

Descartes says that we can be certain about the existence of our minds, which means that certain knowledge is at least possible. Moreover, this conclusion entices him to distinguish sharply between mind and matter, which precisely divides human beings into minds and bodies. The mind is capable of coming to know with certainty what is true. The body is separate, and it is the place for feeling and emotion, which cannot lead to certain knowledge.

This rationalistic approach is one main stream of Enlightenment thought. The other is empiricism, the discovery of truth through experience. The empiricists see objects as having a reality apart from the mind. Plato and Descartes believe that the mind contains certain knowledge; this knowledge is innate. In other words, this knowledge is not learned; we are born with it. According to Plato or Descartes, we know what an object is such as a cat because the concept is part of the human mind at birth. This would allow for perfect and universal knowledge.

The empiricist, however, says that we come to know objects through sense or personal experiences. Experience is necessary for human development and knowledge. We must learn what a cat is since we are not born with the knowledge. John Locke in the seventeenth century argues that the mind is a blank tablet or "white paper void of all characters" (i.e., *tabula rasa*). Upon this blank paper, experiences leave their marks (Locke 1975, 242-251).

Rationalists like Descartes, however, separate reason and experience. For Descartes reason is part of the mind and experience is from the body. As a result, experience is untrustworthy as a means to gaining knowledge about the real world. Descartes sees the world as a creation of a divine mind. God creates the world, and it is orderly in that it works like a machine. It is orderly and predictable. To gain secure knowledge, one has to pursue knowledge in an objective fashion.

The uncertainty of Descartes' times caused the need for such a view. He sought to fight against a growing skepticism. This skepticism came in part after the people in France had gone from a sense of hope to despair. Politically, the people had thought that Henry IV of Navarre was going to end the European wars and bring peace to France. However, he was assassinated before this could occur. This assassination dashed the people's hopes. It pushed Descartes and his entire generation into disorder where chaos became the social reality. According to Walter Brueggemann, Descartes' attempt to gain certainty came out of this disillusionment; it was his response to an approaching chaotic situation (Brueggemann 1993, 3).[1]

On Descartes' view, the *self* (i.e., ego, I, subject, or mind) is capable of being completely objective; this rational self can remain detached, disembodied, and separate from the body with all its emotional baggage. Furthermore, this self/mind can refrain from any kind of personal involvement or attachment with others. Because it can avoid personal involvement or attachment, it can be completely objective, disinterested, and neutral. This self/mind has no reference outside itself. The mind can be completely shut off from the outside material world including the world of experience. The mind is not affected by the social environment. In short, the isolated self is unaffected by social and personal ties. On this view, what we continuously learn from our social environment does not affect how we reason or see the world; it does not affect the mind. This so-called "interiority" allowed the self to create its own certitude. The mind or self, therefore, is the "absolute point of reference" (Brueggemann 1993, 4).

The outcomes of this perspective allow for

- A new model of knowledge grounded in objectivity, which produces a new epistemological security.
- The pursuit of reason, which would be free from personal prejudices or biases. This pursuit meant that one had to escape from all forms of body (i.e., emotions and feelings that are opposed to reason and objectivity) into the purity of the mind.
- The body and earth as the producers of life were seen as peculiarly feminine and material. [This view reflects] the Cartesian masculinization of thought and the flight from the feminine. In this way, the feminine and material were subordinate to the mind, which was capable of rising above the material world (Brueggemann 1993, 4).[2]

Therefore, Descartes' division of the mind and body leads to the elevation of reason above all else. This view ignores or denies how personal motives and personal experiences affect any human endeavor. He does not consider that decisions based on calculations or statistical models conceal deeper motives, commitments, or beliefs that are far from value free. Descartes' perspective requires one to remain skeptical about anything that comes through the human senses or through human feeling or emotion. In practical reality, however, one cannot make an easy mind/body distinction.

The modern perspective based on Descartes' thought only allowed certain types of knowledge. Modernity represented a movement away from the chaos that threatened Descartes' world. On the modern rationalistic view, real knowledge came when there was

- a move from particular to the *universal*, so that real truth is what is true everywhere;
- a move from local to *general*, so that real truth had to be the same from locale to locale;
- and a move from the timely to the timeless, so that the real is the unchanging.
- So, real knowledge is [from the modern perspective] . . . universal, general, and timeless (Brueggemann 1993, 5).

In short, human knowledge has to transcend all boundaries; it must transcend the single individual (i.e., particularity) and apply to everyone (i.e., universality). It has to operate the same in every location and remain immune from the change associated with changing times. In a world based upon these sorts of notions, there was a sense of unity, security and certainty (Brueggemann 1993, 5). Western civilization places a great deal of faith in this belief. However, is this faith well founded?

Regarding morality, the modern perspective attempts to make rules or give specific guidelines for making moral judgments. There are methods that when one applies them properly lead to moral action. For the utilitarians, it consists of determining which acts produce consequences that benefit the most people. Kant's ethic, on the other hand, assumes that it is possible for all rational beings to agree upon moral judgments. Both modern views contend that one can rise above his or her social environment and personal prejudices to make objective judgments based on a particular approach.

As we saw in the last chapter, Marx stood in this modern tradition. Marx and Engels were unrelenting in their critique of capitalism. They provided a grand narrative, which showed how those who were in power used a certain set of ideas (i.e., ideology) to keep the powerless in their places. Therefore, he demonstrated how a person or group perverted *reason and used* it to support the prevailing power structures. Ideology tended to delude people, and it kept people from knowing what was truly in their best interest. Marx, however, thought he could remain relatively unaffected by this ideology. The truth for Marx was that the ideal society would eventually come on the scene because capitalism would eventually fail. The Marxist's task was to enlighten people and convince them to join those who shared their interests. When this occurred, there would be a revolution, and an ideal society could emerge. In essence, then, his view was a very modern one. The goal or movement of history was toward a classless society. His theory described how this revolution would come about.

The Frankfurt School, sometimes referred to as "Critical Theory," represents a step away from the modern tradition. Marx greatly influences this school of thought. Unlike Marx, however, these thinkers concede that it is impossible for anyone to be totally objective. They also contend that intellectuals should not hide behind claims of being objective. They do not attempt to distinguish between fact and value in their work. Their values fuel their work. They vow to take a "critical attitude" toward society. This particular view is a dividing point between the Frankfurt School and analytical conflict theory (Wallace and Wolf 1986, 98). The views of Theodor Adorno, a leading member of the Frankfurt School, anticipate many of the motifs found in postmodern theory (Best and Kellner 1991, 225-233).

Nevertheless, the critical theorists did not break from the Enlightenment or modern view altogether. They agreed there was truth and knowledge. They believed that their way of studying society brought them closer to truth and objectivity than other methods (Wallace and Wolf 1986, 99). Their attitudes placed them squarely in the modern tradition. At the same time, it was a step toward a postmodern perspective, which also rejects one's ability to be neutral and objective.

A TURN TOWARD A MORE POSTMODERN VIEW OF MORALITY

Defining postmodernism is a rather difficult task. It may be easier to offer a description of certain key ideas. In one sense, postmodernism is a rejection of the modern views given above. It rejects the notion that the self or mind can detach itself from the body, which includes its social environment and its prejudices. It rejects the mind/body dualism altogether. It rejects any notion of one's ability to be neutral or completely objective. It also stresses individual differences or particularism. We are not all the same. Everyone is unique in one way or another, but we are also products of our society or environment.

For example, in some postmodern thought, literary critics no longer view literary works as a complete and total creation of an author. The death of the author means that the individual who writes the words is not a creator, as the term "author" has traditionally been understood. The author is deeply shaped by the environment, language, culture, and society so that he or she is not an originator in the sense of creating something entirely new and unique. Various forces work through the author. The author's own experiences are varied. Just as no two people have the exact fingerprints, no two people have exactly the same life experiences. Our life experiences have a part in making us who we are. Postmodernism places a value on plurality and diversity. In that sense, it has a relativistic element. If knowledge is universal, general, and timeless in modern thought, it is largely the opposite in postmodern thought. In postmodernism, knowledge is particular, local, and timely.

Nietzsche challenges the modern perspective. One important aspect of the modern perspective is its reliance on a representational model of reality. Nietzsche calls this model into doubt. The representational model of knowledge refers to the view that I am potentially capable of conveying things as they truly are through reason and rationality. The philosopher, for example, can tell us about the views of Plato. He or she can potentially make Plato's views present to us. That is, he or she can make Plato stand before us with his or her presentation of his thought and convey to us exactly what he means. It would be the definitive word on Plato. The philosopher who becomes detached, neutral, and objective recedes from the foreground and Plato speaks directly through the philosopher. It is Plato as he truly is without the bias or subjectivity of the philosopher. Nietzsche's critique of this view has greatly influenced postmodern thinking.

The representational model goes back to the notion that the mind can accurately reflect the world of objects. The mind of the historian can accurately reconstruct the world of fifth century Greece if there is enough information. Alternatively, the interpreter can accurately provide the meaning of a text if he or she does the job right. Accurate knowledge and representation can make things real or present to us. Nietzsche's critique of this view has two different elements or themes. First, it is

> an attack on realist theories that claims subjects can accurately reflect or represent the world in thought without the mediations of culture, language, and physiology. . . . The first theme assails the *subject-object distinction of modern epistemology where a neutral and objective world is mirrored in the receptive mind of a passive subject* [italics mine] (Best and Kellner 1991, 83).

The second element of Nietzsche's critique concerns the modern tendency to elevate mind over body. Nietzsche counters that we need a "*Lebensphilosophie* [philosophy of life] which privileges the body and its forces, desires, and will over conscious existence and representational schemes" (Best and Kellner 1991, 83). Regarding this theme, postmodern thinkers have followed Nietzsche in denying the mind's ability to represent accurately objects in nature. All we can do is to re-present objects. This re-presenting means that our presentations are not accurate reflections of things in themselves or as things really are. We cannot know things properly and completely through the mind. We know "things" as they are re-presented. In other words, everything we know is mediated or comes through various subjective experiences.

Postmodernism tends to reject the representational model due to its overemphasis on the mind and its neglect of the body. Therefore, postmodern views go on to argue that the "perception of the world is mediated through discourse [i.e., language] written and oral and a socially constructed subjectivity" (Best and Kellner 1991, 83). The key word here is mediated. The word mediated means that our views are the result of a process. We have all kinds of personal and professional experiences that help us to understand the world. Some of the experiences are informal experiences and others formal. Education may come in a formal setting and may shape the way we understand and give meaning to events. Culture and language provide us with the tools for forming views and understandings, but these views are specific to the time and place in which one lives. Our views and our re-presentations of objects are mediated through our culture and language. In short, there is something of us, our culture and manner of speaking and thinking in every re-presentation.

However, it is more than just our social history that influences how we see and understand the world and how we communicate our views of it. How we think and reason is conditioned by the language or discourse of our time. Human language is not the sole product of the individual, but it is connected to the world we live in. The language or discourse we use restricts how we see and understand our world. We can only understand things from the perspective of people living in the late twentieth century in a particular social context. When we observe bizarre human behavior, we think of a mental illness rather than demon possession. We do so because demon possession is no longer a generally acceptable way of describing or understanding behavior, which we perceive to be abnormal. Moreover, if we could travel back in time 100 years, we could not fully understand what is happening. We might understand the words but not necessarily know how to interpret them. Mediation is about making sense of things or interpreting things based on what we know.

What is in question here is the uncritical faith that some people put in the representational model of reality. These thinkers believe that *theory* actually mirrors or reflects reality. Postmodern perspectives reject such assertions. Does this mean that such theories are useless? It would be more accurate to say that models and theories are helpful only insofar as they provide a partial understanding of any given object. In other words, they are heuristic in that they serve as aids to help us understand things at some level. Theories help us to imagine how things might be, not necessarily how they really are. As a result, some postmodern thinkers take a perspectivist position. "Perspectivism" says that theories only provide limited perspectives on objects. As a result, all conscious "representations of the world are historically and linguistically mediated" (Best and Kellner 1991, 4).

So not only do these representational models assume that theories can mirror reality, they assume that *subjects* can study *objects* in an objective manner. Again, it seeks *unmediated* or neutral knowledge, knowledge not connected or mediated through culture and language. A subject, according to Nietzsche, is just a "product of language and thought" (Best and Kellner 1991, 22).[3] Nietzsche's view on "the subject" is quite different than those of Descartes. The subject or self, according to Descartes, is the "I" or the ego or mind. The "I" or ego refers to something real, stable, capable of being isolated and neutral, and capable of thinking. Yet is it? Nietzsche posits the self or subject as a fiction of language. It is not a stable, unified identity. The "I" or subject is a construct of human language, a part of grammar that makes thought possible.

Take for example the scientist. What is the scientist? What is the essence of a scientist? What makes a scientist a scientist? A scientist refers to what people think of when they encounter the word (i.e., the signifier) "scientist."[4] When a person thinks of a scientist, he or she has a mental image of a particular type of individual who performs a particular function. Even though my image of a scientist may be similar to another person's image, it is not necessarily identical.

How do I come by my understanding of who a scientist is? There is no completely stable and fixed concept of what a scientist is. It is an agreed upon concept. It is not a concept present in the human mind from the start; it is a convention dependent upon personal experience, culture, and social learning. Definitions of a scientist describe characteristics or expectations associated with people who work in a particular field of study. According to our everyday view, we assume that our understanding of who a scientist is corresponds to something real. Yet one could say that such subjects are fictions, products of language and thought. Our personal identities, therefore, are not stable and fixed. Subjects are always in process; a subject's identify is not fixed but changes. The "I" of today will not be the exact "I" of a year from now and there is no certainty that the scientist of today will be the same as the scientists of the future.

In addition, the modern view assumes that so-called subjects can come to know what is real and true. An ethicist is one who studies the field of morals. He or she seeks to establish moral rules that depend on certain abstract principles. The representational model, therefore, involves the creation of subjects and objects. Both are part of the language we use. Modern views suggest that the subject can view the object in an objective fashion thus arriving at the truth. This truth is true for everyone and for all times. By this definition, it is universal and timeless.

However, postmodernism rejects this view. Subjects are not passive but active, and this activeness affects how the subject relates to and makes sense of the object of study. Subjects or human beings are not neutral but have preferences and biases that inevitably influence their thinking either consciously or subconsciously. All disciplines work based on certain presuppositions. Therefore, the subject can only be more or less objective. The most objective disciplines such as the scientific disciplines derive from certain presuppositions about the world. Sciences, philosophy, history, and ethics derive from the desire or "will to truth," which itself derives from the presupposition that there is a truth to discover. According to this view, there is an end, a goal to all things that one can discover through one or another means (Nietzsche 1994, 125-128; Scott 1990, 25-39).

Yet, truth is always elusive, and our view of truth is always changing. Even though it may seem unthinkable, some cultures base their worldview on something other than truth. Michel Foucault says that Greek society as depicted by Homer does not seek the "will to truth." Homer's society relies on rituals. Ritual, not truth, is the way one is to react to the world and shape it (Collins and Makowsky 1989, 248-250).

As far as objectivity goes, we can take the historian, the interpreter, and the ethicist as examples of how the subject or individual relates to the object he or she is attempting to study. Historians must be selective in the sources they use for information, and frequently they do not have enough information to write an adequate history. The historian may have access to stories and information, but this information is likely biased. The historian can only try to be as objective as humanly possible. Furthermore, history has to do with interpretation of sources, and historians bring different values and views to their discipline, which may affect their selection of sources and their interpretations.

Likewise, interpretation, which is a universal activity in daily life, must make sense of oral and written communications. The interpreter can only try to be objective. In the area of literature, interpreters disagree over where to locate the meaning of a text. Different proposals locate meaning in the author's intentions, the text itself, the reader, or a combination of the reader and the text.

While there are merits to all these approaches, the last one portrays the reader as an active force in creating a text's meaning. Therefore, interpretation is never free of personal bias.

What does all this have to do with morals? The answer is everything because the ethicist is in exactly the same situation as the historian or interpreter. A person's value system has a great deal to do with his or her particular situation in life. Why would someone born and raised in the ghetto view morality differently from a person who has lived a life of nobility? Even two people educated in the same university by the same professors would not have the same views. They would still be shaped by their life experiences, and this would prevent them from viewing things in an identical fashion. My moral views are mediated through culture and language like everything else. The representational model as a method or path to certain truth, therefore, is insufficient in that capacity.

As a result, Nietzsche and postmodern thinkers reject this representational view of reality. In its place, Nietzsche advocates a perspectivist position. This view indicates, "There are no facts, only interpretations, and no objective truths, only the constructs of various individuals or groups" (Best and Kellner 1991, 22). One might conclude from this statement that Nietzsche is a relativist. Yet, he definitely believes that some views are better than others, and certain types of persons are preferable to others.

Concerning moral values, Nietzsche identifies a number of different perspectives: psychological, physiological, historical, philosophical, and linguistic. In his book, *On the Genealogy of Morality*, he considers each one of these perspectives as important. In a note, he expresses his wish that some Faculty of Philosophy would promote a study on the "*history of morality*" motivated by a "series of academic prize essays." According to Nietzsche, such a study deserves the consideration of "physiologists and historians as well as those who are actually philosophers by profession" (Nietzsche 1994, 37).

This valuing of different perspectives on a topic is a move in the postmodern direction. Nietzsche's comments demonstrate his concern that scholars approach a subject from as many different angles as possible. Each one of these perspectives can be helpful, and together they enrich our understanding of a topic (Best and Kellner 1991, 39).[5] His valuing of diversity of viewpoints instead of reduction to one truth is a step in the direction of postmodernism.

In summary, postmodern theorists reject the idea that the mind/self can develop an objective and universal ethic. It discards this type of universal appeal and stresses indeterminacy or the limits of human efforts to establish a universal moral theory. Postmodernism stresses individualism, but it does not view individuals as autonomous selves capable of discovering moral obligation by the correct application of reason.[6] One must listen to the multitude of individual voices. This perspective could be relativistic, or it could select a set of values or principles to live by. It would not be able to appeal to a higher authority whether a principle or a divine source in order to establish a foundation for morals.

Postmodernism is not a view that one has to accept or reject completely. One could view it as a critique of modernism in its most arrogant form. In my judgment, I think it is correct to question modern notions of Truth, Objectivity, and the Self. In a theological sense, it might steer us away from the pride of knowledge that theologian Reinhold Niebuhr describes so well. It calls us to be aware of our own limitations and prejudices. We need to consider the ways in which our biases affect us, our thoughts, and our actions. Postmodernism is more friendly to pluralism and tolerance of difference. Yet, unlike relativism, it can take and advocate a view or way of life.

The following table sums up at least some of the contrasts between the views of modernism and postmodernism concerning reason, truth, and objectivity.

Table 6.1 Reason, Truth, and Objectivity in Modernism and Postmodernism

Characteristics	Modern	Postmodern
1. Reason	Reason can free us from our prejudices and help us see our world as it truly is.	At best, reason can only play a limited role in the search for truth and meaning, and human beings are always subject to personal biases and prejudices; humans are limited and their reason is limited as well. It is subject to rationalization, bias, formal and informal experiences, as well as presupposition.
2. Truth	One can potentially gain "Truth" in an absolute or certain manner by means of proper investigation and solid research.	It is not obtainable in an absolute manner; truth for humans is relative or limited always falling short. Our view of truth is always changing as the world and social situations change and as new views invalidate old ideas of truth.
3. Objectivity	Objectivity is possible only when one is totally isolated from personal bias and isolated from outside influences.	Objectivity is an illusion because one can never totally isolate oneself from external influences or internal impulses.

In short, the modern perspective adopts Truth, Reason, and Objectivity as obtainable, whereas postmodernism supposes that one can only obtain them by limited degrees. Yet, no one person can speak for postmodernism, which has been defined in various ways. For the modern view, Truth is Universal, General, and Timeless. Postmodernism defines truth as partial, and it relates to a particular location and time. With this brief description of modernism and postmodernism, we now turn to the work of Nietzsche who continues to shape current thought.

FRIEDRICH NIETZSCHE (1844-1900)

Nietzsche was a German philosopher. His father was a Lutheran minister and his mother a devout Christian. Nietzsche was so gifted intellectually that he gained professorship at the University of Basel, Switzerland without having earned a Ph.D. He was appointed to the chair of classical philology at the University of Basel located in Switzerland at the young age of 24. He taught there for ten years. He retired from there due to bad health. Nietzsche's writing style also set him apart. Much of his writing was in aphorisms, which made his work more appealing to a wider audience. *Contains a general Truth — if it aint broke dont fix it.*

Nietzsche's Response to Anti-Semitism

Due to certain misrepresentations of Nietzsche's work, some preliminary discussion about his life and work are in order. After his death, his work comes to be associated with the Nazi movement. This situation continues to generate a good deal of debate. According to a prominent interpreter of Nietzsche's philosophy, Walter Kaufman, Nietzsche is certainly no anti-Semite. In fact, he is opposed to any type of anti-Semitism. Kaufmann quotes from his letter to his sister to underscore his view. In this letter, *Nietzsche* writes as follows:

> One of the greatest stupidities you have committed—for yourself and for me! Your association with an anti-Semitic chief expresses a foreignness to *my* whole way of life which fills me ever again with ire melancholy. It is a matter of honor to me to be absolutely clean and unequivocal regarding anti-Semitism, namely *opposed*, as I am in my writings. I have been persecuted in recent times with letters and *Anti-Semitic Correspondence* sheets; my disgust with this party . . . is as *outspoken* as possible (Kaufmann 1974, 45). *Hatred towards Jews*

In this letter, Nietzsche also remarks that the anti-Semites used the name Zarathustra (the main character in his book *Thus Spoke Zarathustra*) in "every Anti-Semitic Correspondence Sheet," and this usage, he says, "Almost made me sick" (Yovel 1997, 121).

These words are certainly consistent with my reading of Nietzsche's published work. Still, some view Nietzsche's work in a negative fashion. Weaver Santaniello rejects these negative portrayals. She asserts that in the last twenty years, there have been a number of histories on anti-Semitism as well as the Holocaust. Additionally, there have been studies that deal with the "intellectual origins of Nazism." Overall, all these studies clearly indicate that Nietzsche was not anti-Semitic. Santaniello further notes that the Germanic ideology in this regard is "well formed before Nietzsche's works appeared, and that Nietzsche, during his own lifetime, actually opposed many intellectual forerunners of the Third Reich" (Santaniello 1997, 21).

There are passages in his work, however, that are clearly critical of Jewish and Christian thought, and these passages continue to keep the issue alive. His critical views, however, are directed toward priestly Judaism and Christianity. They are not, therefore, anti-Semitic in nature. He also has lavish praise for the Old Testament or Hebrew Bible (Aschheim 1997, 7) as well as for modern Jews. He is only critical of certain aspects of Jewish thought and tradition, which passed on into Christianity.

Santaniello identifies two groups: "anti-Christian anti-Semites" and "Christian anti-Semitism. The first group (anti-Christian anti-Semitic) opposes both Judaism and Christianity. The second group (anti-Semitic Christianity) works with a theological view that identifies ancient Israel as 'deformed Israel.'" They describe Israel as "deformed," and this description casts them into a light that is in opposition to Jesus and Christianity.

The anti-Semitic Christians opposed the Jews because the Jews had not accepted Jesus as the Messiah. These Christians believed that Jesus was the Messiah. Their view was supported by the Old Testament prophesies that foretold the coming of a Messiah. Belief in a Messiah was part of the priestly-prophetic strand that carried over into Jewish-Christian thought. Nietzsche of course rejected this line of thought. Santaniello suggested that this rejection was why the *Übermensch* (i.e., the overman)[7] was central to Nietzsche's thought. This *Übermensch* "represents the Messiah who has not yet come" (Santaniello 1997, 39). The Christian anti-Semites ignored the fact that Jesus was Jewish, and they blamed the Jews for Jesus' death on the cross. Clearly, Nietzsche opposed this whole line of thought (Santaniello 1997, 25).

In addition, many Jews assimilated into German culture (Heller 1997, 194). Europeans expected this assimilation from the Jews into the mainstream European culture. Nietzsche felt that the Jewish people's long history of hardship and suffering had forged them into a great people who could potentially dominate Europe. He felt that if the Jewish people tried to maintain their isolation and their traditions, they would "lose Europe." Consequently, he promoted the view that

> Jews must pour their gifts and power into a new Europe that will be free of the Christian heritage. ... For this to happen, European society must open up to Jews and welcome them, and the Jews must end their voluntary seclusion and involve themselves with all European matters *as their own*: in this way they will, inevitably, attain excellence and end up determining new norms and values for Europe (Yovel 1997, 129).

Yirmiyahu Yovel says that Nietzsche is calling for a "creative assimilation." He is not merely asking Jews to assimilate blindly the values of others. He is not encouraging them to follow the herd mentality, which would be opposed to his own philosophy. He is calling for Jews to become a "catalyst" for a better Europe.

A personal account of Nietzsche's views on contemporary Jews in Europe comes from conversations Nietzsche had with a Jewish friend Joseph Paneth.

Paneth says that Nietzsche agrees with him regarding his views on Jewish assimilation into European culture. Nietzsche agrees with Paneth that Jews desiring to be seen as free individuals rather than Jews are "dangerous to conventional values." Paneth views assimilation as a way for Jews to become "free spirits." Free means freedom to act on self-imposed laws rather than obeying external traditions or conventions (McGrath 1997, 224-225). Certainly, this view of assimilation seems consistent with Nietzsche's philosophy.

According to Santaniello, Nietzsche affirms the ancient Israelites and contemporary Jews of his day. He, at the same time, dislikes "Judeo-Christianity," and he views it as a tradition characterized by resentment. Santaniello argues that a person who wishes to combat both Christian anti-Semitism and secular anti-Semitism in nineteenth-century Germany would take the same position that Nietzsche takes (Santaniello, Weaver 1997, 39). In contrast to the anti-Semites, Nietzsche values tolerance. He says that a strong state can tolerate dissenters (Kaufmann 1974, 251). This statement reflects his misgivings about the German state of his day.

This discussion raises an ethical issue mentioned above. If Nietzsche advocates views that support Nazism and the Holocaust, then there would be little or no justification for considering his view on morality in this book. Are the Nazi anti-Semites justified in using his writings to support their agenda?

We have probably all heard the claim about someone being quoted out of context. Do the Nazis take his words out of context? Do they misrepresent or misinterpret them intentionally? Does Nietzsche hold anti-Semitic views? In my view, their use of Nietzsche does violence to his thought and his texts. Is it ethical for them to twist intentionally his words to their own ends?

Even if one can use and interpret the words of another as support for his or her own view, is that enough justification to ignore the intent of the author? For instance, one can find isolated passages in either Nietzsche's published or unpublished writings that alone might be used to promote anti-Semitic sentiments. Is it ethical to use these words for that purpose if the author has tried to make clear he or she repudiates such views? If intent is what makes the act right or wrong, then the issue is to determine Nietzsche's real intentions.

The problem is that the literary theories disagree over the location of meaning. Historical approaches to interpretation uphold the view that the author's intent determines the meaning of a text. As a result, if meaning is in what the author intends, one can say that the ethical issue also hinges on intent. If this is the case, the author's moral responsibility rests with his or her intent. One cannot hold me responsible for how others use and twist my words.

All the same, other interpretative approaches say that the author is not relevant; the meaning comes from the reading of the text itself. Meaning is located in the text. If an anti-Semitic view is there, then the author is morally responsible for that text. Still others say that the reader creates the meaning of texts. Here too, one might consider the author responsible for the interpretations that come to the mind of the reader when he or she is reading Nietzsche's works.

In the latter two cases, the issue of the author's responsibility is much more difficult to determine. How can we really know what another person intends or what his or her motives are? If one is still living, we could ask them. In this case, however, it is not possible. If motive can be used to answer this question, one could ask, why does Nietzsche write as he does? What are his views and intentions? If he advocates an anti-Semitic view, then one could certainly have the right to question his value for the study of morality.

We could also look at the motive or intent of the interpreter. Is it wrong for the interpreter to use the words of another without regard for the author's own wishes? Alternatively, are the consequences what matter? Is it wrong because the consequences of his work help justify so much evil? Could one cite negative consequences that stem from Nietzsche's works as an argument for saying his writings are unethical?

Derrida, in his book *The Ear of the Other*, is not concerned with intent. Interpretation for him is in no way limited to the intention of the author. Can the text be read in a way that might support anti-Semitic views? He recognizes that Nietzsche's words have been perverted and then comments:

> If one refuses the distinction between unconscious and deliberate programs as an absolute criterion, if one no longer considers only intent—whether conscious or not—when reading a text, then the law that makes the perverting simplification possible must lie in the structure of the text remaining (Derrida 1985, 30).

Derrida seems to agree that it is unlikely that Nietzsche intends to espouse anti-Semitic views, but his work is still open to that exploitation. Can one hold me morally responsible for how another person can interpret my words? If I use language that may lend itself to violence, even though I intend no violence, then am I to blame for the consequences of my words?

Still in my view, I am most responsible for my intentions. There is a limit to my knowledge, and I cannot take complete responsibility for every misreading. In that vain, it seems clear to me that Nietzsche did not take up or support the cause of anti-Semitism. In fact, the evidence is quite the opposite.

Nietzsche's own views on interpretation, however, present another wrinkle in this discussion. Alan D. Schrift identifies an important distinction in Nietzsche's text about interpretation (Schrift 1990, 164-180). If it is not clear by now, I would point out that interpretation and how one interprets a text is a moral issue. If telling an untruth is wrong, then intentionally misinterpreting the words of others is also wrong and dishonest. Nietzsche appears at one point to advocate the view that interpretation should be consistent with an author's intent. One has a moral responsibility to interpret a text in a way consistent with the meaning intended.

Regarding the New Testament writers, Nietzsche noted that they re-interpreted the Old Testament or Hebrew Bible. He disapproved of this re-interpretation because it was not consistent with what the Hebrew writers really intended. As a result, it was historically false. The writer of Matthew's Gospel, for instance, often said that something happened in accordance with something foretold in prophetic texts. If one were to look back at the historical content of these passages in the Hebrew Bible, then it would be clear that the text had been taken out of its historical setting and made to function in a new historical and cultural setting. Clearly, the writers of prophetic texts were not looking to a distant future. They warned their audience about things that were going to happen in the immediate future. He saw such Christian re-interpretation as an act of ripping the Hebrew texts from their historical contexts. Nietzsche disapproved of such interpretations.

Yet, Nietzsche does not adopt a simple view that one has to stick to the author's intent to determine the meaning or value of a work. Schrift suggests that Nietzsche's standard for judging interpretations depends on style. In Nietzsche book, *The Case for Wagner*, he distinguishes between "noble" or "master" morality on the one hand, and "Christian morality" on the other. The former is good and affirmative while the other is bad and world negating (Nietzsche 1967b, 190-191). He also notes that while Nietzsche scolded New Testament writers for reinterpreting the Hebrew Bible or in essence ripping these texts from the Jews and reappropriating them for the Christian community, he approves of Roman writers who reappropriate older Roman texts. How can one reconcile these views?

Schrift finds in this and similar Nietzschean texts a possible standard that Nietzsche employed for judging interpretation. Nietzsche is not interested in correct or incorrect interpretations but style. Some styles (e.g., the style of the Roman writer) contain a grand style that is life affirming and the interpretation from this style does not gain at the expense of the whole. Life denying styles, on the other hand, do gain at the expense of the whole. Regarding the New Testament's reappropriation of the Hebrew Bible, then, the whole (i.e., the Hebrew texts) suffers at the expense of the page (i.e., the re-appropriation). Nietzsche's judgment is not based on one moral interpretation being false and the other correct. His judgments are based on whether a morality embraces values that are life affirming or values that are "hostile to life" (Schrift 1990, 176). According to Schrift, Nietzsche recognizes that "events" occurring in the past are unclear. The meanings that one can find in these "events" depend upon the perspective from which these texts are examined. So when examining these moral texts (i.e., New Testament texts that reappropriated the Old Testaments texts) from the Dionysian perspective,[8] one finds that they are life-negating and a barrier to the advancing of a life-valuing perspective. Nevertheless, when one looks at these texts from the viewpoint of slave morality, one finds a different perspective. He views this perspective negatively. For the Christian writers in the grips of slave morality, the reappropriation is valuable and necessary. The "slave moralists could not survive without them." As a result, Nietzsche's genealogical approach refrains from identifying one valid solitary interpretation as the correct one. Still, Nietzsche does not avoid making judgments concerning the value of different interpretations and reinterpretations (Schrift 1990, 180).

Accordingly, the question for Nietzsche is not intent. Instead, we could try to see if Nietzsche himself or his readers would find an anti-Semitic interpretation of his work life affirming. One indication of Nietzsche's views on anti-Semitic writings comes in his response to such writers. Against Eugene Dühring (whom he refers to as "Berlin's apostle of revenge"), he describes his concept of "equal wills" as a "principle hostile to life" (Santaniello 1997, 27). Hence, Nietzsche would seem to reject anti-Semitism as decadent and life negating.

In short, then, I do not think Nietzsche ever intends to endorse in any way an anti-Semitic view that would lead to the suffering of the Jewish people. He views Jews and many of their writings in a positive fashion; Nietzsche also views Jesus in a very positive way in contrast with the Jewish-Christian priestly view of him as a messiah mentioned above. For Nietzsche, Jesus is a human being, and he is in fact the noblest human being (Santaniello 1997, 29). Jesus was not a messiah bringing in a new wave of apocalyptic violence. Instead, Jesus was a messiah in the sense of bringing about the kingdom of God, which is not in some distant future. Nor is it a kingdom one expects. This kingdom of God is one that is in the individual (Santaniello 1997, 36).[9]

Nietzsche and Morality

Much of Nietzsche's thinking focuses on morality. For Nietzsche, traditional approaches to the understanding of morality are problematic. He identifies two different approaches to ethics. The first approach assumes that there is agreement among civilized nations on moral principles. They take this consensus and try to impose it on everyone else. A second group consists of those people who observe a diversity of morals when comparing one culture to another. From this observation, they conclude that no morality is binding. He considers both approaches "equally childish." Nietzsche sets out to examine the *value of morality*. Does it have any value? What would be the results of people's morality? Are the results of morality helpful for those who practice a particular morality? Does morality make one's life better or does it make one a better person? (Nietzsche 1974, 283-285)[10]

Nietzsche denounces most ancient and modern forms of morality. As human beings cease living in small bands and roving freely, they find themselves confined into larger and smaller communities. These premodern societies come to rely on custom as the foundation for their morality. Customs allow human beings to live together in communities. This situation leads to a *bad conscience*.

These societies or groups no longer accept the old instincts of freedom and unrestrained movement. Group life demands a different set of values. These different values must restrain freedom and movement. They must bring individuals under control. When the individual no longer discharges these old instincts of freedom outwardly, they "*turn inward*" and punish the individual. It is from this process that the bad conscience emerges (Nietzsche 1994, 60-63). The individual's desire to roam freely without restraint clashes with the group's norms and expectations. From this point, when one goes against the group one is bad, and this evaluation on the group's part affects the individual's conscience.

This change shapes the conscience and leads to the *feeling of guilt*. To have a good conscience, one does what others expect. The bad conscience is also prevalent in modern societies; people discourage individuality and creativity when it runs counter to societal expectations. Therefore, the bad conscience occurs before Christianity with the development of traditions and customs. Still, religions like Christianity as well as modern traditions and customs certainly reinforce the bad conscience today. Guilt, therefore, is a by-product of living in community. Even though there may be some positive aspects of guilt, it primarily operates in the present as well as in the past as an instrument of control. If a moral impulse or moral conscience exists as Bauman suggests, then we might assume that a violation of the moral impulse leads to a guilty conscience. It would seem so. Therefore, guilt may be the result of doing what we feel is wrong (violation of the moral impulse) or doing what we know others think is wrong (violation of the social conscience).

Today many individuals and groups play on our guilt. They may attempt to gain our financial support and monopolize our time. To gain what they want from us, they often try to shame the individual or group. Some clergy, for example, often use guilt to motivate people to give money, vote in certain ways, or to support certain causes. Some political leaders can do the same to get votes or accomplish their own agendas.

Nietzsche prefers the morality of the aristocracy who defines "good" in terms of so-called noble individuals. As we shall see below, Nietzsche evaluates morals by considering how they make use of the will to power. He calls for a creative exercising of the will to power that is within each individual.

Will to Power

The will to power is a key idea in Nietzsche's work. It serves as an important basis for his moral views as well. However, it does not become a dominant theme until his later work, and even then, he does not promote it in an absolute manner. Nietzsche describes his views with regard to his proposed book, *The Will to Power*, as follows:

> The Will to Power. A book for *thinking*, nothing else: it belongs to those for whom thinking is a delight, nothing else. That it is written in German is untimely, to say the least: I wish I had written in French so that it might not appear to be a confirmation of the aspirations of the German *Reich*.[11]

Not only does this theme (i.e., will to power) become dominant, it also serves as a way of judging actions. According to Nietzsche, the primary motivation for human thought and activity does not derive from the will to survive, the will to be happy, the will to be successful, or the will to find meaning in life as some suppose. The will to power motivates everything one does whether consciously or unconsciously. It is the one force driving all human existence. Pleasure, for instance, is the result of the "will to power." Nietzsche concludes that the gratification of the will is not what causes or produces pleasure. Pleasure derives from a "forward thrust," which continually strives to become "master over that which stands in its way" (Nietzsche 1967a, 370).[12] Pleasure comes from the "dissatisfaction of the will, in the fact that the will is never satisfied unless it has opponents and resistance" (Nietzsche 1967a, 370). Without exercising one's power to overcome resistance, there is no happiness. Happiness, therefore, derives from our ability to overcome resistance in accomplishing some goal.

For instance, what happiness would a college degree bring if the college merely gives the degree to the student without any work on the student's part? Sure, the student may be happy in a sense if the degree brings about a job and money, but will the degree itself produce happiness? It becomes just another possession. Gaining a degree through an act of hard work and overcoming resistance produces a feeling of accomplishment, which leads to happiness.

The will to power can include many different things. It may seek wealth, reputation, political position, prestige, independence, or freedom. The expression of the will to power differs depending upon the desires of the individual. However, Nietzsche does not consider every expression of the will to power as positive or virtuous. He believes that his former friend, composer, Richard Wagner, has sold out his ideals by trading the creative will to power for the worldly power of fame and success.[13]

Nietzsche feels that many people conform to the expectations of society for personal gain. Those who practice the will to power in a positive way, however, might suffer in some way. The person who attacks the idea or belief of a friend may suffer the loss of that friend as a result. Yet, the person who rightly exercises the will to power must be honest with himself or herself. Being honest can and often does lead to suffering. This suffering can manifest itself in being ignored, hated, and lonely since the majority of people go the way of the crowd. In his book, *Beyond Good and Evil*, he asks the question, "Who has not, for the sake of his good reputation -- sacrificed himself once?" (Nietzsche 1989, 83)[14] Nietzsche's views keep him from achieving popularity during his day. Going against popular sentiment, political views, or religious beliefs can certainly lead to suffering, isolation, verbal abuse, or even worse forms of censure.

As indicated above, Nietzsche does not consider physical force or the force of the state to be the highest form of the will to power. He considers the German state to be relatively weak even though it has great physical strength. Certainly, Nietzsche does not want his view of the will to power to be a legitimation of the German Reich. Instead of sheer might, he values the Persians for their physical and moral strength and the *Jews* for their *moral power*. For instance, the Jewish notion of honoring one's father and mother is striving for moral excellence not physical power. Moral power alone can make a people powerful. A truly strong state can tolerate dissenters (Kaufmann 1974, 197-198, 201-202, 247-248).

The will to power when properly exercised is a creative force. Nietzsche concludes that only weak individuals have to rely on rules made by others. Human beings should be able to create their own standards or rules. The *free spirit* has the power to live by self-chosen principles. However, it takes a strong and powerful individual to be able to live this type of life. Creative individuals transcend the moral codes of their day and live by self-chosen codes that give meaning to their lives (Kaufmann 1974, 250-251).[15]

In addition, the will to power relates to certain political views. These views are sketchy. Clearly, Nietzsche does not approve of socialism or the democracies of his day. He does, however, aspire to a type of democracy that will "'create and guarantee *independence* for as many people as possible, independence of opinions, way of life, and business.' Nietzsche envisages the eventual '*victory of democracy*' and the rise of a 'middle class'" (Kaufmann 1974, 187). However, he does not advocate a society based on equality. Rather he calls for a society that encourages greatness from individuals. Those who have talent and ability should rise to the top. Many people, however, would find themselves relegated to inferior positions.

With regard to value judgments, Nietzsche says that the nobles and aristocrats originally have the power to define or determine what is good and bad. By their power to give names, they are able to qualify some things as good and desirable and other things as bad and undesirable. Those who have power in society can have a great deal of influence on defining the society's system of values. For the Greeks, work or having to work is bad, whereas today, most common people view work as worthwhile and necessary. The Protestant work ethic illustrates the enduring power that values have over people's lives. In our society, we generally tend to define those who do not work as lazy, or we may view them as parasites, whereas in Greek society not working was a sign of one's position (Nietzsche 1974, 258-260). Originally, the aristocrats were the ones who made value judgments about things, and these judgments became standards (Nietzsche 1994, 13).

In short, the "will to power" stands behind the movement of all human history since all creatures seek to dominate their world. The will to power is *the force* that dominates all other forces; it is the driving force standing behind human actions. Therefore, Nietzsche rejects Darwin's view that the *instinct of self-preservation* is the driving force behind human action. He observes that even though there are many different moral codes, they all have one thing in common, the will to power. Adherents of each moral code consider their own code to be the only true one. In these societies, the will to power expresses itself in a "tablet of the good," which dangles over every culture or society. This tablet witnesses to a society's "overcomings," and it is the "voice of their will to power." He observes that:

> Praiseworthy is whatever seems difficult to a people; whatever seems indispensable and difficult is called good; whatever liberates even out of the deepest need, the rarest, the most difficult—that they call holy.
>
> Whatever makes them rule and triumph and shine, to the awe and envy of their neighbors, that is to them the high, the first, the measure, the meaning of all things (Nietzsche 1978, 58).

The most important aspect of the will to power, then, is the notion of self-mastery. Self-mastery comes through the process of self-overcoming.

Self-Overcoming

Nietzsche's ethic focuses on the individual. *Self-overcoming forms the basis of that ethic.* Yet, self-overcoming is something that is inherent in all forms of life. Nietzsche recognizes that "all great things bring about their own demise." This demise or destruction comes about through self-overcoming (Nietzsche 1994, 126).[16] Even nature, for instance, is not a static concept. It is natural for us to strive to become or to overcome and transcend ourselves, to become something that we are not at present. Nature is always changing as a result. The only constant is the will to power.

Self-overcoming, therefore, can have either positive or negative connotations in Nietzsche's writing. For instance, he talks about how self-overcoming can have a negative affect on the individual by making him or her servant to custom. Consider the following quote:

> Concept of morality or custom. -- In comparison with the mode of life of whole millennia of mankind we present-day men live in a very immoral age: the power of custom is astonishingly enfeebled [modern people] and the moral sense [is] so rarefied and lofty it may be described as having more or less evaporated. That is why the fundamental insights into the origin of morality are so difficult for us latecomers, and even when we acquire them we find it impossible to enunciate them, because they sound so uncouth or because they seem to slander morality! This is already the case with the *chief proposition*: morality is nothing other. . . than obedience to customs, of whatever kind they may be; customs, however, are the *traditional* ways of behaving and evaluating. . . . What is tradition? A higher authority which one obeys, not because it commands what is *useful* to us, but because it *commands*. . . . Self-overcoming [italics mine] is demanded, *not* on account of the useful consequences it may have for the individual, but so that the hegemony of custom, tradition, shall be made evident in despite of the private desires and advantages of the individual: the individual sacrifices himself -- that is the commandment of morality of custom. . . . Under the domination of morality of custom, originality of every kind has acquired a bad conscience; the sky above the best men is for this reason to this very moment gloomier than it need be (Nietzsche 1982, 10-12).

Will to power and self-overcoming, therefore, may produce a type of morality that Nietzsche considers inferior and degenerate. Just kneeling before morality or the custom of the day and surrendering one's will to it, may require the will to power and self-overcoming for the individual to conform. Yet creativity would be lacking. It would produce a slave to custom, tradition, and to the current morality. It would not produce a person who could define his or her morality based on his or her own principles and values.

Positively, self-overcoming means that one has power over oneself. The individual should be in control deciding what to do. In contrast to using one's will to power and self-overcoming to follow other people's moral rules, we should create our own standards. The moralists following "Socrates, offer the *individual* a morality of self-control and temperance as a means to his own *advantage*, as his personal key to happiness" (Nietzsche 1982, 11-12). This statement illustrates the positive use of self-overcoming. It means in part to be in control of one's life and not to be afraid or blinded by the power of traditions and customs. More than that, it means to live by one's own self-chosen principles.

In the end, the individual is capable of rising above custom and tradition. From this perspective, one might conclude that it is never enough to say that my tradition or my religion says that I should act in a certain way. Custom or tradition has the power to make individuals forsake their self-chosen principles or self-created values for those of the community. Individuals often sell out their own ideals for the sake of not being rejected by the group. The good person, however, is the one who decides for himself or herself which principles give shape to his or her life.

Completely transcending the constraints set by the community, one can find release. Through this release, one can become a free spirit in contrast to the bound spirit (Nietzsche 1984, 139-143). Is such a transformation possible? For Nietzsche, self-overcoming is the element that distinguishes the moral individual from the nonmoral one. The goal of self-overcoming is not a means of subordinating the interests of the individual to that of the group. Nevertheless, it does seem natural for human beings to impose limits on their behavior, and in that sense we may say that human beings are naturally moral creatures (Kaufmann 1974, 213-214).

Most importantly, self-overcoming means that one can keep his or her passions, instincts, and desires under control. This control is not a mechanism of repression. He associates Christianity as repressive. However, he says that a person should not allow his or her passions, instincts, or desires to control his or her life. Nevertheless, a person devoid of impulses could not do the good or create the beautiful anymore than a castrated man could beget children (Nietzsche 1982, 224-225; Nietzsche 1967a, 205-209). One who acquires self-control is a strong individual, and he or she might obtain greatness. The person, by contrast, who lacks self-control, is weak. It takes a strong person to live according to his or her own self-chosen principles. The weak individual is the one who cannot obey his or her own commands. Nietzsche comments that every living thing obeys someone or something, such is

> the nature of the living. . . . Commanding is harder than obeying. . . . Even when it commands *itself*, it must still pay for its commanding. It must become judge, the avenger, and the victim of its own law (Nietzsche 1978, 114; Nietzsche 1974, 232-233).

Therefore, self-mastery or the desire to overcome the self is an expression of the will to power. He argues that the correct use of the will to power is to maintain power over oneself not others. The desire to have power over others frequently comes from one's inability to have power over oneself. Consider the following aphorism: "He cannot control himself, and from that a poor woman infers that it will be easy to control him and casts her net for him. Soon she will be his slave" (Nietzsche 1974, 211). *Self-overcoming* is what distinguishes the moral from the nonmoral in human thought and behavior. The process of self-mastery begins with the act of sublimation.

Sublimation

Nietzsche refers to a person's success at self-overcoming or controlling his or her own impulses as sublimation. *Sublimation* involves preserving, canceling, and lifting up of impulses. Nietzsche identified ways of combating the violence of a drive and controlling it. One way to control a drive and avoid acting upon it is to stay away from certain situations where one might have the opportunity to act on a particular drive. Another example of controlling or sublimating a drive has to do with his notion of dislocation of forces. By dislocation of forces, Nietzsche refers to the "diverting" one's thoughts and energy into "other channels." One might sublimate the desire for revenge into a positive endeavor that prevents the vengeful desire from being repressed, which would lead to resentment. The negative energy and emotions associated with that desire can then be redirected into something else.

Some examples should serve to illustrate how Nietzsche understood sublimation. In some cases, Nietzsche believes that one can redirect or channel the sexual impulse into a creative action. In another instance, he says that the "barbarian's desire to torture his foe can be sublimated into the desire to defeat one's rival in the Olympic contests" (Kaufmann 1974, 220). In both cases, there is a canceling of the impulse, which is not deliberate. The energy and the underlying essence remain after this canceling, and this is the will to power. After one sublimates or redirects a drive, the objective of that drive, which is the will to power, remains and is fulfilled in other pursuits (Kaufmann 1974, 222-223).

Consider the sex drive. An individual can sublimate or redirect the sex drive in an exercising of power. Through sublimation, one can cancel the sex drive's immediate objective (e.g., sexual desire) and redirect what remains (i.e., power) into other pursuits. The redirection of such energy prevents its repression. This redirection or sublimation allows it to be expressed rather than being repressed. Then it is free to express itself in a positive fashion in some other activity.

Much of Nietzsche's critique of Christianity is directed toward the repression of drives. Concerning sex, Nietzsche does not believe that sexuality is shameful, and many of his criticisms against Christianity derive from his view that Christianity treats sexuality in a negative manner. For Nietzsche, one should control sexuality like any other passion. One should not be a slave to impulses but be their master. In his view, Christianity advocates elimination, surrender, and destruction of the passions and impulses.

Repression and Christianity

The opposite of sublimation is repression. Nietzsche takes a rather dim view of repression. He says that repression of the will to power leads to deep resentment. Resentment is a feeling that is not appropriate for the good or moral person. As he sees it, the goal of Christianity is to destroy the passions, desires, and impulses of the individual. The response of Christian morality as well as many other moral philosophies is to renounce and deny these natural impulses. A morality dominated by an "instinct for life," on the other hand, is the type of morality that he seeks. He identifies almost all morality and not just Christian morality as anti-natural or an "enemy of life" (Nietzsche 1990a, 52-57). He feels we should control our passions but not negate them. It is a sign of weakness for one to avoid the senses, desires, and passions out of *fear*.

Regarding Christianity, Nietzsche defines it as "*resentment against* life, which made of sensuality something impure" (Nietzsche 1990a, 121). Christianity is an "instinct of *resentment*" because it "had to invent *another* world from which *life-affirmation* would appear evil, reprehensible as such" (Nietzsche 1990b, 146-147). Here individuals often direct the resentment that comes from repression against the rich and powerful. Many would direct this resentment against the body, sex, and world.

Nietzsche sees the desire of some Christians who wish to see their enemies punished in hell as a desire that hides behind talk of love for one's enemies. In this regard, he quotes two Christian thinkers: Thomas Aquinas an early church theologian and Tertullian another early church leader. In *Summa Theologiae*, Aquinas writes, "the blessed in the heavenly kingdom will see the torment of the damned *so that they may even more thoroughly enjoy their blessedness*" (Nietzsche 1994, 32).

There is even a stronger statement in the quotation from Tertullian. Tertullian encourages Christians to stand firm and not turn from the Christian faith out of fear for their own safety. He says that if they turn away and renounce the Christian faith, they will lose their salvation. He encourages his audience with a description of Christ's return. He continues:

> That final and everlasting day of judgment, that day was not expected and was even laughed at by the nations, when the whole old world and all it gave birth to are consumed in one fire. What an ample breadth of sights there will be then! *At which one shall I gaze in wonder? At which one shall I laugh? At which rejoice? At which exult,* when I see many great *kings* who were proclaimed to have been taken up into heaven, groaning in the deepest darkness. . . . And when I see those [provincial] governors, persecutors of the Lord's name, melting in flames more savage than those with which they insolently raged against Christians! When I see those wise philosophers who persuaded their disciples that nothing was of any concern to god and who affirmed to them either that we have no souls or that our souls will not return to their original bodies! Now they are ashamed before those disciples, as they are burned together with them. . . . The actors of pantomime will be easy to recognize, being much more nim-

ble than usual because of the fire. Then the charioteer will be on view, all red in a wheel of flame and athletes, thrown not in the gymnasia but into the fire.[17]

This last quotation is a classic illustration of resentment. Tertullian, an individual who was powerless or unwilling to deal with the realities of this life, buried his hatred and it turned into deep resentment. Such resentment leads him to desire revenge for all the ills suffered by Christians of his day. Nietzsche as a rule sees revenge as negative. The type of revenge, however, that is most dangerous is not that which one engages in immediately upon receiving a wrong. Rather, the dangerous type is one put off because the person lacks the power or courage to take revenge when the insult occurs. More often one buries or internalizes the hate or anger, which ends up manifesting itself in resentment and just waiting for a time when he or she can get even. Nietzsche, in contrast to this view, says that the noble person or the free spirit is the one who is free of resentment; this person may be able to love or respect his or her enemies (Nietzsche 1994, 23-24). Resentment, on the other hand, seduces an individual to want revenge as was illustrated above.

Moreover, Nietzsche criticizes the notion of sin, which he sees as a Jewish priestly invention that passes on into the New Testament and Christianity. Sin forms the "background of Christian morality." He describes God as one who sees sin as an offence against God's honor. In turn, God takes pleasure in revenge. Nietzsche remarks,

> His power is so great that nobody could possibly harm him, except for his honor. Every sin is a slight to his honor. . . . Contrition, degradation, rolling in the dust–all this is the first condition of his grace: in sum, the restoration of his divine honor. . . . Sin is an offense against him, not against humanity. . . . Every deed is to be considered *solely with respect to its supernatural consequences* (Nietzsche 1974, 187-188).

It is this view of Christianity with which Nietzsche takes issue. In the hands of the priests, which he calls ascetic priests, the *bad conscience* becomes *sin* (Nietzsche 1994, 110-112). Sin, of course, creates a sense of guilt, and taking care of this guilt is one way the ascetic priests care for the sick or sinner. Nietzsche says that the priests believe that they can help the sick. However, these priests make the sick person a sinner by explaining the individual's suffering as punishment for some transgression. The morality present in this view is for the benefit of the priests or religious leaders because the system gives them power and legitimacy over others. Nietzsche does not reject the value of the Hebrew Bible as a whole or the ancient Israelites. For instance in his book, *On Genealogy of Morality*, aphorism 22, Nietzsche says that he has "every respect for the Old Testament!" (Nietzsche 1994, 113,114; Santaniello 1997, 31) Like any critical reader, he likes some parts but not all.

Moreover, Nietzsche believes that Christianity has led human beings to repress their emotions, impulses, and passions instead of controlling them. Conventional morality tends to command that one obey customs or traditions. For him, being moral in this sense is not true morality. He recognizes that "subjection to morality can be slavish or vain or self-interested or resigned or gloomily enthusiastic or an act of despair, like subjection to a prince: in itself it is nothing moral" (Nietzsche 1982, 59).

Slave Morality

Overall, therefore, Nietzsche sees Christianity as a *slave morality*. Slave morality refers to the situation where religions such as Christianity instruct people that they should value the interests of others more than they value their own interests. It would maintain that we have a duty to help the poor, needy, and weak. This type of morality endeavors to enslave us by creating a bad conscience within us creating the opportunity for resentment in the process. The bad conscience tries to control us by taking control away from us. It controls us by creating a sense of guilt and a fear of censure or even punishment in the next life. Then one may do good things but the motive is not to help the poor, needy, or weak, but to save ourselves. Slave morality involves reversing values making the good (acting from one's own self-chosen principles) evil and making the bad (acting out of conformity to some external force or values) good. In keeping with the slave metaphor, the slave obeys out of fear of the master's whip. Slave morality, therefore, is a breeding ground for resentment, repression, revenge, and guilt.

Nietzsche is not saying that one should be unkind or ignore the helpless. He does not even reject the idea of putting the interests of others ahead of one's own interests. The good person may do good things for others because he or she wants to do so. One might do good things for others because he or she has decided to be the kind of person that helps others. The good person begins with himself or herself instead of beginning with his or her neighbor. Doing good for one's neighbor can be an escape from one's self. Living our lives through other people may prevent us from developing our own moral identity.

We might pause at this point to ask if Nietzsche's views of Christianity are completely adequate. One must keep in mind that Nietzsche is reacting to a certain type of Judaism and Christianity. Certainly, the above quotations from Aquinas and Tertullian do not describe Christian religion in its entirety; it may be a good description of how some Christians view God. Without a doubt, the biblical tradition often portrays God as a jealous and angry God. In the book of Psalms, many laments petition God to take revenge on an enemy. Nevertheless, the reader should remember that the psalmist is being honest about his or her feelings and leaving it in the hands of God. The biblical tradition also portrays God as one who cares for and nurtures humanity. One can interpret the laws and instructions of the Hebrew Bible as God's concern for human well-being; these laws show adherents how to live a happy and meaningful life. A more positive view is that God sees sin as something that poses a danger to others. Many of the laws or instructions are intended to prevent harm to humanity.

In truth, Christianity often does live up to many of the negative descriptions given above. Yet, for many Christians and other religious people this simply is not the case. There are many who strive to live above resentment and revenge and who in their own way attempt to value and affirm life. That is not to say that Nietzsche would accept any form of Christianity, but his criticisms are not valid for the whole of Christianity. In this regard, Nietzsche does say in *Ecce Homo*, "The most serious Christians have always been well disposed towards me. . . . I am far from bearing a grudge against the individual for what is the fatality of millennia" (Nietzsche 1992, 18). In short, repression, resentment, and revenge belong to a slave morality. Religion at its best is not about blind obedience. Liberal Christian theology for all its faults holds that one should not blindly follow the words of the Bible. One could adopt a semi-Nietzschean view consistent with Judaism or Christianity that allows one to be for the other out of a sense of compassion and gratitude and not from any legalistic absolute obligation to follow the dictates of Scripture.

From Good and Bad to Good and Evil

Nietzsche's book, *On the Genealogy of Morality*, attempts to trace the genealogy of such terms as good, bad, evil, guilt, and debt. He notes that the genealogy of these terms clearly shows how moral values change and how we have appropriated, adapted, and manipulated them. In Greek society, good and bad refer to types of persons. People are good or bad depending upon certain characteristics. Nietzsche prefers the values of the ancient Greeks who associate the good with the ways of the nobles or aristocracy. The aristocrats represent those who were powerful, noble, happy, and beautiful. They are the ones who had energy, personal power, and grace to live well, win their battles and dominate their situations. Good people may fail, but they do not blame others for their failures. *Bad*, on the other hand, refers to those who fail, with base and petty concerns, and those who lack the vital energies and therefore end up on the bottom (Collins and Makowsky 1989, 74-75; and Nietzsche 1994, 19).

Greek aristocrats equate good with the beautiful, happy people whom the gods love. Jews and Christians, however, reverse this view of good. Of Judaism and Christianity, he remarks:

> 'Only those who suffer are good, only the poor, the powerless, the lowly are good; the suffering, the deprived, the sick, the ugly, are the only pious people, the only ones saved, salvation is for them alone, whereas you rich, the noble and powerful, you are eternally wicked, cruel, lustful, insatiate, godless, you will also be eternally wretched, cursed and damned!' (Nietzsche 1994, 19)[18]

In Judaism and Christianity, one moves *beyond good and bad toward good and evil*. In this type of morality one endeavors to enslave the strong with their morality.[19] For the Greeks, however, powerful people judge things in terms of good and bad. In short, Nietzsche says that one's life is good when individuals are in "full control of their impulses ... and the *good man is ... the passionate man who is the master of his passions*" (Kaufmann 1974, 280).

Even though Nietzsche admires the Greek aristocratic view of good and bad, he recognized that the so-called slave morality has been successful.

Nietzsche also recognizes some positive in this type of morality. He notes that the leaders (i.e., the priests) of this type morality are some of the brightest intellects who have ever lived. He acknowledges that it is through the priestly class in all religions, including Christianity, that life gains greater depths and human beings become interesting animals (Nietzsche 1994, 16-19). He has a positive view of the "historical Jesus," and he refers to him as a noble human being (Nietzsche 1984, 228-229).

The Metamorphosis

The goal of individual endeavor is to become a higher type of human, a so-called *Übermensch* (i.e., the overman). Humankind is a "rope, tied between beast and overman—a rope over the abyss" (Nietzsche 1966, 14). The beast refers to who we are now. The beast is a product of nature. The human spirit, however, is not satisfied with who we are but seeks more. The overman is the new type of human to come. What is great in beasts or human beings is that they are "a bridge and not an end: what can be loved in man [sic] is that he is an *overture* and a *going under*" (i.e., *untergehen*) (Nietzsche 1966, 15). From this passage, Nietzsche refers to evolution, and the upshot is that present humans should be declining or going under (i.e., *untergehend*) so the *Übermensch or overman* can come to life. One could think of the *über* as transcending and *unter* as descending. So the beast goes under (*untergehen*) and a new type (*Übermensch*) transcends or rises above (*über*) the beast that goes under.

The individual that emerges would be passionate but in control. He or she would be a creative person. He or she would also impose self-chosen standards upon himself or herself. He or she can endure whatever is necessary and strive for excellence. This type person would press ahead in the face of resistance and would not blame others for his or her own failures. He or she is one who lives beyond revenge, repression, and resentment. He or she would be a free spirit. Therefore, he looks for a metamorphosis whereby humans as they are now would go under so that a new type could emerge. Transcending the lesser type entails the will to power. Employing the will to power in the act of self-overcoming shapes or creates the self as a higher type of human being. To become the *Übermensch* would seem to require a Herculean effort.

Assessment of Nietzsche Writings and Ideas

Positively, Nietzsche's will to power as the power to create oneself and to overcome challenges is perhaps his most important and compelling idea. In my experiences especially as a teacher, many people want an easy life with little or no resistance. Mentally, people seem less inclined or equipped to work hard and overcome resistance. People always seem to look for short cuts. Some people say they are happy to be given everything they want without any effort on their part. Nietzsche's work is a welcome voice in the midst of such nonsense. The will to power employed in the act of self-overcoming and in the sense of overcoming resistance does seem to be the way to real happiness. Overcoming what is hard is what most shapes and defines who we are. It brings out our character or lack of character.

Additionally, his life is consistent with his philosophy. He does go against the norms and dares to be different. He questions those notions of good and evil popular in his day. His work contains a wealth of insight. More than this, however, his work points out the destructive nature of resentment, revenge, bad conscience, and guilt. He affirms life and judges the work and ideas of others with regard to this affirmation. In other words, the standard of judgment is whether the ideas of another person or group affirm life or whether they disparage life. His critique of priestly Christianity is insightful and on the mark in many instances. His writing is exciting and a delight to read. By reading his work seriously, one is likely to be provoked. His views also call to our better natures. To affirm life and live above resentment and guilt are wonderful aspirations; it may be a little beyond my capabilities yet I admire it because it challenges me and calls me to improve myself.

In addition, his work has made many contributions to postmodern thought. Nietzsche's insights are helpful in pointing out the weaknesses of modern ethical. For example, the modern view of seeing the ethical subject or self as a stable, potentially neutral, and objective entity is wrong. As Nietzsche notes, educated individuals have rightly concluded that people from all historical settings believe they understand what is good and evil, what actions we should praise and punish. Yet even the educated or learned person is biased. He identifies their prejudice as thinking they know better than people of the past (Nietzsche 1982, 9).

Perhaps his greatest contributions are the notions of the will to power as self-overcoming or self-mastery, the affirmation of life, as well as his examination of resentment, repression, and revenge. His views of good and bad also have value. Would one not be better off to take full responsibility for his or her actions? A good person would be one who upon working hard and overcoming resistance would experience satisfaction and pleasure. If the good person works hard and fails, he or she would take full responsibility for his or her own failures instead of blaming others. Being such a person would require great effort and would be a worthy endeavor. I would add one last thing to my list of positives. I agree with him that the uncritical acceptance of customs and traditions is undesirable.

Still some might reject his assertion concerning the will to power on at least two levels. First, using this concept in a negative sense, one can claim the will to power as the right of the strong to exploit the weak. It could justify horrible acts. It could lead to a contest of strong wills, which is not always bad but could be in certain situations. Second, is he correct that the most basic drive in human beings is the will to power? Nietzsche's views must contend with others. Some scholars argue that the basic drive of human beings is the will to meaning. Others might argue that it is the will to survive. We might even question whether there is just one basic force.

One might characterize Nietzsche's views as elitist. Perhaps, he puts too much emphasis on the noble or aristocratic individual. In a later chapter, I discuss the work of John D. Caputo who affirms the "law of the other" (*heteronomy*). Nietzsche might characterize this law as part of a slave morality. Caputo wants to find a way to affirm both the Jewish and Greek sides of morality. For Caputo, Nietzsche is too one-sided. Some notion of community or hospitality is important, and I discuss this notion further in the final chapter. Any healthy perspective must contain both elements. Ethics should foster cooperation and hospitality as well as self-control and self-mastery. Overall, his thought contributes significantly to the current discussion of morals.

CONCLUSION

Before continuing this present discussion by examining contemporary writers, I would digress and examine moral values from social and psychological perspectives. In chapter seven, I explore the changing nature of moral values and its implications for our study. Chapter eight discusses the psychological aspects of human nature. Here, I examine views that portray ethics as a matter of human beings working for or against their own nature. Egoists, for instance, say that human beings are naturally selfish and ethics ought to proceed on that premise. The discussion of ethical perspectives in chapters seven through nine prompts the ensuing questions: Can we develop a normative ethic? Is a normative system of ethics even desirable?

NOTES

1. Walter Brueggemann's discussion of Descartes draws upon two studies: (1) Stephen Toulmin 1990; and (2) Susan Bordo 1987.

2. Brueggemann is drawing from Bordo's book *The Flight to Objectivity.* On the connection between a woman's body and evil, see Nell Noddings 1989, 35-58.

3. Also see Paul A. Bové 1986, 22-23, 35-37. These sources also discuss Michel Foucault's views on the subject. Best and Kellner point out that Foucault's views on the subject change over the course of his career. See Steven Best and Douglas Kellner, 41-42, 50-52, 60-68.

4. Signifier refers to the image or sound image produced by a word.

5. On Nietzsche's views of perspectivism, see Nietzsche 1974, 297-300.

6. One can find this view throughout Nietzsche's work (e.g., Nietzsche 1982, 10-12).

7. In some cases, this word has been translated as Superman. It has the notion of transcending who we are at present to become a higher type. For a clear and helpful discussion of *Übermensch,* see Ansell-Pearson 1992, 309-331.

8. Dionysus is the Greek god of wine. Dionysus is the god of dance, excitement, and creativity. This god, for Nietzsche, stands in contrast to the more rational and critical aspects of thought. This god knows that absolute or fixed truths are just illusions.

9. She is referring to aphorism 29 in Nietzsche's book the *Antichrist.* The Gospel of Thomas makes this point explicitly. The kingdom of God is within a person. In saying number three Jesus says "If those who lead you say to you, 'See, the kingdom is in the sky,' then the birds of the sky will precede you. If they say to you, 'It is in the sea,' then

the fish will precede you. Rather, the kingdom is inside of you, and it is outside of you."
(The Gnostic Society Library "The Nag Hammadi Library—The Gospel of Thomas"
http://www.gnosis.org/naghamm/gthlamb.html (accessed September 20, 2010).

    10. Also see Nietzsche's statements in 1994, 4-5, 7, 11-14.

    11. This quotation comes from one of Nietzsche's drafts for a preface to the *Will to
Power*. However, Nietzsche never finishes the book, and the book we have entitled *The
Will to Power* is actually a publication of Nietzsche's notebook. See the editor's introduction by Walter Kaufmann in Friedrich Nietzsche 1967a, xiii-xxiii. The above comes from
page xxii.

    12. For an overall discussion of the will to power, see pages 205-206, 238-239, 341-
453.

    13. For more on Nietzsche's break with Wagner see Kaufmann 1974, 30-41, espe-
cially pages 36-37.

    14. Also, compare his aphorism on reputation in 1974, 238.

    15. The emphasis on the great individual was not unique to Nietzsche. Fydor
Dostoevsky's novel, *Crime and Punishment*, published in the year of 1866 tells the story
of Rodion Raskonikov who wants to see himself as a great individual like Napoleon who
can make and act on his own rules. Søren Kierkegaard puts great stress on the individual
making choices. For Kierkegaard, Abraham was a knight of faith because he freely decided to trust God even if it meant the death of his only son, Isaac. Unlike Kant's stress
on autonomy of the self, these views allow for subjectivity. Great individual's do not all
do the same things. They stand out from the crowd, which is governed by expectations
and rules of others. There is no absolute or universal law within these individuals that
make them march to the same orders. Nietzsche's will to power in a positive way is a
creative force allowing one to define oneself in many possible ways.

    16. Also, see Scott 1990, 49.

    17. The quotations of Saint Thomas Aquinas and Tertullian come from Nietzsche
1994, 33-34. Nietzsche quotes them in Latin, and the translation comes in the footnotes
by Carol Diethe. I have quoted the section on Tertullian in part. It is interesting that
Tertullian goes on in a similar vein about the Jews responsible for Jesus' death. Compare
also aphorisms 12-15 on pages 27-33 of *Genealogy of Morality* as an entrance into these
quotations by Aquinas and Tertullian.

    18. Also, see Nietzsche 1989, 108.

    19. Compare to Nietzsche 1994, 19-37.

Chapter Seven
Moral Values and the Social Sciences

The practical function of morality is to make society possible, to help people live together without too much harm or conflict, to safeguard, in a word, the great collective interests (Émile Durkheim 1993, 65)

In this chapter, I examine values from a societal perspective. Remember that most views of ethics have a communal component. The philosophy of Socrates and Plato stresses the importance of reasoning. Socrates in particular assumes that correct belief on the part of the individual would ensure correct action. Furthermore, he believes that acting morally is in an individual's own self-interest since correct action leads to individual happiness. Still, Plato defines a state, in his book *The Republic*, as a place where the moral individual serves the interests of the whole. This chapter examines moral values from a social perspective with awareness of how the individual relates to the larger society. It examines moral values to determine their social significance.

Most modern moral theories evaluate intentions or actions in connection with what is beneficial for society as a whole. Even Kant's categorical imperative assumes that ethical subjects (i.e., rational creatures) should be able to universalize their rules. This notion assumes that the universal rule is in the best interest of everyone and not just the individual. In a different way, utilitarianism also calls for the individual to consider what is best for the larger society. The social aspect of morality is also a concern of the relativist. The relativist sees morality as a tool, which holds a community together. For them, truth and morality depend upon a particular location and time. What is good for today may not work tomorrow, and what works for a small community in one state would not work for a large city in another region of the country. Moral values are in fact relative, and according to the relativist, one should not attempt to impose the values of one culture on another. The relativist then must talk about what is moral and immoral in the context of a particular community and a particular period in time.

In total contrast to Kant's universalism, relativism says that particular societies determine what is morally right and wrong for themselves. A relativist position logically assumes that as a society grows and develops, customs and values change. Therefore, relativism does not try to eliminate change, but it attempts to minimize the pace of change. Relativism shares the view of Auguste Comte who says that the lack of harmony between society as a whole and its parts is pathological. Relativism views a static and functional society as preferable. Change can be dangerous, and if it occurs, a society must manage it.

The 2006 Baylor University Religion Survey shows how views differ across different geographical regions of the country. The analysis of this survey data indicates that views of God fall into four basic categories or types: God as authoritarian, benevolent, critical, or distant. The authoritarian view and the benevolent view of God share the belief that God is active in one's life; they differ in that the first one views God as angry and the other does not. The critical view says that God does not interact with the world. God observes the world and views it with disapproval. God shows displeasure in the next life. The distant view sees God as uninvolved in this world. Additionally, God is not angry.

In the survey, 43.5% of people from the South identify with a view of God as an authoritarian while in the West 20.8% view God as authoritarian. In the South, 16.9% view God as benevolent as opposed to 27.4% in the West. The percentages are similar for those who see God as critical (15.9% in the South compared to 13.6% in the West). Finally, 21.5% of those surveyed in the South see God as distant versus 30.3% in the West (Table 7).[1] The different views of God correlate to moral beliefs. Those who see God as an authoritarian are more likely to view abortion as always wrong even when the baby may have serious birth defects. 48.1% of this group view abortion as always wrong when there is a possibility that the baby would have a serious defect. 34.6% of those who identify with a benevolent God see abortion as always wrong in these circumstances, 13.6% who identifies God as critical considers it wrong, and 7.4% who view God as distant view it as wrong. This survey demonstrates that views on God and morality differ from place to place.[2]

Time of course is another factor. Observing television shows from the early days of television and comparing those television shows with today's television programs, one can clearly see a considerable change in values. What is acceptable now would not have been acceptable in the 1950s. I am not arguing, however, that values of the past are better or worse than those of today, just different.

Continuing this line of thought, I begin this chapter with a discussion of society and morality in relation to the work of sociologist and relativist, Durkheim. Durkheim sees the role of the sociologist as one who can help modify society when necessary to keep it functional. His view affirms the relativist observation that societies and values are not fixed, but they change over time. These values are not universal either. They differ from region to region. Consequently, one should keep societal change to a minimum. After a discussion of Durkheim's ethics, I focus on the changing nature of morals over time. The discussion draws on functional and conflict approaches to sociology. The functionalist side notes how morals have changed and how societies have adapted. Conflict sociology brings out the other side by examining the dynamics of conflict in relation to a society's morals. It focuses on the sources of power and authority. The remainder of this chapter, therefore, focuses on three areas. First, I consider how one might study and modify a society to make it more functional in the future. Second, I examine changing values, and look at how they affect cultures in relation to family structure and the public sphere of employment practices. Finally, I discuss ethnocentrism and the strengths and weaknesses of cultural and ethical relativism.

ÉMILE DURKHEIM AND SOCIOLOGICAL STUDY OF MORALS

Durkheim (1858-1917) was a French sociologist who identified a need for the sociological study of ethics in his book, *Ethics and the Sociology of Morals*. Robert T. Hall who translated the book into English also wrote the introduction. In it, he described Durkheim as a "social relativist" as well as an ethical relativist (Hall, Robert T. 1993, 48). Durkheim recognized a diversity of norms in society, and he suggested that morals differ depending on gender, age, social status, religious status, and occupation (Hall, Robert T. 1993, 26). Consequently, Durkheim recognized multiple perspectives as opposed to universal moral norms of Kant and other moral philosophers.

For Durkheim, morals are connected to particular societies and particular places. For instance, he says that one cannot say that slavery is universally wrong. It serves a useful and necessary purpose in some societies. One might object to this view, but it illustrates one of Durkheim's key ideas. For some societies to free its slaves may inadvertently lead to a destruction of that society (Durkheim 1993, 70). One can improve a society's morals, but one must pay close attention to the moral structure of society in doing so. Later he modifies his views on ethics in a way that is less definite. One can study society and make recommendations on what changes are needed. So, one can eliminate certain flaws and irregularities in society making it possible for that society to develop to a "higher stage" (Hall, Robert T 1993, 22).

For Durkheim, the pragmatic role of morality makes its continued existence possible. Morality enables people to "live together without too much harm or conflict, to safeguard, in a word, the great collective interests" (Durkheim 1993, 65). He feels there is a need for a study of ethics different from the philosophical study of ethics. In his view, the study of ethics needs to be examined as a part of sociology; it should constitute a sub-discipline within the field of sociology. The nature of this study should be empirical; it is a science.

For Durkheim, morality is the product of society. Laws by themselves are not enough to keep society functioning smoothly. One of Durkheim's contemporaries, Rudolf Jhering, says that a person obeys the law out of fear; the motive, then, is self-interest. However, fear alone is not enough. Durkheim says that for society to be possible there must be more than fear; there must be "some unselfish feelings in us" (Durkheim 1993, 86). Love and duty are two types of such feelings. They go beyond the sphere of law and "belong to the domain of pure morality" (Durkheim 1993, 86). Morality is not based on a selfish self-gratification. Morality is by nature directed toward the other members of society who are similar, "'the affinity of like for like'" (Hall, Robert T. 1993, 42). In other words, morality is a social matter and not a private one.

In his early work, Durkheim pays close attention to the existing norms in society (i.e., the average or statistically normal conduct). Under normal circumstances, these norms provide an orderly society, and this type of society benefits the whole. He does recognize that change occurs. The sociological ethicist must endeavor to discover anew the circumstances of normalcy in a society (Hall, Robert T. 1993, 28). To accomplish this task requires the sociologist to project the "development of a society with enough accuracy to determine a future state of equilibrium" which in reality turns out to be extremely difficult (Hall, Robert T. 1993, 29). It also means that what is morally right depends upon the norms of that society. In his view, it would be the role of the politician to maintain the status quo. If the status quo is going to change, he or she should seek to find a cure that helps society readjust.

Eventually, Durkheim gives up on this type of naturalistic ethic. He recognizes that societies often disregard their morals and need someone to remind them of the norms. Other times new norms emerge that are related to societal change, and these new norms are beneficial or functional for a society. Some practices become outdated and need to be discarded. In his revised view, the sociologist who studies morals can reflect and perhaps make recommendations (Hall 1993, 29-33).

For Durkheim, what is moral is not timeless, general or universal. What is right for one society is not right for another. The problem with such a contextual moral theory is its overemphasis on order and maintaining order even at the expense of the individual. Slavery, for example, is morally acceptable in some societies. I would agree that it may be functional for the whole, but can one ignore the individual's suffering? King eloquently notes in one of his letters from a Birmingham jail that the cry for freedom cannot wait.[3]

> For years now I have heard the word 'Wait!' It rings in the ear of every Negro with piercing familiarity. This 'Wait' has almost always meant 'Never.' .... We have waited for more than 340 years for our constitutional and God-given rights. ... Perhaps it is easy for those who have never felt the stinging darts of segregation to say 'Wait.' But when you have seen vicious mobs lynch your mothers and fathers at will ...; when you have seen hate-filled policemen curse, kick and even kill your black brothers and sisters; ... when you suddenly find your tongue twisted and your speech stammering as you seek to explain to your

six-year-old daughter why she can't go to the public amusement park that has just been advertised on television, and see tears welling up in her eyes when she is told that Funtown is closed to colored children, and see the ominous clouds of inferiority beginning to form in her little mental sky ... then you will understand why it is difficult to wait (King 2000, 69).

Before saying more about relativism, we need to expand on the implications of social change.

THE FLUID NATURE OF MORAL VALUES

Some moral philosophers want to find a reliable method to discover a set of universal standards. All the same, these desires are not obtainable. First, we will not find universal agreement, and second there is no way to establish beyond doubt any universal standards. We live in a pluralistic society that fosters many different views of what is desirable. Even if universal moral laws of right and wrong exist, how can we know them? Will society ever be able to reach a consensus on right and wrong? Moral values belong to the world of becoming, to use Plato's words. In reality, views of all kind including ethics change over time. Our truth today may be tomorrow's error. Some might settle for attempts to build a consensus as a means to bring diversity to a halt or slow its pace and introduce uniformity. Some want to do this on large scales. What will such plans lead to? Conflict theory in sociology would see in this desire an attempt to control, to spread our brand of morality, and to create a consensus to our liking.

Change is not always change for the better. Societies grow and develop but that does not mean that we are progressing toward a higher sense of justice or morality. It just means that our situation in life changes and our way of understanding the world changes. Our values assist us in coping with new and changed situations. When moral values are no longer able to give meaning or guidance for everyday living, they eventually tend to lose their grip on a society. Therefore, these older values have a tendency to undergo transformation and change. While some moral values may lose their appeal altogether, others may survive in modified form. There are always those who feel strong convictions to maintain traditional values. Traditional or religious forces always try to preserve or conserve certain traditional values. As a result, tension exists between those who hold onto traditional values and those who accept new or modified values. Today, more than any other time, we have come to realize the changing nature of moral values because of the rapidity of change.

In a previous chapter, we discuss the development of moral thinking from different historical times and cultures. Admittedly, this sketch is selective. We look at traditions that have affected Western thinking. Now I want to look at how the nature of moral thinking has changed over the centuries. One cannot really describe this change in evolutionary or progressive terms. Values change but not always for the better as the term "evolution" might imply. Changes are often rapid and represent a break with the past rather than continuity.

The terms "ethics" and "morals" mean fundamentally the same thing, at least in a historically descriptive sense. They refer to custom or habit. Clearly, the customs and habits of the past are different from the ones today. Consequently, customs change throughout human history. With the increase of technology and communications, values in our society today are changing at a rather rapid pace. We can now look at how values have changed in the past and how they continue to change.

Changing Societal Values

The work of Ferdinand Tönnies helps us distinguish between the moral values of premodern and modern societies. Tönnies identifies values associated with community (*Gemeinschaft*) from those associated with the larger society (*Gesellschaft*). The community values depend upon a social order that derives from the "consensus of wills." For Tönnies, communal relationships closely follow family structures. Folkways (i.e., rules), *mores* (i.e., morals), and religion are important for they provide a foundation for this collective view, which stems from the agreement of the community (i.e., the consensus of wills). Common and binding norms govern the relationship between individuals and particular communities. These norms have their origins in family life. Religion upholds such norms and gives them their validity (Tönnies 1971, 146). In this social setting, morality is an ideal for the community. The moral ideal is primarily a product of "religious beliefs and forces, [which are] by necessity intertwined with conditions and realities of family spirit and the folkways and mores" (Tönnies 1971, 146-147).

Gesellschaft (i.e., society, city, or state) seeks order based on convention and agreement. This order is "safeguarded by political legislation, and finds its ideological justification in public opinion" (Tönnies 1971, 146). Therefore, *Gesellschaft* (society) is purposive and goal oriented. It derives from the "conventional order of trade and similar relations but attains validity and binding force only through the sovereign will and power of the state" (Tönnies 1971, 146). Morality can be an ideal or a "mental system of norms for the life of the community." As a mental system "it is entirely a product and instrument of public opinion, which encompasses all relations arising out of the contractual sociableness, contacts, and political intentions" (Tönnies 1971, 147). In short, Tönnies describes *Gemeinschaft* (community) by its close personal ties and by its kinship relationships. He describes society, on the other hand, as "more impersonal or business-type relationships" (Wallace and Wolf 1986, 23). Morality functions in both settings.

Tönnies' ideas have also influenced Durkheim's description of mechanical and organic solidarity. Mechanical solidarity (associated with premodern societies) refers to a society that has a clear consensus of beliefs, ideas, and morality. In this type of society, there is a strong *collective or group conscience*. People tend to agree on right and wrong, and there is less diversity. There are ancient societies where diversity would exist, but people could easily isolate themselves in their own smaller groupings. As societies grow, however, this consensus becomes more difficult to hold together, and it may give way to diversity. This shift is the result of an increase in the *division of labor*. This increase in the division of labor coincides with the modern era. It follows that ideas, beliefs, and morals also become more diverse and flexible in modern industrial societies and consensus becomes more difficult. The division of labor, therefore, becomes a new social bond that replaces the older one based on unity of thought and belief. Dependency on others becomes a new bond. In modern societies, people must cooperate to obtain goods and services necessary for survival. This type of society tends to weaken the collective conscience (Durkheim 1933).[4]

Sociologist Talcott Parsons has further developed the work of Tönnies. Parsons develops the work of Tönnies in terms of *expressive* and *instrumental values*. *Expressive values* refer to the values of traditional society (i.e., Tönnies' community) where relationships are personal and stable. These relationships are still, however, present in modern societies. We find them most readily in one's home or family life. *Instrumental values* refer to relationships that are more modern, impersonal, and businesslike (Wallace and Wolf 1986, 22-28).

Parsons identifies five opposing sets of values. They include ascription versus achievement, diffuseness versus specificity, affectivity versus neutrality, particularism versus universalism, and finally collectivity versus self. The first term in each pair represents the expressive side, whereas the second term constitutes the instrumental side. These differences further develop the ideas of Tönnies. A brief look at the contrasts can show how modern thinking in the public sphere differs from the private or communal sphere.

1. *Ascription* means that people judge or relate to others in a community or family setting based on the other person's age, gender, and race. In addition, political associations and one's economic status can provide an individual with a privileged place in society. People and groups in most premodern societies hold their elders in higher esteem than the young, and in the vast majority of cases, they automatically favor men over women. Moreover, premodern societies may judge people solely based on their race. On the other hand, an individual may gain status in the community because of the political or economic status of his or her own family. Modern societies, on the other hand, see these judgments as unethical. In a modern society, Parsons says we expect individuals to judge people on their abilities or *achievement*. It is no longer acceptable to discriminate against people due to their ascribed status.

Concerning elders, many people still feel that we should relate to them with due consideration and respect for their age. Some people feel that society no longer gives them proper respect. In times past, societies would hold their elders in high esteem; they would see them as a source of wisdom. Today one is much more likely to make negative associations with old age. Besides age, we also struggle with the issue of equality where race and gender are concerned.

2. *Diffuseness* refers to the types of demands that one can expect from a relationship. In a community or family setting, a person could expect other members of his or her group to have a personal interest in his or her affairs. In modern societies, outside the home and a small circle of friends, we relate to

others based on *specificity*. For instance, an individual's health is typically the only concern of the doctor. The doctor may become irritated if the patient asks questions or makes conversation that is not consistent with the roles and expectations of the doctor and patient relationship.

3. *Affectivity versus affectivity neutrality* refers to the expected stance toward another person. We expect family members and married couples to relate to each other with affection. One expects parents to take special interest in their own children. Showing affection in a family context is acceptable. The same is not true in modern public life. While it may be acceptable for parents to show affection for their own children, it is not acceptable for a teacher to show special attention to just one or two students. A show of affection or preference in public is inappropriate. A teacher must relate to a student in an *affective neutral* or non-emotional fashion.

4. *Particularism* means that we relate to or associate with others based on their membership in a particular group. In communities where groups tend to isolate themselves from others, there is an inclination to distrust outsiders. Those members who form the group or community are of primary concern. From this perspective, the community tends to judge a person by the norms of the group. Particularism is a way of relating to others, and in its negative form, it can become a mechanism of exclusion and discrimination. In a modern society, however, we expect people to judge others on *universalistic* grounds. Universal means that we should treat people equally. It expects us to be impartial.

5. *Collectivity versus self* concerns the role of the individual in society. Does he or she merge into the whole or remain distinctive? In communal societies, individuals see themselves in relation to the larger group. They are part of a larger collective. Collective or community values stress the moral obligation one has to the community. One's identity comes from the community to which he or she belongs. Modern societies, however, stress individuality and autonomy. This type of society encourages people to pursue their individual *self-interest*. One can legitimately pursue one's own advantage in modern societies. Our capitalistic system, for instance, encourages one to pursue profit vigorously.[5]

Parsons proposes this model of societal values in 1951. He describes how society works to move and to prepare children to leave home, the location of expressive values, and enter into the public arena, the home of instrumental values. In this way, instrumental values help to resocialize the child so he or she can function in the public realm. Before examining ascription versus achievement and affectivity versus affectivity neutrality in relation to education and hiring practices, I need to add one other aspect of Parson's social analysis to our discussion, societal evolution.

Evolution of Societies

Like Spencer and Durkheim, Parsons describes societal evolution as moving from a simple societal structure to a more complex one over time. Once a society develops beyond the "primitive stage," it naturally matures. As it becomes more diverse, it requires more organization. As a result, societies become more stratified. According to Parsons, social stratification has four specific processes, which he identifies as differentiation, adaptive upgrading, inclusion, and value generalization.

Social stratification refers to the various types of divisions in society. A key process accompanying social stratification is *differentiation*. Differentiation is the process whereby different people or groups can play specific roles within the larger society. Parsons notes that as societies grow they become increasingly differentiated, and as a result their population becomes increasingly stratified. Therefore, societies become more complex and differentiated over time. As this evolutionary route continues, some roles are more essential to a society's survival than others. As a result, society values these roles more highly. Consequently, there is a ranking of positions according to their importance. In this fashion, certain professions command more respect and confer higher status than others because only a limited number of people have the intellect or skills to fill these positions (Wallace and Wolf 1986, 40-41). Additionally, as societies grow and become more complex, specialization of roles occurs. Over time, we can see a historical progression from the "medicine man" in some premodern societies to nurses, pharmacists, and surgeons in modern societies.

The other three processes are *adaptive upgrading, inclusion,* and *value generalization.* According to Parsons, evolution progresses in this particular order. As societies become more diverse, adaptive upgrading follows. Adaptive upgrading refers to a society's ability to adapt, foresee, and deal with potential problems that might endanger or disrupt the order and stability present in a society. Society rewards those people who can help it overcome problems that might threaten its continued survival (Wallace and Wolf 1986, 41, 43).

Inclusion is a process by which individuals obtain fair and equal opportunities, and so it has important moral implications. To obtain fairness, societies establish universal norms. The purpose of these norms is to protect one from exclusion due to ascriptive factors such as age, sex, or race. Yet, Parsons says it is appropriate to differentiate between people based on modern instrumental values. For instance, it is acceptable to distinguish between people because of a person's achievement level. For Parsons, it is proper that doctors have a higher status than factory workers. Nevertheless, it is not acceptable to prevent a qualified person from gaining a position because of ascriptive factors such as age, sex, or race. Inclusion involves breaking down boundaries or barriers and providing opportunities to everyone. In an inclusive society, medical doctors are no longer just white males; any qualified individual regardless of race, gender or class can become a doctor (Wallace and Wolf 1986, 38-44).

The final process is value generalization, which suggests that as societies progress they need a religion that is more general in nature. It needs a general religion not associated with any particular type of religion like Catholic or Baptist or Islam. According to Parsons, a general religion could do a much better job in legitimating a wider range of moral values since it would appeal to a broader group of people. For instance, a society might evolve away from Protestantism or Catholicism to a civil religion. Civil religion would espouse the values of life, liberty, and the pursuit of happiness rather than specific doctrines associated with a specific brand of religious faith.

Because of the above processes, societal evolution leads to progress. According to Parsons, modern societies have moved away from expressive values because they are inefficient and narrow. Modern society is a more productive and fair society. Today people can go as far as their abilities can take them. At least, this is the modern dream, or one might argue it is the modern delusion. As noted earlier, evolution is not equivalent with progress. We can see problems with this view when we examine a sample of Parsons' work on education and hiring.

Expressive and Instrumental Values in Education, Hiring Practices, and the Work Place

Now we can examine the areas of education and work in connection with Parsons' thought and other more recent studies. We can see a number of Parsons' notions concerning societal values in his discussion of education. In 1959, Parsons writes an article in the *Harvard Educational Review* on elementary education. He is examining school systems as socializing agencies. In the home, parents and children relate to each other differently than they relate to people in the public domain. Elementary schools are the primary agency for socializing children, and they have the responsibility of moving the children away from expressive values toward instrumental values associated with modern society. Consequently, the values that schools inculcate are different from the values one receives and expresses at home.

Performance in elementary school, he says, is the primary determinate of who goes to college and who goes straight into the work force. Parsons observes that the records of elementary school children are

> evaluated by teachers and principals, and there are few cases of entering col-
> lege preparatory courses against their advice. It is therefore not stretching the
> evidence too far to say broadly that the primary selective process occurs
> through differential school performance in elementary school, and that the
> 'seal' is put on it in junior high school (Parsons 1967, 649).

His claim is that the whole process works on *achievement* and that *ascription* does not play a significant part. Therefore, the educational system *differentiates children* according to their abilities.

Affectivity versus affectivity neutrality also relates to schools. Specifically, the teacher should refrain from relating to a student or child on an emotional basis. At home, the parent can relate to his or her child in this way. A child can certainly expect his or her parents to give him or her more attention than they would give to the neighbor's children. In the school system, however, things are different. At school, children learn that they must relate to their teachers on a non-emotional basis. Teachers must not become emotionally engaged with their students; they are to be neutral and objective.

Schools must judge children based on their achievement. As a result, the classroom is divided into low and high achievers. Such a division is necessary for the school to meet the needs of society. Some children are simply not college material. Moreover, schools cannot overly concern themselves about the negative psychological impact on those children whom they identify or label as low achievers (Parsons 1967, 656).

Response to Parson's Functional Approach

Parsons' views on the educational system reflect modern instrumental values. Like Parsons, many people feel that the values of achievement and impartiality ought to be the ideals for any modern society. The modern ideals represent the apex of societal evolution. However, one could question these ideals. Just how desirable are they? One may question whether achievement and impartiality have ever really functioned as the basis for judging people in the areas of education, economics, or business. Parsons and many others in the functionalist tradition see society as a great machine. Individuals, on this view, are cogs in this machine we call society. Society has needs, and it produces institutions and individuals to meet those needs. This view of society is rather naïve and static by today's vantage point.

Recall that Parsons and those who follow the functionalist approach see education as a way of obtaining the most gifted individuals. These gifted individuals are necessary because they fill the most important jobs in our society. Parsons says that the educational system judges students on their personal achievement and not on ascriptive values. The educational system should be designed to educate the most highly qualified individuals to do the most prestigious and important jobs. The people who fill these positions, therefore, are due higher social and economic status because of their abilities. However, society needs other less gifted individuals to fill the less prestigious jobs.

In 1971, Randall Collins analyzes and criticizes this functionalist view of education. According to the functionalist approach, societal needs govern the individual's rank in the larger society. Those who have skills in demand become more important, and their rewards are greater than those with lesser sought after skills. One gains a job, on this account, because of one's achievement in obtaining special skills. However, Collins argues that "demands" of any occupational position are not fixed, but represent whatever is settled upon in the bargaining process. This process is between the people who fill the positions, and those people who attempt to control them (Collins 1971, 1007).

In contrast to Parsons, Collins says that ascriptive factors continue to play a significant part in one's advancement. Discrimination due to one's ethnicity and class still occurs. Here discrimination goes beyond skin color, gender, or class to include the way a person dresses, his or her manners, his or her attractiveness or lack thereof, and his or her conversational abilities. One's *educational level* can also be a way to discriminate. The status or level of one's education can limit those who have an opportunity to gain employment. Often, the job requirements are not necessary for doing the job satisfactorily. The skills for doing a job in many cases do not come from formal education but on the job training.

Certain ascribed groups (i.e., white males in positions of power) may use education as a way to obtain employees who fit in with their own value system. Some employers, for instance, may select employees only from elite universities. In this way, they are getting employees who are in similar social situations as themselves. In other words, they are obtaining employees who most likely share their own values. Collins attempts to show that these selections do not correlate to the fact that these schools turn out more highly skilled employees. A study of

> top executives in nationally prominent businesses indicated that the most highly educated managers were not found in the most rapidly developing companies, but rather in the least economically vigorous ones, with highest education found in the traditionalistic financial and utility firms (Collins 1971, 1014).

Education, therefore, is not important solely because it teaches needed skills. Education is an instrument for narrowing or limiting the competition for jobs (Collins 1979, 48).

Compared to Collins' work, Parsons' view seems rather naïve by today's standards. Parsons suggests that modern society has evolved to the point where discrimination is no longer acceptable. Inclusion is the legitimate goal of civilized societies. Whereas *expressive societies* may exclude people based on sex, age, or race, *modern societies* do not. Modern values do not allow for distinctions between people based on ascription but on achievement. These modern views expect people to judge others based on their performance. Expressive societies may show nepotism (i.e., affectivity), but not modern ones. While expressive societies may exclude those who are outsiders (i.e., particularism), the values of modern societies oppose discriminating against people; modern societies should be inclusive. However, conflict theorists, feminists, and others have convincingly shown that achievement and inclusion are goals far from being reached.

The functionalist approach to sociology, of which Parsons is a major contributor, values conformity. For Parsons, an ideal society is one where everyone knows and performs their assigned roles. Society has needs, and it is up to individuals to play their roles in society to meet those needs. This view usually means that people should accept their place in the social order and see themselves as part of the larger collective. If they have a poor paying job, it is because they have not prepared themselves to achieve or that they just do not have the ability to achieve. Still, society needs these people to do jobs that are less desirable or jobs that others do not want.

More Recent Responses to the Functionalist Approach

I do not mean or wish to imply by my critique of Parsons' views that some jobs are not worthy of respect. People who work at such jobs, jobs that many people might classify as undesirable, are essential and their work is deserving of respect. Yet, should society label these individuals and the value they have for society as in anyway inferior? The person with special abilities plays an important role in society, but that does not make him or her worth more than one with no special talents. I am not suggesting that Parsons' hold the view that one group is inferior to another. Yet, his view can lead one to that conclusion.

The current system for evaluation and selection of individuals for certain tasks is not a neutral one; it often judges people on an ascriptive basis rather than on achievement. Generally, the modern view believes that it is possible by means of reason to be neutral and impartial. However, this belief does not lead to an ideal society based on achievement and inclusion. One can conclude that modern society with its emphasis on reason, rationality, objectivity, and trying to treat everyone the same has failed to create a fair and just society. Parsons' functionalism sees people as parts of the larger mechanism, and their role as the parts of that mechanism is to serve the good of the whole. There is also an individualistic emphasis on the self in modern life. A society should operate where a person receives rewards for playing by the rules of the game. The individual should seek his or her own self-interests within the context of instrumental values. The interests of the individual depend upon the good of society as a whole.

Conflict analysis and postmodern thought see things differently. Postmodernism rejects modern theories that try to suppress pluralism, diversity, and difference. Conflict investigations indicate that instrumental values do not necessarily lead to inclusion or equality. They often overlook the role of power that actually subverts equality and inclusion. This omission masks inequalities and exclusivistic practices as well as practices where one with power takes advantage of those who have little power. Parsons' functionalist system views individuals as parts of a whole whose purpose is to serve society. He does not consider the abuses or injustices necessary to uphold and maintain existing political and social institutions.

According to a study by James N. Baron, *ascription* still operates as an instrument of selecting employees. Baron's study indicates that there is a tendency to evaluate positions filled by women and minorities differently from those held by white males. For example, "members of high-status social groups (e.g., males, especially whites) are substantially more likely to be allocated to unique job titles in organizations" (Baron 1994, 73).[6] Interestingly, he also finds that companies established before the concern for equality make slower progress toward redressing gender inequities than companies established during the time when equality had become an important issue (Baron 1994, 76). Baron concludes:

> In the organizational world I have described, the extent of ascription is affected not simply by employer tastes, labor supply, the legal environment, and economic transaction costs, but also by psychological, political, and normative factors shaping organizational change and sustaining the status quo in a given setting. Drawing on my research, I have described how some of these factors affect three facets of discrimination: how ascriptive characteristics figure in the way jobs are defined, evaluated, and staffed in organizations (Baron 1994, 81).

Baron's essay appears in a collection of essays dealing with discrimination such as gender and race. Therefore, Parsons is certainly wrong to suggest that modern values place achievement over ascription. As we have seen, people in today's job market are judged in relation to age, sex, race, appearance, and social status. We could likely add other items to this list as well. One may ask if it is ever possible to get beyond judging others on an ascriptive basis. Is it possible for humans to be impartial? We can have all manners of policies, but do they ensure that everyone will receive equal opportunity in practice? As Baron notes, there is a discrepancy between policies and practice (Baron 1994, 79-81).

Observations

Is our society gradually progressing toward some sort of ideal as the modern view suggests? Parsons believes that modern society is making progress toward an ideal democratic society (Wallace and Wolf 1986, 43). According to Parsons and others who adopt an evolutionary view, modern society and its values are better than the values of so-called "primitive societies." Yet, this notion of evolution is highly questionable. Is it justifiable to claim that today's values are superior to the values of our ancestors? (Best and Kellner 1991, 37)

Sure, there has been progress made toward inclusion, and I would certainly value the notion that everyone should receive a fair opportunity to obtain their goals. Nevertheless, we have not reached that stage, and we are unlikely to ever eliminate bias. Human beings are not perfect creatures by any definition, and there seems to be a natural human tendency to look out for one's own interests. This human tendency often tempts us to act with little regard for the welfare of others.

Moreover, every generation redefines the notion of what is good and desirable. To say that societies are progressively evolving for the better is a highly questionable. Societies change, and some may improve only to decline again later. When things go badly people may abandon concern for the welfare of others and revert to a survival mentality. Even when oppressive systems of government are overthrown, it is likely that the oppressed may become the oppressors. Societies and moods often swing back and forth.

Modern values (i.e., the values that Parsons advocates) are certainly different from the values of previous generations, but on balance, they are no better or worse. Abuses and injustices in communal societies have occurred in past generations that lived according to the expressive set of values, but we still have abuses and unfairness today in modern societies. People can always find ways to harm others or take advantage of them.

Durkheim's dismissal of universal norms comes from a recognition that societies evolve in different ways. This view also realizes that evolution does not necessarily lead to constant progress toward instrumental values. His view that we should not actively reform society in accordance with certain ideals, however, is questionable. For instance, should we not try to make society more just? If a society practices discrimination against a particular group, should we just accept that practice?

In short, there is no correlation between the evolution of societies and progress. Societies must adjust to new conditions. Societies are always changing. The change is not always in a positive direction. Societies must always strive to create and maintain a just order. The remainder of the chapter focuses on the changing nature of the family from premodern times to the present, and a brief discussion of culture and ethnocentrism.

CHANGES IN FAMILY LIFE AND VALUES OVER TIME

In chapter ten, I look at issues of gender and equality. An important background for this discussion comes from an understanding of the moral worldviews that derive from the family or community settings. These worldviews continue to impede equality and openness to difference. The views that shape us originally, therefore, come from our primary socialization. I begin this discussion with a brief sketch of premodern families. This description entails an examination of rural families that are dependent on agricultural production. I also describe urban family life in preindustrial societies. Before going on to modern family life, I examine how patriarchal values are the norm not only in the family setting but also for the state. The Greek philosopher Aristotle and his Roman counterparts allow women a limited role in those societies. Their views represent a vision of how society should be structured and what place parent, child, wife, and slave should play within that structure. This discussion concludes with an examination of family life at present, which entails a discussion of both the modern and the postmodern family.

Rural Premodern Family Life

I begin with the family structure of *poor agrarian peasants* living at or just above the level of subsistence. Teodor Shanin defines peasants as small agriculturalists who work primarily for their own benefit. They must create a surplus to distribute to the state, to landowners, and to anyone else to whom they are obligated. Family farms are the main "units of social organization" and farming is the main way they earn and sustain their existence. These groups or communities are neither highly stratified nor completely egalitarian. Differences in power relations occur even within peasant families and communities (Frank 1994, 555-556).

These agrarian societies tend to be less open to outside influences than their modern counterparts. Consequently, they tend to resist change that comes upon them from the outside even though they may be easily overpowered. Families within such a community would be able to control the family environment and keep a firm hold on their children. With limited outside influence, children know one set of values. These are the values adopted by the members of the community. A modern example of this type of social isolation can be found within some Amish communities. Socialization in these communities would be more successful. The nuclear family teaches its children moral values that are rein-forced by the community. This analogy leads one to suspect that authority fig-ures are much more important in these types of social societies than they are in modernistic ones.

In this agricultural type of society, the entire family has to join forces in the struggle for survival. There is no differentiation of roles. For the most part, chil-dren have to do whatever the situation requires. Each child has to help with the daily chores. These families have a patriarchal family structure, which means that the husband/father makes the decisions and is primarily responsible for the family's well-being. By family, however, I do not mean the modern nuclear family consisting of the mother, father, and dependent children. In many pre-modern communities or tribes, the extended family functions in place of the nuclear family. The extended family refers to a large household related by mar-riage and blood. This means that the children have ready access not only to their parents, but also to other adults such as their grandparents. This family structure creates a large network of social support for the children and parents. In some rural societies, however, the land is insufficient to support a large family. Such a situation might force some members of the family to leave their agricultural pur-suits and go to the city to earn a living.[7]

Authority relates to this notion of patriarchal family structure. Males cer-tainly have more authority in this type society than females. In addition, the elder son is important in these societies. He is the one who would receive the decision-making role in the family as well as property at the absence or death of his father (Wolf 1966, 69-71). The ideal family then is one where there are a number of children, particularly male children, surrounded by other family members outside the nuclear family.

The moral values of such a family would consist in traits that allow for the survival of the family and community. Peasant families or families that depend on agricultural pursuits would value hard work and land. Survival would depend upon having some land from which they could make a living. That land is their primary and often times only source of life. Accompanying hard work, family ties and cooperation are necessary. This cooperation must occur both within the family and within the larger community. It may at times have required more than the extended family to survive. Some societies would band together form-ing a larger group to resist threats of bad weather or even outside enemies. These societies would also value security and stability. Moreover, they would avoid violence if possible. Since they were not necessarily a strong group in a military sense, they would associate violence with insecurity and a danger to their way of life. Finally, they would value tradition and respect for elders and parents (Redfield 1956, 105-139; Wolf 1966, 67-71; and Shanin 1990, 72). In short, cooperation and community are the two things that stand out most, and presumably, they would not have valued individuality that highly.

Urban Premodern Family Life

Families in the preindustrial city have values that are not completely different from those outside the city. The major differences have to do with the fashion in which one makes a living and the type of existing influences. Rural areas primarily make their living off the land, and they can limit outside influences to a large degree. City dwellers, on the other hand, do not make their living off the land. Being in the city, they are much more likely to encounter people they consider outsiders. As a result, city life would expose them to a wider variety of influences. Values such as hard work, the desire for peace and security, and patriarchal authority over the family would still occur. The importance of family would also be significant, but it would not retain exactly the same value in city life as it would outside the city. In the rural areas, the families must cooperate to work the land whereas in the city the extended family depends upon the income of several family members and not just the head of the household (Sjoberg 1960, 160). After marriage, the bride becomes part of her husband's family, which makes up the extended family. This extended family

> includes a man and his wife (or wives), their unmarried children, married sons, and the latter's wives and children, and perhaps other relatives such as widowed daughters or sisters of the family head, as well as numerous servants (Sjoberg 1960, 157).

The roles within this extended family are hierarchical. Ascribed traits such as age and sex are quite important, as they would have been in peasant families. This type of society is patriarchal in its power structure. Women have few social or legal rights. Gideon Sjoberg describes the roles of males and females in the following manner:

> In childhood, she is dependent upon her father, after marriage upon her husband, and in widowhood upon her sons. The men are the family's representatives in the external world; their primary duty is to support the women, children, and the aged and infirm[ed] [*sic*] in the family. . . . In essence a woman's lot in life is determined first by the kind of family she is born into, and then by the family she enters through marriage (Sjoberg 1960, 163).

According to Sjoberg, this society expects women to serve their husbands and to bear his children. Giving birth does bestow a higher status on women, and a male child is preferable. Her status in the household, however, does not go with her outside the household. Age also brings higher status and older women certainly gain status because of their age. Producing offspring, especially sons, is of utmost importance in both the agricultural family as well as for the family living in the city. Parents raise their children to respect the roles and values dominant in their particular community. Children should, if all goes well, learn and transmit these values to their offspring. Usually, values associated with the preindustrial city and those associated with the rural areas do not appear to be radically different.

However, before continuing, I need to make a few comments regarding social class. Scholars do not agree on how to determine one's social class. Do we put someone in a social class according to income level, social status, political status, perceived status, or some combination of the above? This becomes a rather complicated task, which goes beyond the scope of this discussion. Sociologist Gerhard Lenski has organized the Mediterranean population into nine different classes (Lenski 1966, 190-290). His study shows that there is a wide gulf between the five upper classes and the four bottom classes. Most of the population falls into the four lower ones. Given his view, our description above would hold for the majority of people. There would be some exceptions particularly regarding the elites of society.

Therefore, typical poor agrarian families or those families living in the cities share certain views. This sharing indicates that one's values and beliefs depend in part on social forces and conditions. We can conclude that one's *social location* plays a vital role in shaping one's morals. One's economic situation is also important. A peasant living 2,000 years ago would certainly see life differently than a mobile entrepreneur of that same age. The dominant views of a particular geographical location or of a particular period can have a great impact upon how individuals feel and think about their world. Premodern family values differ from modern ones. Premodern views vary quite noticeably regarding the place of children and the roles of men and women. Traditional gender and social roles in relation to the family continue to have a significant impact on Western culture and continues to shape and mold views about the role of women in today's society.

We can see the philosophical and religious underpinnings of this way of thinking in the work of Aristotle, Jewish religion, and Christian religion. The ascriptive values related to gender are consistent with fundamentalist and conservative Christian thinking today. In essence, views on gender expressed by Aristotle, the Romans, fundamentalists, and the traditional views of the most cultures from ancient times to the present limit women's sphere of influence to the home and family.

Premodern Views on the Family in the Greco-Roman World

Aristotle's views on the family revolve around the *household code*. Aristotle says that something is good if it fulfills or performs its proper function. Everything has a function and when it performs this function, it is good. Consequently, Aristotle's goal is to define the function of the household in relation to the larger state. He also defines the roles of each member of the household. The household is an integral part of the state for Aristotle and later for Rome. In this light, Aristotle sees the state as a natural outgrowth of households or earlier associations of people. The goals of each household are to provide for the needs of society. The family or household, then, is an important aspect of the state.

The notion of "pairs" is significant for Aristotle. Things exist in pairs. Procreation depends upon pairing of the male and female. Likewise, society depends upon rulers and the ruled (i.e., slaves) for continued existence. According to Aristotle, *nature* itself leads to the formation of households. A household derives from the

> association formed by men with these two, women and slaves . . . and the poet Hesiod was right when he wrote, 'Get first a house and a wife and an ox to draw a plough.' (The ox is the poor man's slave.) The association of persons, established according to nature for the satisfaction of daily needs, is the household (Aristotle 1981, 58).

From the formation of households, villages come into existence. Further development leads to several villages, and this in turn to the state. The state, therefore, is a natural outgrowth of the household. The purpose of the state is to secure the "good life." The state, therefore, is the goal or the purpose of these other associations. The household and village lead to the formation of the state. The state has priority over the household and individual; in this instance, there would be a clear hierarchy (Aristotle 1981, 59-61). Consequently, Aristotle closely relates the family or household to the state, and he says that humans are "political animals."

Aristotle's view that things naturally exist in pairs and that one of the pairs is the ruler and the other is the ruled determines the shape of the household. Aristotle breaks the household down into three pairs: master-slave, husband-wife, and parent-child. In each one of these three pairs, the first in the pair is superior to the second. The first is the ruler and the second is the ruled. Society simply takes it for granted during Aristotle's day that slavery is natural. Still, Aristotle attempts to justify slavery. According to him, slaves are "live tools," and slaves are property of their master (Aristotle 1981, 63-69). Not only is the master the head over the slave, but he is head of the household, which means that he is in authority over his wife and children as well. He assumes that men are naturally more fit to rule than females.

In terms of morality, each person in the three pairs has to perform their function well. If they do so then they are virtuous. One could even ascribe a minimal amount of virtue to a slave who serves his or her master well. The ruler or head of the household must have "moral virtue in its entirety; for his function is in its fullest sense that of a master-craftsman, and reason is a master-craftsman" (Aristotle 1981, 95). The wife and child must also have the appropriate virtues. For example, silence is a virtue for a wife, but not for a husband.

It is also significant that Aristotle believes there is a connection between the household and the state. Just as the husband is head of the household, the ruler is head of the state. Each household is part of the state and so it is important to connect the roles in the household with the state. The state, therefore, has the responsibility to regulate the relationships in the household.

In *Ethics*, Aristotle makes analogies between the state and the household. The father is like a monarch in relation to his sons. As the so-called ruling monarch of his household, the Romans expect the father to provide for the needs of his children. The association between husband and wife is an association based on an aristocratic model where the husband rules the wife by "virtue of his merit." He gives her responsibilities and authorities that are suitable for her. He is not to rule over everything. Brothers should resemble timocracy (i.e., a government based on military value of honor) since they are equals, except for the differences in their ages. Democracy occurs when there is no head of the household or the head is weak (Aristotle 1976, 276-277).

The Greco-Roman world took this connection of the household and state seriously. Like Aristotle, "Greco-Roman political writers understood the household to be the basic building block of the state" (Stambaugh and Balch 1986, 123). By the time of the Roman Empire, some women were gaining economic power. As a result, they gained some independence, and this in turn led to a growing uneasiness in the Roman city and household. John E. Stambaugh and David Balch conclude that the

> Romans feared sedition when their wives followed barbarian Dionysus, Queen Isis, the lawgiver Moses, or Jesus. These foreign religions experienced persecution by the Roman state partially because Romans feared a restructuring of the Roman patriarchal household (Stambaugh and Balch 1986, 124).

Nevertheless, the basic idea present in Aristotle and Rome is also reflected in the Hebrew Bible (i.e., Old Testament) as well as the New Testament. The household code appears in part or in its entirety in three New Testament passages: Colossians 3:18-4:1, Ephesians 5:21-6:9, and 1 Peter 2:18-3:6. These writings instruct people on the proper household. Likewise, Jewish writers of the time such as Josephus and Philo defend the Jewish faith with regard to its household structure. They argue that Jewish women (e.g., Abraham's wife Sarah) are properly submissive according to the Law of Moses (Balch 1974, 120, 134-138, 176-179). According to Balch, the household code (1 Peter 2:18-3:6) functions as a defense of the Christian community in Asia Minor, which includes its views on the role of wives in the home.

The New Testament passages that contain all or parts of the household code (i.e., Colossians 3:18-4:1, Ephesians 5:21-6:9, and 1 Peter 2:18-3:6) defend Aristotle's view of the household in that they maintain the same power structures. The New Testament discusses the roles and functions of master and slave, husband and wife, and parent and child. Colossians 3:18-4:1 and 1 Peter 2:18-3:6 address master and slave and husband and wife relations. In Ephesians, the author[8] discusses all three: master and slave, husband and wife, and parent and child. In these passages as well as in Aristotle's writings on the subject, it is always the first in the pair that has power over the second. Therefore, slaves are to be submissive to their masters, wives to their husbands, and children to their parents. Some scholars have suggested that the New Testament writers maintain these distinctions out of fear of the Roman authorities. The Roman authorities expect the household to function according to the household code.

Yet as Josephus and Philo maintain, Jewish women are subject to their husband's authority. Jewish children are also expected to obey their parents. Generally, property goes to the oldest male in the family, and the elder son would seem to take over for his father upon his father's death. Of course, there are cases where this does not happen. Upon David's death, Adonijah has a claim to the throne due to his status as the elder son, but Solomon is the one who actually becomes king. In relation to 2 Samuel 9-20 and 1 Kings 1-2 (commonly referred to as the Throne Succession Narrative), Claus Westermann contends that this text expresses a close relationship between the family structure and monarchy. The family element precedes the political one. The ancient Israelite monarchy takes shape in this text, and Westermann argues that the expectation of the elder son inheriting the throne after his father's death is based on the model of the household or family as presented in the Genesis patriarchal stories. For example, he connects the continuity of generations in the patriarchal stories with the continuity of the dynasty (Westermann 1971, 611-619). So, the patriarchal structures present in the household relate to the state.

It would be surprising to see church leaders, who were males, go against this code regarding gender distinctions since it provides them legitimacy for their high status in the Church hierarchy. That does not mean, however, that there is no opposition to the patriarchal system in the Bible. Paul may have dissented from this view to some extent. In Galatians 3:28, Paul says, "There is no longer Jew or Greek, there is no longer slave or free, there is no longer male and female; for all of you are one in Christ Jesus."[9] Much recent New Testament scholarship paints Jesus and Paul in a more favorable light concerning their attitudes toward women and the place of women in the Christian community or church. There are also emancipator tendencies in the Roman Empire during the first century C.E. (Fiorenza 1984, 77-79).

Therefore, in Aristotle and Rome as well as in Judeo-Christian writings there is a strong emphasis on male dominance of the family. For households to function properly as a vital part of the state, families are to follow Aristotle's views on the subject. If masters and slaves, husbands and wives, parents and children fulfill their proper roles, then a strong state exists. In summary, Aristotle and the Roman authorities believe that the household code is essential for a peaceful and productive state. It is the state's job to provide for its citizens, and it is the job of the husband to provide for the household. This basic view of the household is also the dominate view in traditional or conservative Jewish and Christian communities as well.[10]

Modern and Postmodern Family Values

The modern and postmodern periods show changing attitudes concerning the family. I examine the modern family in relation to the postmodern one to highlight the contrasts between the two views. David Elkind describes the differences between modern and postmodern families. The modern family tends to focus its attention around the child. Elkind relates this orientation to the ideas of Darwin who stresses the need for a parent's offspring to survive.

Postmodern families, on the other hand, revolve around the parents. Mother and father enter into the work force. In many cases, a single parent works to provide for the needs of the child or children. In either case, there is a need for childcare. As a result, parents entrust their children to other caretakers. In a sense, this need for someone to take care of the children is just the logical movement toward inclusion, a modern instrumental value. Women have traditionally taken care of the children even in the modern family. When they enter the workforce and there is no extended family to take care of the children, the only option is to employ caretakers for the children.

In modern and postmodern families, parents may not be able or willing to provide the child with the security available to earlier generations of young people. Often, parents have to choose between career and family. Elkind is not judging parents today, but only noting an imbalance (Elkind 1994, 5-14).

The family structure in modern family life stresses boundaries, limits, authority, and specific roles associated with gender. Parents and children know their place since their roles are well defined. Mothers often stay home and play the role of caretaker while the fathers work outside the home as the "breadwinners." At this time, the ideal family consists of a married couple with children. This ideal when followed leads to a stable home life. This type of family structure makes for a certain stability of family life (Elkind 1994, 26-30).

The postmodern family, however, is not nearly as well defined. Family structures are diverse. Parents do not have well-defined roles. The mother may now be the breadwinner instead of the husband. Some fathers now take their children to the doctor when they are sick and help do many other things that society once considered a woman's job. In most cases, men have begun to play roles that society once considered feminine, and women have come to perform roles that society previously defined as masculine. Parents are more likely to define their roles within the family as opposed to accepting already established ones due largely to pragmatic concerns.

Another interesting aspect of postmodern life concerns scheduling. The irregularity of schedules today may mean that the father has to prepare the meals while the wife works. Even children may find themselves having to take on responsibilities and roles that once belonged to adults (Elkind 1994, 30-35). Work schedules are more flexible and allow many people to work from anywhere at anytime day or night. The days of steady hours is gone for many. Now one cannot get away from work. Cell phones, internet access, emails make it difficult to simply disconnect. In a sense, we might not want to lay all this at the feet of postmodernism. Much of the way things are today have to do with the advance of technology and the natural evolution of society based on it.

Elkind also examines changing family attitudes. There are at least three major changes. To begin, modern families replace the old norm of arranged marriages with the notion of romantic love. Elkind says that romantic love derives out of the "notion that a woman was relatively helpless and dependent, in need of a prince charming" (Elkind 1994, 41). Once this hero arrives on the scene, the view is that the woman would be happy to devote her life to him and their children. However, women become tired, for whatever reasons, with the limited roles of wife and mother. Again, the modern notions of inclusion and equality lead to significant changes in society that Elkind describes as postmodern.

The second change in family attitudes has to do with marital love. This type of love would often lead to the union of a couple. The expectation for a modern couple was to have children. Society expects mothers to be the ones responsible for the care and nurture of the child. Men, on the other hand, are there to provide strength, leadership, and financial resources to the family.

Third, the home is the place that shelters the family from the community. It is the place where parents teach values and attitudes, which children need so that they can become good citizens. It is the place of primary socialization. In many instances, this privacy may belie the notion that all is well. For example, since society frowns on divorce, many women stay in abusive situations. Many parents continue marriages for the sake of the children.

In contrast to the ideals of romantic love, marital love, and domesticity, postmodern life more often engages in consensual love, shared parenting, and urbanity. Consensual love relates to the so-called "second sexual revolution." After the 1950's, it becomes more acceptable for sex to occur outside the realm of marriage or between couples. Since the 1960's, many people accept sex between two consenting participants. The notion of "living together" becomes popular. In enduring relationships that produce offspring, responsibility for the child's care falls on both parents. That is not to say all couples share the parenting role, but many people today expect parents to share this role. This sharing of responsibility also is the result of postmodern values. If mother and father both work, the traditional roles must change.

Finally, postmodern families do not protect their children in the way modern families do. Divorces are common, and they typically have an emotional impact on children. Elkind describes this as urbanity in contrast to domesticity. He aptly describes today's family life as a

> railway station, with parents and children pulling in and out as they go about their busy lives. In many homes, family meals are a relic of the modern nuclear family ideal. In middle-class homes, one parent comes home late from the office while the other parent is driving one or more children to piano lessons or scouts (Elkind 1994, 57).

Two other characteristics of family, the nature of authority and family values, have changed. In premodern societies, we have already seen that authority is patriarchal in nature. This means that the father is in charge or at least thinks he is in charge. The same is true in the modern family. Elkind defines this authority as unilateral. Unilateral authority typically refers to white Christian males. For instance, white males have dominated Congress, the Senate, and major corporations. In addition, males have been in charge in the religious sphere. The family also conforms to this pattern. Schools reinforce these values on the children. Generally, there would be higher expectations for boys than girls. Postmodern families, on the other hand, operate on *mutual or shared authority* (Elkind 1994, 59-62).

The modern family also stresses the ideal of togetherness. Schedules allow many families to share at least one meal together each day. Schools, media, and other social institutions reflect and reinforce the values parents teach at home. The modern view discourages divorce and people often stay in bad relationships for the sake of the children. The child is the center of attention in the modern family. Like the premodern family, the modern family stresses boundaries and limits along with a clear sense of right and wrong. It also teaches respect for parental authority.

The postmodern family, on the other hand, is autonomous, which means in effect "that each family member is empowered to place his or her need for self-realization and self-fulfillment before the needs of the family as a unity" (Elkind 1994, 63). What is important to the postmodern family is that each member is competent (i.e., achievement-oriented) and independent. With two parents working and many working much more than forty hours a week, there is not as much time for the family to come together. Things are even more difficult for some single parents. Elkind concludes that the conditions created by two working parents have been harmful for children (Elkind 1994, 76-78).

According to Elkind, postmodern families are parent centered. Daycare workers or other substitute parents meet the needs of children for much of the day. Parents today generally want their children to be independent. Postmodern families often exhibit a diverse family structure. Limits and boundaries are not always well defined. Daily schedules and work habits have drastically changed traditional parental roles. Now we expect both parents to share the responsibilities of raising children and providing for the family's economic and other needs. Finally, parents today are more likely to share authority.

I have just highlighted a few of the points made by Elkind. Moreover, this discussion of the family is brief. Much of what Elkind discusses simply reflects the evolution of society. The changes may not always be healthy for children or parents. Family structure today is often a pragmatic approach. Postmodern life may not be what is best for the child. However, do we expect parents or mothers to sacrifice their goals for a fulfilling career so they can do what is best for a child? I say mothers because traditional modern life left the care of children to mothers. Postmodern life is a compromise in a sense; it is doing the best one can to meet the needs of self and children.

Clearly, the postmodern family is no more of a perfect arrangement than the modern family. The postmodern family exists as a pragmatic arrangement. The arrangement allows flexibility rather than already established norms and roles. It is not ideal for parents or children. It has advantages and disadvantages. It is a balancing act. Nevertheless, the postmodern approach is better suited to approach the goal of true equality than the modern one where expressive values still play a role.

One thing seems clear from our discussion about the changes in family life. Premodern values in the family or community continues to mold and shape the larger society even today. Primary socialization is affective. Changing it is neither easy nor always desirable. The role of women is one example of where the old views on gender continue to affect people's lives in the present. One could conclude that for change to occur in wider society, things must change in the way people think and operate in family and community settings. Many communities continue to teach patriarchal values and worldviews that produce fear of outsiders. As a result, gender, ethnic, and cultural biases continue. In addition to gender, ethnocentrism is another harmful aspect that exists in most all cultures past and present.

CULTURE AND ETHNOCENTRISM

Anthropologist Margaret Mead has described culture as the hand of the dead upon the shoulder of the living. Our identity is largely the results of culture. Mead argues that Westerners are mainly Christian because they have been born to families who practice Christianity. She concludes that if we had been born in India we would most likely be Hindus. Children simply adopt the religion into which they are born. Generally, this view is correct.

It is true that some individuals convert to a different religion, but this conversion usually causes great trauma to the convert as well as to his or her family. Families and friends may ostracize someone who converts from one religion to another. Culture, therefore, is a powerful force. It shapes our attitudes about the world in which we live, and it molds our character. In addition, we tend to feel comfortable with those whom we share a common cultural heritage. This feeling of commonality leads to a sense of belonging to a larger group, which offers security, protection, and personal identity.

Unfortunately, however, this common identity has negative as well as positive consequences. Just think of hearing people speak in terms of "we" and "they" or "us" and "them." Culture tends to instill the view that our views and beliefs are correct and those who have different views are misguided. Often it is not merely that they are misguided but that they are evil, and they are a threat to us and our way of life. This thinking leads to a view known as *ethnocentrism*.

Ethnocentrism refers to a culture's tendency to view its beliefs and practices as superior to those of other cultures. Sumner says that ethnocentrism directs a group of people to overstate and exaggerate "everything in their own folkways," which is unique to that group and helps to distinguish them from other groups or outsiders. As a result, this process makes the folkways stronger for the group (Sumner 1975, 87).

Examples of this attitude are common. The crusades force many Muslims or Christians to convert or face violence. Christians see it as their duty to correct or kill the so-called "pagans." Likewise, the

> Greeks and Romans called all outsiders 'barbarians.' . . . The Arabs regarded themselves as the noblest nation and all others as more are less barbarous. In 1896, the Chinese minister of education and his counselors edited a manual in which this statement occurs: 'How grand and glorious is the Empire of China, the middle kingdom! She is the largest and richest in the world. The grandest

men in all the world have all come from the middle empire.' In all the literature of all the states equivalent statements occur (Sumner 1975, 88).

It is common, therefore, for members of one culture to have an attitude of superiority with regard to others. They may believe that their nation, religion, values, and ways of life are the best and all other ways are inferior. Such an attitude can and often does lead to intolerance, bigotry, and violence.

Before moving on to modern examples of ethnocentric attitudes, I offer an example of ethnocentrism that comes from our country's early history. This account reflects a mixture of motives. Part of the issue is greed and land. The white settlers want the land of the Cherokees. Yet, there is also distrust and dislike for them because their culture and values are different. The Cherokee people did more than any other native people to "adopt Anglo-American culture. In a remarkably short time they transformed their society and modified their traditional culture in order to conform to United States policy" (Anderson 1991, vii). The United States policy results in the Cherokees' loss of land, which comes about as a slow process. In the early years, the policy of seizing land turns into a policy of "civilizing" Native Americans. This policy is first defined by Henry Knox, George Washington's Secretary of War. The policy attempts to change the

> wandering hunter who owned land communally, governed himself by barbaric custom, worshipped spirits, and spoke a 'savage' language into a sedentary farmer who owned land individually, governed himself by written law, worshipped the one true god, and spoke English learned in proper schools. . . . The Indians had to give up 'only' their hunting, language, religion, tribal organization, and customs. After all, making civilized men out of 'savages' would benefit the Indians and the new nation as well as ensure the progress of the human race (Anderson 1991, viii).

Note some of the language used here: "governed himself by barbaric custom, worshipped spirits, and spoke a 'savage' language." Settlers were turning them into an evil presence, which helped to justify their own desires to take their lands. The Cherokees tried to accommodate the white culture, but this attempt resulted in a disruption of their social and spiritual lives. It also produced great psychological trauma for these people. The accommodation to United States policy was a defense against further abuse directed against them.

However, when the civilization program failed to work over night, many people began to see the Cherokees removal to the West as the only preferable option. Therefore, in 1817, the government offered the Cherokee Indians land west of the Mississippi in exchange for their own land in the Southeast. The government also promised to help them resettle. About 1,500 to 2,000 Cherokees went west. The Cherokee leaders, however, opposed these migrations (Anderson 1991, ix).

Due to this pressure, the Cherokees increased the pace of accommodation to American culture. About this time, however, the belief emerged that people did not obtain their culture through learning, but that culture was something innate.

Whites began to believe that Indians could not change their culture; they might appear civilized, but they really were not. Along with this ethnocentric attitude toward the Cherokee people, the issue of states' rights surfaced. Many in the state of Georgia believed that the Cherokee constitution, which claimed power over tribal lands, violated the United States Constitution. As a result, the state of Georgia itself took action by passing laws outlawing the Cherokee government and began to enforce "state law in Indian country, and authorized a survey of Cherokee land that was to be distributed by lottery to Georgia citizens" (Anderson 1991, xii).

The Cherokee people were unable to get support from the federal government so they took their case to the Supreme Court who ruled in their favor, but Georgia ignored this ruling. Andrew Jackson, the president at this time, chose not to enforce the court's ruling. He did not want to divide the Union. Even supporters of the Cherokees sided with the President on a utilitarian basis. They thought it better to preserve the Union than to prevent harm to one Indian tribe. This struggle ended in 1835 under the Treaty of New Echota. The Cherokee people had two years to go west or be removed by force. Those who did not go west were

> rounded up at bayonet point and herded into stockades. The Indians were allowed little or no time to gather their possessions. As they turned for one last glimpse of their homes, they often saw them being ransacked for valuables by whites or put to the torch (Anderson 1991, xii-xiii).

According to one estimate, this removal caused a loss in population of as many as 8,000 Cherokee people (Thornton 1991, 75-93).

In this century, ethnocentric attitudes are still alive and well. Today ethnocentric attitudes might surface when an Afro-American family moves into an all white neighborhood or when a poor family attends a church made up of rather wealthy and influential people. It can also happen in reverse, when a rich family attends a small church made up primarily of blue-collar workers. It seems to be common for people to exclude other individuals or groups because they perceive them to be outsiders.

One can observe a good example of modern ethnocentric attitude in interdenominational strife within Christianity. Fundamentalists within the Southern Baptist denomination, for instance, see their views of the Bible as correct and all other views as dangerous and heretical. They are unwilling to accept others who differ with them significantly on religious doctrine. Members within a congregation who do not share their views must keep quiet or run the risk of sanctions. To hold views contrary to the party line can be the basis for exclusion. The differences may be small by outside standards, but even small differences distinguish right belief from wrong and dangerous belief. Many nonfundamentalists Southern Baptists have lost positions in the denomination due to minor differences in belief.

These kinds of attitudes tend to divide people into categories. Instead of treating each person on an individual basis, we generally place people in some preexisting political, religious, or ethnic category. In some political circles, one may even distinguish between normal Americans and everyone else. By doing so, we know how to relate to these individuals as either friend or foe. For some reason, societies tend to have trouble handling diversity. Currently in this country, we are in the process of dealing with a wide diversity of beliefs and values. The present controversy of building a Muslim center and mosque near the site of where the World Trade Centers once stood prior to 9/11 in New York City reveals some of these emotions.

One way to improve relations between peoples is to downplay the negative aspect of political, religious, and ethnic differences and try to focus on the individual. For instance, it can certainly be harmful to evaluate a member of the opposite sex with regard to existing notions and stereotypes about gender. It is even worse to take these stereotypes and categories as a measure of how to treat people by valuing masculine attributes and devaluing nonmasculine ones (Best and Kellner 1991, 207). The key is to learn how to live with difference and avoid devaluing those with whom we differ.[11]

People can also use academic studies in ways that might devalue difference. Sociological and psychological studies, for example, are important and helpful in determining what we think about such things as race and gender, and why we think the way we do. Some people, however, can take these kinds of studies, which describes normal or typical behavior as support for their own view that anything falling outside this norm is immoral. Those with "alternative" life styles" may be seen as defective. This judgment does not just fall on same sex marriage, but it would include any nontypical arrangement such as a nonkinship group who chooses to live together in a small community setting. A relativistic or postmodern emphasis on difference can counter these pressures for everyone to be the same.

Things have changed in recent times. There has been an increasing awareness that we cannot force our values on others. That is not to say that everyone feels this way, but that this view is more prominent now than in the past. Today, many of us place a high value on tolerance and pluralism. In a so-called postmodern world, we can no longer assume that our values are the correct ones even though many still make that assumption. As a result, the notion of tolerance and openness has become more popular.

CONCLUSION

A sociological examination of moral values has a great deal to offer. It reminds us of the variety of different ways people conceive of their morals and how they practice them. It teaches us the following lessons. Culture gives one a sense of belonging and continuity. It tells one what his or her place is in society, and it provides guidelines on how one should act. Culture offers us a script about role expectations. We become comfortable with those whom we are in regular contact. This familiarity leads to comfort and resistance to those with whom we are not familiar. It seems, therefore, to be a common occurrence for human beings to view their culture, values, religion, and political parties as superior to those of strangers. Ethnocentrism is not a rare happening.

These lessons alert us to the pressure on individuals to conform to family and community values. It provides the individual with a wider perspective from which to determine how to respond and act. It also points up a rather different view of ethics than one finds in most textbooks on ethics. While most modern ethical theories focus on ways of determining right or wrong, the social study of ethics shows that there is no one universal set of morals. Personally, it helps us to keep our options open.

Moreover, cultural relativism can caution us about the negative and dangerous affects of ethnocentrism. In response to an ethnocentric view in Western thinking, *cultural relativism* calls one to value tolerance for difference. Not every society has to be the same. Not every family has to be the same. Social approaches can help us understand cultures on their own terms.

So far, we have looked at a variety of different ethical perspectives, and none offer a completely satisfactory means of identifying good and bad. I do not say that to suggest that such a perfect ethic is possible. It seems that every ethical approach has weaknesses. However, we must forge ahead looking for additional elements that may prove useful for the development of a satisfactory, but not perfect, ethic.

evaluation of other cultures according to preconceptions originating in the standards customs of one's own life

NOTES

1. American Piety in the 21st Century: New Insights to the Depth and Complexity of Religion in the US http://www.baylor.edu/content/services/document.php/33304.pdf (accessed August 25, 2010). See Table 7: America's Four Gods and Demographics.

2. Ibid. Data on different moral views can be found in Table 9 "Four Gods and Sexual Morality."

3. This letter comes after his arrest in Birmingham Alabama for demonstration against civil rights' abuses.

4. I might add that Max Weber's distinction between legal and traditional authority is also influenced by Tönnies. In premodern societies, traditional authority prevails whereas in the modern state legal authority (e.g., bureaucracy) dominates. See Weber 1971, 170-175.

5. The information for the discussion of these values comes from Ruth A. Wallace and Alison Wolf 1986, 22-28.

6. See also in the same volume the essays on "Discrimination Against Minorities and Women: Some Historical Background," 1-4 by Paul Burstein, and "Assimilation in the United States: An Analysis of Ethnic and Generational Differences in Status and Achievement," 27-37, by Lisa J. Neidert and Reynold Farley.

7. See, for example, John Dominic Crossan 1992, 19-20. Crossan tells of a peasant who has to leave his wife and travel to the city of Alexandria to find work.

8. It is also important that Paul's authorship of Colossians and Ephesians is questionable.

9. See Elizabeth Schüssler Fiorenza 1983, 205-236.

10. I am not saying that Jewish and Christian communities share all of Aristotle's views about the relation of the household to the state and politics.

11. I will discuss these later.

Chapter Eight
Psychological and Ethical Perspectives

In this chapter, I raise several issues and examine views on human nature. I present the following questions for the reader's consideration. (1) Are human beings free to choose how they act? (2) Are we innately selfish creatures? (3) Is it at all possible for us to act in an unselfish or altruistic manner? Many of the views I address in this chapter answer no to the first and third questions above. Behavioral psychologists would say we are not free; human action is determined by certain environmental forces. We are conditioned to act in certain ways. They would also say that human beings are rational creatures. We are selfish creatures always trying to maximize our profits and cut our losses.

I also reexamine individualistic consequentialist ethics such as psychological and ethical egoism in this chapter. The major concern in this type of ethic is self-interest. In other words, does an individual have a moral obligation to put the interests of others ahead of his or her own personal interests? Hedonism and egoism stress the viewpoint that we should only concern ourselves with what is in our own best interests. Yet even if one rejects this viewpoint, the discussion raises a moral dilemma. What should one do when his or her own individual interests are in conflict with the interests of others?

The last part of the chapter examines the issue of moral development. Do we progress through stages of moral development while we get older? This view is very different from the view discussed in the last chapter about how values change over time. From a psychological viewpoint, some argue that human moral development is related to the aging and maturing process.

BEHAVIORAL PSYCHOLOGY: FREEDOM AND ALTRUISM

The views of the psychological behaviorists put altruism and human freedom in doubt. Simply put, altruism refers to the unselfish concern for another person's welfare. It would entail putting the welfare of others ahead of our own. It would mean that a person acts on behalf of another person without selfish motives or selfish intentions. Is such altruistic behavior possible? To answer this question we need to examine the claims of the behavioral sciences.

The second important issue concerns human freedom. Are we free beings? The behavioral sciences would answer these two questions in a negative fashion. They would say that a person's social environment conditions and determines one's behavior. Furthermore, behavioral psychologists can condition individuals to respond to stimuli in certain ways. In short, we do not make free choices because human beings are not free. Most ethical theories, however, assume that we are free and responsible for our actions.

Behaviorism is a school of psychology, which asserts that psychology should be a totally objective discipline. The only thing that is admissible as scientific data is what the psychologist can observe. John B. Watson develops this position. This view also denies altruism and human freedom. Human beings act on the pleasure/pain principle. That means that human beings, like other animals, try to avoid pain and do things that produce pleasure. Watson uses this principle to elicit certain types of behavior out of his subjects. Watson says:

> Give me a dozen healthy infants well formed and my own specified world to bring them up in and I'll guarantee to take any one at random and train him to become any kind of specialist I might select—doctor, lawyer, merchant, chief, yes, even a beggarman and thief, regardless of his talents, penchants, tendencies, abilities, vocations, and race of his ancestors (Watson 1926, 10).

Behavioral modification or conditioning is the method he advocates for accomplishing this amazing achievement. We see this general principle at work today in all areas of life from the parent who gives his or her child a reward for appropriate behavior to employers who provide material incentives for workers. This psychological perspective, therefore, assumes that the behavioral scientist can control a person's behavior by rewarding the behavior he or she wants to promote and punish undesirable behavior. We act to increase and ensure our own happiness and avoid pain. Another psychologist who adopts this view is B. F. Skinner. Skinner experiments with animals and applies that research to explaining human behavior.

Behaviorism and Social Exchange Theory

Skinner is a behavioral psychologist following in the line of Watson. Operant conditioning is Skinner's term that refers to the reinforcement principle. Reinforcement can be either positive or negative. Reinforcement of behavior is a way of modifying an individual's behavior. In Skinner's novel, *Walden II*, written in 1948, he describes a fictional society based on the laws of behaviorism. This society is for Skinner the ideal society. In this book, Skinner clearly recognizes the practical possibilities of behavioral psychology. The notion is that the behavioral scientist in an ideal situation could conceivably produce the right kind of people and therefore create a perfect society.

He furthers this view in his book, *Beyond Freedom and Dignity*, written in 1971. Here Skinner denies that human beings have either "freedom" or "dignity." In most respects, humans are like other animals. We respond to stimuli in predictable ways. Skinner believes that various environmental forces combine to condition and to determine human behavior. We do the things that produce pleasure or reward, and we avoid those things that cause pain or punishment. Therefore, the pleasure/pain principle determines a person's reflex or response to a certain stimulus.

Skinner points out that in the past people typically follow the moral standards of the majority. They follow certain rules and laws to avoid punishment. According to Skinner, this approach has now lost its power. He remarks that

> young people are beginning to ask some embarrassing questions: Why should I serve my fellow man? Why should I seek to be admired by other people? Why should I avoid censure or criticism? Why should I die for my country? (Lindzey, Hall, and Thompson 1978, 216)

Skinner realizes that one cannot respond to these questions by pointing to "absolutes." He continues by observing that

> there is no absolute truth in value judgments. No one has that kind of truth or can answer questions by appealing to it. It is not a question of what people should do or ought to do, or what is right. The question is why certain cultures have made certain things reinforcing or have failed to do so. If these values are now being challenged, it is presumably because the culture has engineered them badly (Lindzey, Hall, and Thompson 1978, 216).

Skinner argues that it does not matter what is on the inside of a person. The behavioral scientist can control and make any person act in certain ways by regulating certain aspects of a person's environment. Unlike many philosophers, Skinner does not necessarily view control as a negative idea. He looks for a type of control that does not have hostile effects. Skinner maintains that life is impossible without some sort of control over the population (Skinner 1971, 41, 168-169). Laws, for instance, can control most people's behavior and, therefore, protect the general population. Moreover, dispensing rewards and punishments in a deliberate fashion is the way of controlling and manipulating behavior (Skinner 1971, 60ff).

He concludes that the behavioral scientists ought to guide the direction of human behavior in a society. Skinner admits that no utopian vision has ever worked in the past, but he contends that this fact does not justify giving up on a planned society. Behavioral scientists could develop a plan for society that could be obtained by operant conditioning. This plan would entail rewarding appropriate behavior and punishing unwanted types of conduct. Following such guidelines would lead us to an ideal society (Skinner 1971, 145-183).

In chapters six through eight of his book, *Beyond Freedom and Dignity*, Skinner discusses values and ethical injunctions. He says that scientific investigations can tell us how to change human behavior. They can also tell the behavioral scientist what changes they need to make (Day 1977, 11-14). The purpose of change is for the survival of a particular community. Skinner finds the society of his time sick and in need of repair. He says that society does not carry out rewards and punishments in a rational and consistent way. If rewards and punishments are rational and consistent, we could produce desirable behavior and control it. Society does not need less control, but it needs more control. It also needs control of a different kind (Skinner 1971, 91-92, and 182-183).

The purpose of these controls is to reach certain goals. Survival is the most important value. In other words, he would justify or legitimate such control based on the survival of the species or the culture. There must be a compromise between the individual's desires and the needs of society. The compromise allows for the continued survival of the individual and the community (Skinner 1971, 182-183; Richell 1993, 210-211).

George C. Homans is a sociologist greatly influenced by Skinner's work. Homans and Skinner, both professors at Harvard, become good friends. Homans makes use of Skinner's work in his book, *Social Behavior: Its Elementary Forms*. In this book, he examines the process of human exchange. Human exchange is a well-known principle. Today it is often referred to as rational choice theory. Anthropologists have long noticed the importance of gift giving in premodern societies. The notion is that human beings expect to get something in return for their efforts.

Homans develops several propositions about human behavior. The first proposition simply states that when a person receives a reward for a particular action he or she is more likely to repeat that behavior in the future. He calls this proposition the success proposition. Another proposition concerns human rationality. It states that a person is "more likely to perform an action" if the person values the consequences of that action (Homans 1978, 135-138). Moreover, desirable consequences bring pleasure or reward. On the other hand, bad consequences bring punishment. There are many types of rewards and punishments. Rewards and punishments depend on one's perceptions. Perceptions differ from person to person. This complexity makes explaining, understanding, and predicting human behavior difficult.

Another important component of Homans' work relates to his notion of value. His value proposition suggests that the "greater the profit a person receives as a result of his action, the more likely he is to perform the action" (Homans 1978, 139). This proposal assumes first that human beings are rational creatures who behave in a rational manner. Second, it assumes that human beings always consider the price of their action and calculate which action is in their own best interest.

One might object. We often do irrational things. For Homans, however, we do what we want to do so there must have been a rational reason for what we do. It only has to be rational for the person performing the action. Spending a great deal of money for a sports car may seem irrational to me, but it only has to make sense for the person spending the money. He puts it this way: "In choosing between alternative actions, a person will choose that one for which, as perceived by him at the time, the value, V, of the results, multiplied by the probability, p, of getting the result, is the greater" (Homans 1978, 145).[1]

In simple terms, Homans argues that individuals tend to calculate the possible rewards and costs of an action, and they try to make their rewards greater than the costs. Therefore, he is suggesting that a person weighs the REWARDS against the COSTS of any potential action, and he or she then endeavors to gain a PROFIT (i.e., R-C=P). Homans defines the cost of any behavior as the rewards an actor has lost in forgoing alternative action. Anytime we interact with others, it costs us something, and someone else receives a benefit from the action. One gains a profit when the reward he or she gains outweighs the cost that one acquires. In short, we always expect to make a profit for our actions (Homans 1978, 139-141).

For example, one may attend college for any number of reasons. According to Homans, a person who chooses to go to college without being coerced would do so because he or she believes it is to his or her advantage to do so. In other words, that person would conclude that the profit of going to college outweighs the costs. The *costs* could include such things as time studying, time away from family, hard work, and financial burdens. The *rewards* for one person may be the satisfaction of being the first person in his or her family to obtain a college degree. For another person, the reward may entail getting a job, receiving a pay increase, or even obtaining a better job. As a result, one may consider the higher status or knowledge gained from the educational experience as a sufficient reward for his or her labor. Since human beings are rational, they will not act unless there is a profit. The *profit* may mean that the financial expenses and hard work are more than compensated for by the gains in social status, money, or receiving the job of one's dreams.

Correspondingly, Homans introduces the notion of distributive justice. This view would explain justice in terms of his work on human behavior and expectations of rewards or compensations for performing certain actions. Distributive justice refers to receiving what one expects to receive for an action. It is part of the calculation or formula R-C=P. If people receive what they expect then they receive justice, which results in their satisfaction. However, if they do not get what they expect then they do not receive justice. As a result, the person who does not get what he or she expects may become angry or upset and feel he or she has been treated unjustly. For example, the individual who goes to college thinking that a college degree will open up doors for his or her professional career expects to find a job consistent with those goals. What happens, however, when that person is completely unsuccessful? Most likely, that individual feels that potential employers have treated him or her unfairly. Alternatively, perhaps the college has failed to prepare him or her for that career.

On a more mundane level, if I open the door for an individual and that person does not acknowledge my act then my act goes unrewarded. As a result, I might feel some injury. When we do not receive an expected reward, we feel cheated. So, we expect, he says, to receive a reward for our good actions. Why, for instance, would fundamentalist Christians go to church and sacrifice a great deal of their time, money, and possible pleasure if they do not believe that their personal sacrifice would receive some reward that would more than make up for the costs? Belief in the afterlife and eternal reward and punishment serve as powerful motivations in this case.

This notion of distributive justice accompanies his sixth proposition, the so-called "Aggression-Approval-Proposition." This proposition builds upon the premise that people want social approval, and they behave in certain ways to gain their friend's approval. However, when a person's actions do not receive the expected reward, or when the person receives punishment that he or she did not expect, anger is the result. Consequently, the person is more likely to perform aggressive behavior, and the results of such behavior become more valuable to the person.

A second part to this statement declares that when a person's actions receive an unexpected reward, especially a reward greater than expected, he or she would be happy. Correspondingly, when the person does not receive an expected punishment he or she would be pleased. Imagine that the person obtains a better job than he or she expects to receive based on his or her college education. Then he or she feels life is just. This person, therefore, becomes more likely to act in an approving manner. The action he or she performs is more fulfilling (Homans 1978, 141-143). According to Homans, then, human beings define justice solely upon their own personal expectation. Justice occurs when one is rewarded for good actions that reap the proper reward. Injustice is being punished for actions that should bring reward but do not.

We can conclude from Skinner and Homan's work that human action is rational, and it seeks rewards and avoids punishment. From this perspective, one would rule out the possibility of altruism or unselfish behavior. If I do anything that seems altruistic, it is because there is a profit in it for me. Perhaps, I help someone else, but the pleasure from helping is my reward. I would not do it, on this account, without some expectation of payback. Payback could be a mere smile, some kind words, or a show of gratitude for my help.

There is much truth to the statement that human beings naturally seek their own self-interests. It is much more questionable to say that we always seek our own interests. Often and perhaps in most cases there is a mixture of good will and self-interest that is involved in our actions. In most cases, I doubt that actions are purely selfish or altruistic. The problem for the altruistic argument is that if we receive any reward for our acts, whether a feeling of having done something nice for someone or if we receive money, altruism is lost.

Nevertheless, just because we receive pleasure out of doing something for others does not necessarily mean that our actions are selfish. Tom may give his parents the money to take the trip of their dreams. Sure, he gets a great deal of satisfaction out of their pleasure, but does this mean that he does it only for the satisfaction or pleasure?[2] It is unlikely that we can ever find an act completely free of self-interest. Human actions fall on a continuum between selfish and altruistic. I would not rule out pure altruism, but if it does occur, it would be rare. I return to this idea below.

Now we turn our attention to the issue of human freedom. The work of Watson, Skinner, and Homans supports the view that human beings are creatures who are controlled by their own self-interests, and as a result, they have no freedom. Homans argues that one can explain human behavior in relation to human rationality and human craving for pleasure. We are governed by the environment. We are conditioned to act in particular ways and are prisoners to our desire for pleasure.

One might think that doing something for reward is the mark of a free person. On the contrary, a person whose nature compels him or her to seek a reward is not free. Since we are predetermined to act selfishly, it is the social environment and the conditions that we face that shape us and make us who we are. Using behavioral principles, behavioral scientists could control the environment, the rewards, and the punishments to create a particular kind of society and person. To use a simple analogy, humans would be like a blank hard drive on a computer, and the behavioral scientists would be the programmers. They could manipulate the environment or program it in a way to provide rewards for desirable behaviors necessary for society and punishments for behaviors detrimental to society. The key to being successful is consistency in rewarding and punishing.

Watson, Skinner, and Homans all assume that human beings are rational animals. Like the psychological egoists, they would maintain that the human animal always seeks its own pleasure or self-interest, and it attempts to avoid pain. If we are rational beings without freedom, the behavioral sciences should be able to condition us and predict how we react to stimuli in the environment. Subsequently, they could control our responses to a given stimulus. If they are correct, and we are not free then who is accountable for the actions that harm or benefit society? Is it the individual or the behavioral scientists or others who are in control of shaping society? If it is not the individual, then why should we condemn the individual for some actions and praise him or her for others if he or she is simply responding to stimuli in a way that is not the result of human free will? It is like praising the genius for his or her intellectual capacity. It is meaningless because nature produces the genius. If we are not free, why criticize one who does wrong or praise one who does right?

Do Ethics Depend Upon Human Agents Having Freedom?

As we said earlier, freedom and responsibility go together. If we are to punish criminals, we must assume that they have a choice. Why should society punish an individual who has no free choice? (James 1975, 150-158)[3] Without some measure of human freedom, the whole notion of punishment becomes morally problematic. Is it just to put someone in jail for stealing if he or she cannot control his or her actions? I would maintain that we are not completely free. On the other hand, we are not simply at the mercy of biology or the social environment. The answer to whether humans are free or whether human actions are determined by various stimuli is not an "either or" answer but a "both and."

We are not completely free. There are things over which we have no choice. We cannot do anything about when, where, and how we are raised. We may have some control over our tendencies and personality. Some people, for example, have a positive outlook and others do not. A negative person may try to change and embrace a more positive view, but that does not mean that he or she can eliminate the negative. Still the negative person can make choices to act in a positive manner.

Exercising free will and living as an individual rather than as one of the crowd are not easy things to do. Søren Kierkegaard notes that the person

> who believes it is easy enough to be the individual can always be sure that he is not a knight of faith, for vagabonds and roving geniuses are not men of faith. The knight of faith knows, on the other hand, that it is glorious to belong to the universal. He knows that it is beautiful and salutary to be the individual who translates himself into the universal. . . . He knows that it is refreshing to become intelligible to oneself in the universal so that he understands it and so that every individual who understands him understands through him in turn the universal. . . . He knows very well where he is and how he is related to men. Humanly speaking, he is crazy and cannot make himself intelligible to anyone (Kierkegaard 1954, 86)

Kierkegaard in this quote is speaking in a religious context. By knight of faith, Kierkegaard is referring to one who acts as an individual, one who makes decisions and acts according to his or her own free will. His reference to vagabonds is interesting. Just because one might live outside normal society does not necessarily make that person an individual in the sense described by Kierkegaard and other existentialists' philosophers. The person of faith knows that the universal (i.e., what most all people expect and want) is desirable. He or she feels its attraction. Still, the knight of faith is the true individual. He or she ultimately stands alone. The emphasis of Kierkegaard on the individual in some ways is similar to the view of the individual in the work of Fydor Dostoevsky and Nietzsche.

One can find a measure of freedom in the work of some behavioralists. Herbert Blumer contends that human behavior consists of more than a simple stimulus-response-reinforcement model as defined by Skinner.[4] There is an important process going on between stimulus and response that prevents the scientist from knowing how one might respond with certainty. In response to behaviorists such as Watson, Skinner, and Homans, Blumer describes a three-stage process made up of *stimulus-interpretation-response*. Human beings interpret the meaning of a particular stimulus before acting or responding. In other words, our response depends upon the interpretation we give to a particular stimulus. One cannot always know or predict how others are going to interpret a stimulus.

For example, two very similar individuals do not share the same exact experiences. Personal experiences distinguish one individual from another. These experiences are always mediated through culture, language, or social interaction. In other words, all of our experiences occur in particular cultural and social settings, and we can only relate or understand these experiences based on spoken or written language. Additionally, the unconscious desires or impulses play a role behind the scenes influencing our understanding of a particular situation. We interpret and value stimuli differently. Consequently, our behavior is not always predictable or a matter of conscious choice (Wallace and Wolf 1986, 193-195).

As a result, humans are capable of a measure of freedom, but we may fail to exercise this freedom. Blumer's work suggests that humans usually have more than just one available option. Consequently, a particular stimulus would not always produce a certain result; it is not simple cause and effect. Individuals must choose between many different options. At minimum, Blumer's approach means that we decide based on our interpretation. However, I would add that our decisions and actions are commonly done without much thought and based on what is expected. In most cases, we may not exercise our freedom at all, and some people may rarely exercise their freedom. This view would be consistent with the views of Kierkegaard mentioned above.

I agree with those who stress the limited nature of human freedom. Many societal influences limit one's freedom. Berger views most human beings as prisoners of society. The objectified world (i.e., the worldview that members of a society take-for-granted) holds people captive. Kierkegaard, Berger, and others would still view it as a prison from which the individual can escape.[5] Simone De Beauvoir and Nietzsche consider human beings who blindly accept and follow the customs and values of their society as lacking something valuable (De Beauvoir, 1994; Nietzsche 1982, 10-13). In short, one can speak about human freedom to the extent that a person can interpret various situations and consciously select between various options. One may also be able to create new and unexpected options where none previously existed. In short, the thief could decide to obey the law. On the other hand, this thief could take what does not belong to him or her.

PSYCHOLOGICAL EGOISM

Psychological egoism, like the behavioral psychologists above, declares that human beings are only capable of acting according to their own self-interest. In all we do, we promote our own interests. Bernard de Mandeville is an eighteenth-century writer and a proponent of such a view. He contends that human beings are typically unsuited to live without some external force to suppress their natural inclinations. He concludes that government is necessary. Mandeville says that those who govern society must make citizens believe that it is to their advantage to obey the state and to concern themselves with the public rather than the private interests of the individual (Mandeville 1975, 114).

Earlier, Thomas Hobbes (1588-1679) says that in the state of nature, humans are selfish, and as a result, they all seek their own interests. This situation leads to a constant state of war. The "social contract" is an agreement made between the governing and the governed. This contract implies that the governed will freely relinquish some of their rights in return for protection that the governing powers can provide. Keeping such a contract is really in the best interest of every individual (Hobbes 1970, 133-150).

This implies in effect that if individuals pursue only their own personal interests, they will not do as well as if they cooperate with others.[6] Therefore, some cooperation is to their advantage. In essence, the state can force the individual to look at his or her long-term interests and not just at his or her short-term interests. However, is contract the correct term for what happens in past societies? It seems more likely that those who gain power in society find ways of wielding that power to their own advantage. From this perspective, order is not derived from a mutual agreement between parties of equal power, but the stronger elements in society impose an order on the weak.[7]

In short, psychological egoists believe that human beings are naturally selfish. They deny the possibility of altruism. These egoists stress that self-interests determine everything we do. However, suppose that an individual risks his or her own life to save a drowning child. Why would a selfish person do so? The egoist might reply that the individual just wants to escape the guilty feelings or public scorn. Additionally, one may save the child for the good feeling such an act produces or to escape the bad feelings associated with the death of a child. For anyone committed to such a view, there is no sufficient proof to the contrary; we are simply incapable of acting without some selfish motivation. Moreover, how can we deny that we receive some pleasure or good feeling from saving a life? Does a good feeling, however, explain the motivation of the person who acts as being selfish? It would be difficult to deny that most actions involve a measure of reciprocity, that is, we receive or expect to receive something in return for our actions.

No one, however, can deny that people do sometimes sacrifice themselves and put their own lives at risks for the sake of other individuals. Along these lines, there are some interesting new studies regarding altruism. These studies suggest that altruism has a basis in the evolutionary process. Altruism would not survive unless it serves some useful purpose. It would have eventually been bred out of humans. So, some have tried to show that altruism has a basis in biology, and we sacrifice our own good for those with whom we share genes. The reason for such sacrifice is that one wishes to make sure that his or her genes survive. As I commented above, this view is not strictly speaking altruism, but "genetic self-interests." In this way, therefore, "sharing, cooperation, [and] generosity were nature's way for an individual to help his relatives. By helping them he helped himself genetically" (Fisher 1982, 111-114).

This view is interesting, but how can one explain that humans are willing to risk their life for strangers or even pets? (Wallace and Wolf 1986, 293) This fact may go beyond biological explanation. One may often give something to others to place them in his or her debt. The reasoning may be that one person may want another to owe him or her something. This situation may work to his or her benefit in the future (Fisher 1982, 113).

Another explanation, which derives from Nietzsche, is that self-sacrifice or non-egoistic actions stem from a bad conscience. Bad conscience results from the fact that one can no longer discharge the "*old instincts of freedom*," and as a result, they turn inward. Now the person has to look out for the welfare of the group. When one does not, there is guilt. At this stage, group survival depends upon cooperation of its members. Cooperation often requires that the individual sacrifice his or her needs for the sake of the community. Nietzsche would not call this altruism, however, since there are selfish motivations behind such actions. Typically, society tends to teach us that the interests of others take priority over our own self-interests. Nietzsche even says that we can take pleasure out of hurting and denying ourselves of certain things for the sake of others (Nietzsche 1994, 63-64). Concerning intention, therefore, doing something for the "pleasure" it produces, removes the act from the realm of altruism.

Similarly, Helen Fisher notes the role of cooperation in the survival of the human species. Survival requires the individual to sacrifice for the sake of the group. Fisher remarks that

> through natural selection, man came to walk erect, to bond, and to live in tiny family groups. And via the very same evolutionary process, it would select for certain types of personalities—personalities with an innate disposition to share, to cooperate, to divide work, and to behave altruistically (Fisher 1982, 118).

This view seems plausible. The need for cooperation requires that individuals put the interests of the group ahead of their own. By going against the interests of the group (i.e., acting selfishly), one could endanger the group, which in turn might lead to group censure. Laws, morals, or customs, therefore, would be the next logical step. The group can ensure that people remain loyal by creating policies and views that are to varying degrees binding.

In conclusion, it is still debatable whether human beings are capable of altruism if by this we mean doing something for others without any regard of personal reward. Additionally, defining altruism as the exact opposite of egoism is questionable (Nietzsche 1992, 45).[8] Frequently, actions have elements of both selfish and unselfish motivations. In most cases, people probably consciously or unconsciously calculate the advantages and disadvantages of any action, and it would be rare that individuals would act in a manner that is not profitable in some way. While there may be those who do their good deeds in private with no desire for public recognition or reward in this life or the next life, this person is the exception and not the rule. Such an individual may simply enjoy or feel compelled to act for others, and so his or her motives may still prevent us from identifying him or her as a purely altruistic person. What we can say is that people vary in their motives from obviously selfish to sincere. It is problematic, however, to go a step further and label some actions as altruistic. Altruism may be an extreme or ideal that cannot ever occur in pure form. However, it is beyond question that some people act on the behalf of others and often even at great expense to their own well-being.

I suspect that all the above explanations of self-sacrifice are necessary for understanding why some people deny themselves for the sake of others. On a family or kinship basis, the biological view makes sense. Yet, there are also sociological and psychological forces that play a part. Since people in premodern societies have to cooperate to survive, they come to depend upon each other. This dependence means that sometimes one has to sacrifice oneself for the good of the group. If individuals are unwilling to contribute to the common good, the community may put them outside the group and its sphere of protection. This punishment or isolation would certainly pose a danger to the individual and his or her family.

It is just as true that humans often do things for others out of a sense of compulsion; we do things because the group expects us to do them. To disappoint the group or a significant other is wrong and the result of doing so is punishment or a guilty conscience. There is no way of knowing how many individuals sacrifice their time, money, and talents just because they feel that others expect them to make that sacrifice. We have described both the positive and negative aspects of self-sacrifice. Now we need to take a closer look at two ethical theories, which describe one's moral obligation in relation to the consequences of an act.

ETHICAL EGOISM

Ethical egoism is a consequentialist ethic. It judges an act on its consequences for the person performing the act. We could distinguish hedonists from ethical egoists. The hedonist considers how the consequences of an act affect his or her own self-interests. A pure hedonist might not calculate his or her long-term interests the way a true ethical egoist would.

For the ethical egoist, an act is good if its consequences make the actor happy. What would a thoroughly hedonistic husband think about cheating on his wife? He or she might say that it is perfectly all right so long as it does not cause more pain than pleasure. He would need to consider if the pain of a guilty conscience would outweigh the pleasure. Alternatively, would the risk of being caught and losing his family outweigh the potential pleasure of the act? If either is the case, then he might decide not to cheat on his wife. From this perspective, whatever increases one's pleasure is the correct behavior. Hedonism totally concerns itself with an individual's happiness; they say that only pleasure is desirable or an end in itself. However, they disagree on the nature of happiness, whether it has to do with the absence of mental distress as the Greek philosopher Epicurus[9] argues or whether it involves sensual pleasures. This later form of hedonism is the one that most people probably have in mind when they think of the word hedonism. This philosophy or view of self-gratification seems to concentrate primarily on the present not necessarily looking at how an act affects one long term.

Ethical egoism advocates acting in ways that would promote one's own self-interests. It says that human beings ought to act according to what is in their own best interests. William K. Frankena defines ethical egoism as follows: it instructs one to do that which "will promote his own greatest good." Further it says "that an act or rule of action is right if and only if it promotes at least as great a balance of good over evil for him in the long run as any alternative would, and wrong if it did not" (Frankena 1973, 15).

This view is also consistent with the views of the behavioral scientists. We naturally do the things that bring us pleasure and avoid those things that cause pain. Ethical egoism says that an act is morally correct if it is in the individual's best interest (Kalin 1970, 64-87). An individual can advance his or her own interest in either the short or long term depending upon the particular situation. The act is good if the consequences are good for the individual performing the act and bad if they are not.

In a particular situation, the ethical egoist may say that if an act is to my advantage in the short-term, and no significant long-term effects make it to my disadvantage, then the act is desirable. Nevertheless, if the act is good in the short term, and the potential risk of future negative results is high, then the act may be wrong. Breaking a promise, for instance, may be expedient in the short term, but it may produce many bad effects in the future. In this case, breaking a promise is wrong.

The ethical egoist may also help others if he or she calculates that the act will produce more pleasure and happiness than it produces personal sacrifice. To put it in the words of Homans, acting for the other person may bring a profit for the individual performing the act. In other words, the rewards of helping another person may outweigh any costs. A man may be a good father and a good husband because of the satisfaction he gets from seeing his wife and children happy. A wealthy woman may leave money to a university, not because she feels that it is her duty, but rather because of the pleasant feeling it gives her, which might include the recognition that comes with such an act. Therefore, the egoist may certainly act on the behalf of others.

Moreover, the ethical egoist can agree that often such things as keeping a promise or being honest, which may cause some displeasure, is moral. One could point to the negative consequences for the individual if he or she breaks a promise. For example, breaking a promise could cause another person to lose trust in the promise breaker, and it could as a result hurt the promise breaker's credibility. This act may later have significant negative consequences for the one who breaks the promise. Breaking a legal agreement may result in punishment. Therefore, the egoist could say that frequently one can satisfy his or her own happiness by obeying certain guidelines. In short, keeping one's promises or being honest may be in the individual's best interest most of the time.

The psychological egoist is one who holds the view that we are incapable of acting without selfish motivation. If the psychological egoist is right, we are all egoists whether we admit it or not. Therefore, we all act on this basis whether we call ourselves Christians, followers of Kant's moral philosophy, or utilitarians. I have argued that we are not slaves to self-interests, and that we have some measure of freedom. This view means that we have some measure of freedom to ignore our own self-interests so that we can act on behalf of others. Regardless of whether we receive pleasure from self-sacrificing acts, the acts may cause us to sacrifice something important to us so we can help others.

Assessment of Psychological and Ethical Egoism

Brian Medlin contends that ethical egoism is inconsistent. He argues that one's moral rule has to convey one's true attitudes. Additionally, Medlin requires the ethical egoist to universalize his or her ethical principles. These two requirements are not met by ethical egoism. Medlin argues that if we say that a person ought to do something, then we must actually desire for that person to do it. Likewise, we must say that if one person ought to do something, then everyone ought to do it (Medlin 1970, 59-63).

Jesse Kalin a proponent of ethical egoism rejects Medlin's contention that a moral principle has to express one's attitude. There is a difference between what one ought to do and what one desires. I may feel that the other team should do their best to win the game, but that does not mean that I have to desire for them to be successful or for them to play their best (Kalin 1970, 74-75). Kalin does not accept the notion that everyone should strive toward one "supreme principle" or one single attitude that everyone shares (i.e. universalization). What is good, according to Kalin, differs from person to person. He maintains that each person's happiness is an end or goal of his or her action. He also holds that every person should be inclined to his or her own happiness (Kalin 1970, 75-79). Going back to behavioralism, we could conclude that pursing one's own happiness is consistent with one's natural tendencies.

By taking an ethical egoist approach as one's only ethical guide, one could justify any type of attitude or behavior so long as it is in one's best interests. In essence, this view says that what is good for the individual is good or moral. While there may be times in which it is justifiable to put one's own interests above the interests of others, it is not persuasive to say that one always has a moral obligation to do so. Just to say that it is natural for one to pursue one's own happiness does not settle the issue. Even if true, humans are not slaves to nature. We can decide to act in ways we believe to be consistent with our moral responsibilities. What we perceive as our responsibilities may not be the same as what is in our personal best interests. This mode of thinking is too narrow.

So is there a point at which one should look beyond his or her own personal happiness? Do we have a responsibility to act in ways that may not maximize our own personal happiness, but that enhances the security and well-being of another person or the larger community? What would life be like if everyone endeavors to maximize their own good without regard or consideration for the good of the other person? We may often encounter or experience this tension in our interaction with others. How do we balance our interests with those of the other person?

In summary, ethical egoism does not say that a person should not ever help another person or group. It just points out that we have no fundamental moral duty to promote other people's happiness at the expense of our own happiness. From this point of view, one person should not expect or require another person to act for the good of other people unless it is to his or her own advantage. One should only what is in his or her own best interests. To reiterate, psychological egoists say that human beings just naturally act selfishly; it is simply impossible for us to act in any other way. In doing so, they deny human freedom; we are subject to natural inclinations to seek our own pleasure. Acts that appear to be unselfish, they might say, really derive from other motives such as guilt or the wish for recognition for some good act. One can even interpret the act of saving another person's life from this vantage point. Everything we do could be described as seeking our own happiness or satisfaction.

CONFLICTING INTERESTS

We are now at the stage where we can consider the following question: What should we do when our self-interest clashes with the interests of others? One of the major problems in defining how one should act is to determine when and under what circumstances an individual has a moral responsibility to set aside his or her self-interests to help another. One might legitimately inquire whether we are under any moral obligation to consider the interests of others except when our actions adversely affect others. One option is to say that we should consider our own interests as no more or no less important than the interests of any other person. Even though this neutral approach appears sensible, I wonder if it is possible. We are not able to be neutral if that means setting all our subjective impulses aside. Our decisions are always colored by feelings and social environment.

Moral values function in a society to undergird and uphold the worldview of a given society. Moral values, therefore, can serve to unite people and encourage them to promote the common good. Group survival may depend upon cooperation and belief in a common set of values and principles. Today's moral values tend to function in much the same way as they have always functioned in the past. The two main differences are that (1) modern societies are more diverse so their power is weaker, and (2) individuality is seen as more important. In the modern world, there is a popular tendency to focus on the self apart from the group. This focus leads many people to turn inward. Overall, it appears that people today spend a great deal more time, energy, and money in pursuit of personal or individual happiness.

Moral values today can take on one of two extremes. In some circles, they may focus on the welfare or common good of the larger community rather than the interest of the individual. Perhaps more commonly, they focus exclusively on the self or individual. As we have seen, there are modern ethical perspectives that justify either emphasis. So should we focus our morals on the interests of the individual or the larger community?

The answer to this question depends largely on one's own personal ethic. In other words, the individual has to decide. For instance, basing an ethic on biblical traditions could lend support to either position. It could stress one's moral obligation to the larger society, or it could encourage one to pursue one's own personal salvation. Pursing one's own personal salvation might entail doing good works or helping other people.[10] Utilitarian and nonconsequentialists ethical approaches consider the interests of the individual as well as the interests of the others. There are situations, however, where it is difficult to define what I ought to do in cases where I must choose between acting on my own interests or acting in accordance with the interests and needs of others. This difficulty stems from our limited human knowledge, our limited ability to be neutral or objective, and the limited nature of human ability to use reason to settle these types of conflicts.

Exclusive focus on either the other person or on the self seems excessive and possibly harmful. Do we have a moral obligation to put the interests of others over our own interests? Undeniably, many of those systems of ethics that encourage people to do so make a positive contribution. Many different individuals across the globe have benefited from this impulse. As a group, we have accomplished a number of worthy goals in large part due to the desire to put the needs of others ahead of our own. Whether this desire is an unselfish act is debatable. Yet for whatever reason, the impulse to help others is vital, and without it, society would collapse. Such a concern for the interests and needs of the other plays a positive part in society.

However, what should I do when circumstances force me to make a choice? Sure, it may be admirable to sacrifice one's own happiness for the other, but does morality require it? On the other hand, is it an "either or" situation? Is my well-being tied to the well-being of others? To a large degree it is. We are largely dependent on each other. It is often in our best interests to consider the needs of the larger community of which we are a part. A society depends upon a certain amount of cooperation to survive. For example, one's ultimate survival on this planet may require cooperation of people in this country and abroad. In addition, we must admit that we are not self-sufficient. Today's population is probably more dependent than any other in our history. What would we do without electricity, communication, or modern transportation? What would we do without stores where we can go to buy food and clothing? We have grown quite dependent on technology and most people do not even know how it works.

As a result, we are interdependent upon each other. Charles Taylor tries to hold the two together. His "ideal of authenticity" clears space for both the individual and the community. Authenticity generally has to do with self-fulfillment. The ideal of authenticity takes on a "dialogical nature." We become what we are in relation to others. There are "significant others" for instance who have a hand in shaping and molding our lives (Taylor, Charles 1992, 1-41). Things gain importance or significance not because they are important to individuals alone, but because they transcend the particular feelings of the self or individual (Taylor 1992, 32-33). We can view peoples' significance as part of their interaction with their fellow human beings. Therefore, any meaningful ethic has to consider both the personal and social nature of existence.

There may be no one answer to the question, "what should I do when my interests conflict with those of another?" The decision finally rests upon personal beliefs or ethics. Certainty is not possible. It seems fair to say that our own happiness is just as important as the happiness of others. There are times when one might be able to compromise or give up certain rights for the sake of another. We cannot live our lives free from all restraints. Cooperation is often in everyone's best interests.

One suggestion in cases where interests come into conflict is to find a way in which both parties can win or have their needs addressed. In other words, when one's own personal interests clash with the interests of others, the ideal, which is not always possible, is to look for solutions where both parties gain something they need. We should look for solutions or ways of acting where both parties gain some benefit.[11] If one person's gain is harming another individual, then there may be compelling reasons for him or her to sacrifice his or her interests for the sake of the other person or the common good.

MORAL DEVELOPMENT

A different psychological view on morality derives from those who look at the moral development that takes place in individuals. Earlier, I discussed morality in relation to socialization. A child learns his or her morals from parents, friends, teachers, and from the larger society. On this view, a child's moral development has to do with social learning. Freud associates conscience with his notion of the superego. The superego is a product of the social environment. It is the superego or conscience along with the general moral codes that determine how children think and act concerning what is good and bad. Children generally act in ways that family members find acceptable because not doing so results in some sort of punishment. The punishment might come from a feeling of guilt or from some form of physical punishment. The thought of receiving disapproval or rebuke from a significant other serves to keep children in line. This social-learning approach to moral development explains how children seek to avoid guilt. Children may first attempt to control guilt by avoiding behavior that produces the guilty feeling. Later they may attempt to rationalize or justify their behavior or reduce the guilt by apologizing. The social learning approach says that children learn moral behavior through a combination of rewards and punishments (Hall, Perlmutter, and Lamb 1982, 454-455).

Other psychologists study the nature of moral thinking and reasoning. This cognitive approach considers the justifications given for moral reasoning. The two leading proponents of such an approach are Jean Piaget and Lawrence Kohlberg. Piaget identifies stages of moral development. In one stage, the morality of constraint, young children obey rules and authority figures. Disobedience inevitably produces punishment. At this stage, the child judges an act good or bad depending upon its consequences. This reasoning changes with the next stage of moral development where intentions become more important. He calls this stage the morality of cooperation, which begins about age 7 or 8 and lasts until age 12 years old or older. At this stage, the disobedient girl who falls down and hurts herself may blame herself for the accident (Hall, Perlmutter, and Lamb 1982, 460-463).

Kohlberg extends Piaget's work. Whereas Piaget's stages cover children from an early age until 12 years old, Kohlberg's theory includes all ages. Kohlberg identifies three levels of moral development: preconventional morality, conventional morality, and postconventional morality. The preconventional level refers to a period in a child's life where he or she judges an act based on the physical consequences of the act. In the conventional level of morality, children conform to social rules to gain social approval and to avoid social disapproval. The final level is the postconventional level where morality depends upon self-chosen principles and rules that have a "universal logical validity and therefore can be shared" (Hall, Perlmutter, and Lamb 1982, 463). These stages are fairly well known and one can find them described in many psychology textbooks. Therefore, these brief comments should be enough to convey the general idea.

Kohlberg's general thesis is that children go through these stages in sequence. Furthermore, the sequence relates to the age of the child. The child has to understand the typical reasoning associated with one stage before he or she can continue to the next stage. Each new stage requires a reorganizing of the child's thoughts and feelings. Still, not everyone reaches the postconventional level of moral development.

Children may go through stages of mental development affecting the ways they think about what is right or wrong. Nevertheless, the notion that stage six is better than stage four is certainly less than obvious. These stages reflect Kohlberg's view that a healthy person moves toward abstract ways of thinking and reasoning. The movement is toward ways that value universal aspects of moral reasoning over a more personal and caring approach.

Along these lines, Kohlberg's theory shows that women do not move through the stages as expected; they do not reach the postconventional states in the same percentages as men. This situation may have to do with socialization since girls learn from society to be caring and compassionate. These values fall into the conventional level (Hall, Perlmutter, and Lamb 1982, 466). Carol Gilligan has maintained that Kohlberg's work is gender biased. She rejects his conclusion that women are somehow morally lacking. Difference for her does not mean that male morality is better than female morality (Gilligan 1982, 19). She sees the two types of morality as complementary.

This last point also raises the following concern. To what extent is Kohlberg measuring cognitive development as opposed to measuring one's social learning? If Kohlberg is correct and these stages are universal, then social environment should not make any substantial difference in the cognitive development. However, studies indicate that culture makes a difference. Kohlberg has revised his theory due to some of these criticisms.

Still, he seems committed to the view that moral thinking that comes out of abstract rules or universal norms are always on a higher level than moral thinking established on other considerations. Elizabeth Simpson and Sarah Harkness comment that

> Kohlberg's theory is culturally biased and not universal, because it is based on a social organization and values that fit only Western culture. Simpson argues that because Kohlberg's approach focuses on issues of equality, rights, and justice, moral reasoning at a principled level [i.e., a postconventional level] fits only a constitutional democracy. In addition, it is probably beyond most of the people in the world. It may be that formal, abstract reasoning requires formal education for its development (Hall, Perlmutter, and Lamb 1982, 466).

I would say that moral development in reality is both a cognitive and a social phenomenon. To sort out what comes from cognitive development and what comes from social environment seems impossible. Some of Kohlberg's work may suffer from mixing up social influence with cognitive development. While we may move from concrete to abstract levels of thinking, social environment or socialization has a lot to do with whether one derives his or her values from the abstract or the concrete. A person may act out of care and compassion, but this does not mean that he or she cannot also reason in an abstract or impersonal way. It may just mean that he or she chooses to value compassion and caring over abstract reason and notions of universality.

CONCLUSION

In short, this chapter has discussed various aspects of morality primarily from the perspective of the individual. The work of Watson, Skinner, and Homans shows that human behavior is predictable because we are rational, and because we always attempt to gain reward and avoid punishment. Altruism, therefore, is impossible. Likewise, freedom is unattainable. Human beings are controlled by the environment. Skinner even proposes a society where the social scientist would control one's behavior through operant conditioning. Ethics for Skinner means producing an ideal society through behavioral modification. Since humans are selfish and rational creatures, the behavioral scientist could in theory control human behavior by controlling the environment. The controllers, therefore, have the ethical task of creating an acceptable society.

Psychological egoists agree with behavioral scientists that we are selfish and rational creatures. They do not necessarily agree, however, that a few elite behavioral psychologists have the right to dictate what society ought to be like. The ethical egoist says we have a moral obligation to advance our own interest. Moreover, he or she argues that we do not have an obligation to advance the interests of others at our own expense unless we receive some reward.

In many cases, we may be able to discover ways in which one can meet his or her own needs as well as the needs of others. We can often find mutually beneficial solutions to ethical problems that meet the needs of the self and the other. However, does one have a moral obligation to put the interests of others ahead of his or her own interests? Certain religious or ethical perspectives may call on one to do so. I have suggested that individuals have to decide for themselves what to do when their interests come into conflict with the interests of others. I do attempt to provide a rationale for this conclusion in the last chapter.

Finally, I look at different psychological theories related to moral development. These theories focus on behavior and cognition. The former theories are similar to the views of conscience and socialization I describe in an earlier chapter. The cognitive theories of Piaget and Kohlberg focus on moral thinking and reasoning. One's social environment and one's cognitive abilities have a bearing on how a child thinks and acts.

The question that remains, however, is how can we distinguish between what a child learns from the environment as opposed to one's normal mental development? Our inability to distinguish the social from the cognitive development would weaken arguments that talk about universal stages of moral development. Finally, why should we consider abstract notions such as universal rules or standards as morally superior to tendencies to care for people in particular situations? This issue resurfaces in the following two chapters.

NOTES

1. For George C. Homans, this proposition is the sixth one, but I place it here to explain his views on rewards, costs, and profits, to follow.

2. See Joseph Butler 1975, 122-133; William K. Frankena 1973, 21-23.

3. William James contends that only a belief in free will is compatible with morality. For the opposing view see John Staurt Mill 1975, 136-149. For Mills, our actions are determined by past events.

4. See Marc N. Richelle 1993, 29-30.

5. See Berger 1963, 54-150.

6. See *Introduction* 1970, 17.

7. Compare to Nietzsche 1994, 62-63.

8. Nietzsche contends that one must love oneself before he or she can love others, which he defines as friendship. He sees so-called altruistic actions as often proceeding out of dislike for one's own self. See Kaufmann 1974, 363-371.

9. Not all hedonists, however, would advocate unlimited self-gratification. Recall that Epicurus says that the best way to be happy is not an unrestrained indulging in sensual pleasures, but the avoidance of anxiety.

10. While Christians often decry legalism, many who cling to an emphasis on personal salvation and act as if they believe in works salvation. Legalism is just as prevalent among most Christians as it is in other religions or the public.

11. This strategy has been used in bargaining situations. See Roger Fisher and William Ury, *Getting to Yes: Negotiating Agreement Without Giving In.* (New York: Penguin Books, 1981), 41-98.

Chapter Nine

Contemporary Ethical Perspectives

Chapters five and six introduce modern and postmodern ethical thinking. Among other individuals, these two chapters discuss Kant, Marx and Nietzsche. The perspectives of these thinkers continue to influence modern and postmodern thought. In this chapter, I look primarily at the continuing impact of Kant and Nietzsche's ideas on morals in relation to more contemporary thinkers. I might add that the Marxist tradition is also still a viable position in modified form. Habermas, for instance, develops an ethical theory that draws significantly from the Kantian ethical tradition, but the influence of Marx is also present in his work. Kant, Marx, and Habermas all stand in the modern tradition that sees truth as something obtainable by means of reason. Nietzsche's work, on the other hand, has gained a wide appeal largely from those favorably inclined toward postmodern thought. Another ethical theory, the ethic of care, sits on the borderline between modern and postmodern thought. It is a feminist ethical view. I discuss Rita C. Manning's version of this ethical theory. Concerning postmodern thought, I focus on the views of Foucault concerning reciprocity, Edith Wyschogrod's view on the ethical person as a saint, and Caputo's opposition to ethics. The purpose of this discussion is to show how many of the concerns already addressed in earlier chapters are still pressing matters for us presently.

KANTIAN STYLED ETHICS

W. D. Ross

The modern debate concerning morality has a great deal to do with diversity and plurality. Kant's ethical perspective as stated in the categorical imperative appears too rigid considering current thinking. His absolutist position on morality does not fare well today. W. D. Ross has helped to make Kant's views less rigid. He introduces the notion of *prima facie obligation or duty*. Ross recognizes that there are times when there is not one clear or absolute right or wrong. There are instances when our duties or our obligations can come into conflict with one another. In cases of conflicting duties, one duty must take priority over the other. Ross recognizes that we must sometimes choose when life presents us with conflicting obligations. Ross maintains that when I am faced with two competing obligations "I have to . . . study the situation as fully as I can until I form the considered opinion (it is never more) that in the circumstances one of them is more incumbent than any other" (Ross 1975, 192).

Using this line of reasoning, we could consider the following situation. Joan is a single mother with two small children. She feels that taking a life is wrong regardless of the circumstances. One night, however, someone breaks into her home. Suddenly, she has to weigh her obligation not to harm another person, possibly by taking his or her life, against her obligation to protect her family. If she chooses to protect her family, then she considers that response or obligation to be her *prima facie* duty.

On the other hand, consider a less drastic situation. I promise to take my son to the football game in a couple of weeks. The game is on Saturday. Two days before the game, my employer tells me I have to work on Saturday. It is a situation where a job must be completed by Monday morning, and my position at work is probationary. Without the job, I could not support my family. Consequently, I have two conflicting obligations. I have an obligation to keep my promise to my son, and I have an obligation to provide for him and my family. Under these conditions, I would determine that my obligation to provide for my family outweighs my obligation to keep my promise to my son.

Ross agrees with Kant that consequences have nothing to with one's *prima facie* duty. My intent or motive determines whether my action is moral or immoral. One's duty may not always generate happiness for the individual or for the greatest number of people. The value of this ethic is that it is flexible enough to deal with real life situations. It maintains Kant's notion of duty and obligation without having to make it an absolute. For Kant, one must keep a promise regardless of the consequences. For Ross, there are conflicting obligations and duties. When that happens, one must determine which obligation is primary (i.e., more important) and which is secondary (i.e., less important).

Habermas' Proposed Ethic

Habermas is another prominent contemporary figure who has drawn on the Kantian tradition. His ethic is not one, however, that derives from the rational individual in isolation. This ethic is at home in a pluralistic environment. Habermas is a contemporary German scholar whose work is important for philosophy and sociology alike. His work has been influential in both areas.

Habermas is a vital participant in the current discussion of modern and post-modern values. In his book, *Moral Consciousness and Communicative Action*, Habermas bases his ethics upon his previous theories relating to *communication theory*. For Habermas, the location of truth is not in the isolated self but the social self. He considers a statement objective if it derives from *social discourse*. Habermas is content with the notion that social agreement constitutes the basis for objective truth, and that we can reach this agreement through communication. He, therefore, draws an ideal picture of what communication should be and do, even though he realizes that this ideal most often goes unrealized.[1]

Like Kant, he stresses rationality as a way of discovering what is right or just. Both Kant and Habermas want to make formulations that have universal appeal. Reflecting Marxist's concerns, Habermas limits the scope of moral theory to the issues of justice and fairness. Moral questions that fall outside these two considerations are no concern for his ethical theory. The issue of what constitutes a good life is not necessarily the domain of moral theory unless "good" means the life or self that creates a fair and just society for everyone. Therefore, the things that fall outside the scope of justice and fairness do not belong to the concern of moral theory (McCarthy 1990, vii).

Unlike Kant, Habermas recognizes that we live in a pluralistic age where there is often little agreement over what is fair or just. However, he does not give up on the idea of some type of a universal ethic. He finds the solution in what he calls *discourse ethics*. A discourse ethic replaces Kant's categorical imperative with the procedure of "moral argumentation" (Habermas 1990, 195). In addition, a discourse ethic considers consequences as a part of the deliberation over what is fair and just. Universalization is the main key in this type of ethic as one can see from the following quote where he discusses the central principle of moral argumentation.

> Only those norms may claim to be valid that could meet with the consent of all affected in their role as participants in a practical discourse.
>
> While retaining the categorical imperative after a fashion, discourse ethics scales it down to a principle of universalization (U). In practical discourses (U) plays the part of a rule of argumentation.
>
> (U) For a norm to be valid, the consequences and side effects of its general observance for the satisfaction of each person's particular interests must be acceptable to all.
>
> Finally, an ethic is termed *universalist* when it alleges that this (or a similar) moral principle, far from reflecting the intuitions of a particular culture or epoch, is valid universally. As long as the moral principle is not justified . . . the ethnocentric fallacy looms large. I must prove that my moral principle is not just a reflection of the prejudices of adult, white, well-educated western males of today (Habermas 1990, 197).

In short, for a norm to be valid, its consequences, which are for the satisfaction of everyone's interests, must be acceptable to everyone engaged in the discourse.

Habermas lands squarely in the modern tradition. For instance, he concludes that the "moral point of view" is the viewpoint characterized by fairness and justice. From this point of view, one can judge moral questions *"impartially."* He describes his discourse ethic as an instrument of "argumentation" which "insures that all concerned in principle take part, freely and equally, in a cooperative search for truth, where nothing coerces anyone except the force of the better argument" (Habermas 1990, 198). Habermas suggests that practical discourse as a communicative process encourages all participants in the discourse to put themselves into the place of the other person. Likewise, it urges them to see the issue from the other person's point of view. The issue is whether a certain proposal is fair or just to everyone affected. This process must take place publicly and not in private (Habermas 1990, 198).

I must admit that this sounds good. It stresses universality, justice, and fairness. In addition, it avoids the Kantian view that allows one to determine in isolation what one's duty entails. Yet is this type of ethics realistic? Can we ever free ourselves from biases and prejudices? Are issues clear-cut enough to allow everyone to agree? Do we all operate on the same notions of justice and fairness? What stops a person from engaging in the process in bad faith? Will the better and more rational argument win or will the better rhetorician win? Can we really put ourselves in another person's place and see the issue from their perspective? Finally, can we take power and authority out of the discussions? In other words, are we ever truly equals? Some people always have more power, authority, or status in a relationship.

The practice of putting ourselves in another person's shoes is good idea, and it would no doubt help us understand others better. However, our ability or willingness to do this is limited. No two people are exactly alike since no two people have the same life experiences. To even approach an understanding of the other person's views in this way would require a long personal relationship. I am skeptical that two people can ever fully understand each other especially when they come from different cultures and different social environments. For example, I could go live a week in poverty like a homeless person, but there is still a big difference between a homeless person and me. I can go back home in a week to my comfortable lifestyle, and I cannot imagine what it is like to live that way without hope of a better life.

Can communication resolve the different positions or ideas between parties? Differences in race, gender, nationalities, and geographical locations clearly create significant difficulties for the proposal of Habermas. These differences prevent us from really understanding another person whose subjective reality is different from our own. All the good will in the world cannot change the fact that we do not all see and understand the world in the same way.

Habermas' proposal is an advance over Kant's categorical imperative. As I stated earlier, Kant assumes that all rational beings would agree on what is moral and immoral (i.e., the categorical imperative). If I am rational and I follow Kant's categorical imperative (i.e., I can will that the rule on which I act be followed by everyone) then I can know what is moral and immoral for myself and everyone else. Therefore, I have a duty to do what is moral. Furthermore, once I determine that breaking a promise is wrong, I must accept that it is always wrong to break a promise. There are no exceptions. The consequences of an act have nothing to do with the morality of an act.

Habermas, on the other hand, calls for a consensus among all parties affected. Even though I am skeptical about his views, I do agree that the notion of discourse on important matters of justice and fairness is important. He is right that trying to understand an issue from the viewpoint of another person is helpful. Unlike Kant, people engage in public discourse to hammer out an agreement. In this way, the rule of fairness does not come from the mind of a single private individual far removed from those who are going to be affected by the decision. Habermas instructs those who are engaged in this discourse to put themselves in the place of the other person. While this makes his proposal more acceptable, it is still idealistic. Sometimes agreement is possible, but often it is not possible. No amount of good will or discourse would change that fact. It also seems to assume, which is highly unlikely, that coercion can be eliminated.

Finally, nonconsequentialist ethics such as the one Kant proposes depends upon *a-prior knowledge of morals*. However, this type of knowledge is hardly an adequate basis for constructing an ethical theory since one cannot even prove that such knowledge even exists. What seems apparent to one culture at a particular moment in history may not be so evident to other cultures. In other words, it seems rather unlikely that there is a common moral view that all rational creatures share or can agree upon. Habermas' approach, however, is not dependent on this view. It simply seeks consensus based on rational dialogue. He wants to maintain rationality, but the rationality is no longer located in the isolated individual. It is part of the social arena, and it can be evaluated by everyone.

Still, one must realize that rational thought is a tool, and this tool is not a means to certainty. Rational thought can occur in the service of ideologies, theologies, and numerous worldviews. The ideology, theology, or perspective one takes provides the framework from which reason functions. Reason is not free of bias. It cannot guarantee that our views are fair or just. It is based on assumptions. Based on Marxist assumptions, reason may provide guidance in how to organize a society in the absence of capitalism. A fundamentalist Christian may use reason to argue against human evolution and for scientific creationism. The liberal Christian may use reason to argue for human evolution and against scientific creationism. Reason then is a tool. One can employ it to support widely different views. In other words, it functions in extensively different worldviews.

This discussion also leads to a realization that we are easily deluded. Marx falls in the modern tradition because he felt that he could see beyond ideologies and determine what type of society is best. Other thinkers in the Marxist tradition, those associated with the Frankfurt School, recognize that ideologies are pervasive and affect everyone. American theologian, Reinhold Niebuhr, points out that we, as human beings, are prone to claim more for ourselves than they have the right to claim. He comments that a person wishes to have certain knowledge. As a result, he or she is "tempted to deny the limited character of his knowledge and the finiteness of his perspectives" (Niebuhr 1964, 182).[2] This realization in some ways represents a shift to a more postmodern attitude, which recognizes that there is no way to be totally neutral or objective; in other words, we cannot completely break free from current ideologies.

Some Movements in the Direction of Postmodern Thinking

As we said earlier, the work of Nietzsche has prepared the way for what many people call postmodernism. Postmodernism stresses diversity, the timely, and the particular in contrast to unity, timeless, and universal truths or norms. Modernism stresses the use of reason as a way to obtaining Truth. Modern philosophical systems claim that they can lay a foundation for knowledge. This foundation provides "absolute bedrock of truth that could serve as the guarantee of philosophical systems" (Best and Kellner 1991, 21). Modernism makes claims of being neutral and impartial whereas postmodernism recognizes such claims as mere fancy. In some cases, this recognition leads to a relativistic point of view. Nietzsche, however, presents a view that allows for other possibilities.

What would a postmodern ethic appeal to? Some regard postmodernism as a relativistic worldview that calls ethics into question. I am using the term "ethics" in this context as a philosophical normative discipline. In other words, postmodern views would tend to undermine the belief in modern ethical systems of thought since truth is not timeless or universal, but it is rather timely and particular (Wyschogrod 1990, xiii). Still, one could develop a postmodern ethic from a perspectivist position, a position that does not claim universal or absolute truths.

In chapters five and six, I briefly discuss the decline of the modern view, and the rise of a postmodern one. Nietzsche's work plays an important role in the development of postmodernism. Generally, a postmodern approach to ethics recognizes that values, thoughts, and cultures are always shifting, changing, and adapting to new situations. From this perspective, a timeless, changeless ethic is unrealistic. Yet, postmodernism is not exactly relativistic in nature since it can make claims. A postmodern ethic is most often described as always being open to the other. Other refers to the other person. It can also refer to the unforeseeable, what is coming that is not easily seeable or predictable. It is openness to the other, what is different, what cannot always be foreseen ahead of time or anticipated. In some cases, it is about responsibility or obligation to the other. In the remainder of the chapter, I explore some of the avenues of ethical thought shaping current discussions. I begin the discussion with a feministic ethic known as the ethic of care. Then I move more into the domain of postmodern thought.

An Ethic of Care

The ethic of care may fit somewhere between modern and postmodern perspectives. It shares the postmodern critique of modern moral theory. This ethic derives from a feminist perspective known as the ethic of care. An ethic of care differs significantly from the modern ethical theories discussed above. An ethic of care, as defined by Rita C. Manning, has two aspects. The first aspect asserts that we have an inclination to care. Our ethical obligation is to be a caring person. The second feature of this ethic is a practical one; it calls not for adherence to moral principles but to moral action. We should "care for" others. This caring for others "involves acting in some appropriate way to respond to the needs of persons and animals, but can also be extended to responding to the needs of communities, values, or objects" (Manning 1992, 62).

The objects of care include "persons, animals, ideals, values, institutions, and objects" (Manning 1992, 65). She associates the ethic of care with human nature. For her, it is natural for one person or group to enter into relationship with other human beings; we are social animals. From this perspective, she then can develop an ethic consistent with this view of human nature. One should be sensitive to the suffering of others and try to help if possible. In the absence of natural caring, one must remember that there is an ethical obligation to care for others. This perspective engages the human imagination. When a stranger is suffering, we should try to become aware of their particular situation. Then we should allow this awareness to produce an "emotional response" in us so that we can act (Manning 1992, 69). Therefore, an ethic of care embraces emotions and personal feelings in the act of caring for another individual or group of individuals. It can also be directed toward nonhuman objects listed above. It does not view the presence of human emotions as a reason an act lacks moral worth.

Still, are there any limits to my responsibility to care for other persons, animals, goals, ideals, or institutions? Manning says there are limits. She defines these limitations to our obligation to care for others, and she argues that we cannot establish fixed rules for this type of ethic.

Regarding the limits of this obligation to care for others, she does not believe that we have an unending obligation to care for everyone and everything. She defines the limitation in relation to other persons. We have a *prima facie* (i.e., primary) obligation to care for one in need under the following three circumstances. First, we have an obligation when a person has a legitimate need, and he or she cannot meet that need without our assistance. Next, we have an obligation when we can care for another person as a part of a reciprocal relationship. Finally, we have an obligation to care when we play a particular role such as a parental or job related role that requires us to care. This helps to provide concrete guidance for one's actions.

She notes that caring for others is often draining and certainly could lead to one's exhaustion physically and otherwise. Therefore, we must also allow others to care for us. Reciprocal relationships are best because they give the person doing the caring a source of strength. A total commitment to care can lead to burnout, which lessens one's ability to care for others in the future (Manning 1992, 72-73). Concerning rules, Manning says that we can only employ general principles or rules of thumb. Her rejection of rules has a great deal to do with her misgivings about modern moral theories discussed earlier.

There are numerous applications of such an ethic. I conclude this discussion with an example related to education. Another advocate of this type of ethic, Nell Noddings, has advocated that we should organize our schools around themes of care. She says, for instance, that

> our society does not need to make its children first in the world in mathematics and science. It needs to care for its children—to reduce violence, to respect honest work of every kind, to reward excellence at every level, to ensure a place for every child and emerging adult in the economic and social world, to produce people who can care competently for their own families and contribute effectively to their communities (Noddings 1995, 365).

This view is a shift from an ethic based on reason and abstraction to one based on emotion that comes to humans naturally. In short, humans are social creatures by nature, and this implies that we have an ability and obligation to care for each other. The obligation goes both ways; we often should care for others and at times we need the care of others. The inclination to care is contextual and not abstract. We do not care in the abstract but in specific situations. In fact, she notes that an ethic of care calls for "institutions [that] support and sustain caring while simultaneously reducing the need for care by eliminating the poverty, despair, and indifference that create a need for care" (Manning 1992, 62). Clearly, the approach as she defines it is idealistic, but it also has some very practical value. It can serve as a general guide for one's actions. It limits one's obligation to care to certain situations. This limiting trait makes her view a good practical and workable ethic.

An ethic of care has ties to modern and postmodern views on morals. This ethic, as described by Manning, has connections to modern ethical systems in that it allows some small place for rules, and because it defines one's moral obligation. It shares with postmodern thought a critical view of modern moral and ethical thinking. Manning, for instance, expresses some mistrust for rules, and she shows a reluctance to adopt rules as a sufficient basis for her ethic of care. She also notes the harmful effects of binary oppositions, which hold so-called masculine traits higher than their opposite feminine traits.

POSTMODERN MORAL THINKING

Many people see postmodern views, particularly deconstruction, as incompatible with ethics. They describe it as a relativistic philosophy. The reason for this is that postmodernism rejects ethics as a system of moral thinking. Certainly, it rejects ethics as a normative enterprise for determining right and wrong in a complete manner. It recognizes the changing nature of the world and the subjective aspect of all human endeavors. New perspectives emerge as times change and as our knowledge and understanding of the world changes. This process is an ongoing one, and there is never a point when it ceases. One can develop a postmodern perspective on morality. Yet from a postmodern perspective, one would not be able to establish a set of rules or norms to prescribe moral behavior.

To explore moral thinking from a postmodern perspective, I begin with a look at perspectivism. In some ways, it can serve as an introduction to the postmodern mindset. Next, I have chosen to discuss three individual postmodern thinkers: Edith Wyschogrod, Foucault, and Caputo. Wyschogrod's book, *Saints and Postmodernism*, is one of the first in-depth discussions of ethics from a postmodern view. Wyschogrod's ethic focuses on the altruism of saints. Foucault offers a different viewpoint. He points to the danger of normative ethical systems. He sees ethics as an issue of power, and he advocates a view consistent with Nietzsche entailing the exercise of power over oneself and not others. Wyschogrod and Foucault represent two different possible ways of construing a postmodern ethic. Then I move to the work of Caputo. I will spend more time with his views since I think they provide a way of drawing on Jewish and Greek traditions. By looking at perspectivism and considering the ideas of these three writers, we can observe different possibilities for postmodern moral thinking.

Perspectivism

Postmodern thought is widely recognized to be thinking from a particular perspective. This view begins, as far as I know, with Nietzsche who talks about viewing things from one's little corner of the world. One might view this view as relativism. Yet, it does not have to deny truth. It simply recognizes that whatever we know and understand as truth today largely depends on a number of different things such as culture, education, discourse, political views, religious views, or one's own personal experiences and biases. It cannot claim any transcendent view; perspectivism finds itself situated down below in a particular social setting, and it cannot take flight to rise above human thought and develop a Godlike understanding of our existence.

Perspectivism is a predicament we find ourselves in, and it is a view chosen consciously. Part of being human is that we are limited in knowledge, understanding, ability, imagination, and power. Humans are caught in a web from which many spend their lives trying to break free. Yet, we can never break completely free. Nevertheless, an individual may embrace this predicament and make the best of it. He or she may desire to be an active force in choosing, embracing, or creating his or her moral values.

Regardless of the way one's life unfolds, the individual experiences external forces as well as internal ones that shape his or her outlook on life. One's perspective is always limited. Personality or physical limitations can partially determine one's views or outlooks on life. No matter how hard we may fight, we always have to live within certain confines, and these confines blind us to other possibilities or ways of thinking. I could never live and think as a person born and raised in India because that is not within my ability. My place of birth and socialization within a small Alabama county is part of who I am. I might add, modify, or try to change that, but it is there in my memory. It lingers unconsciously inside me shaping some of my attitudes. It is both a positive and negative force; one I cannot neutralize. Therefore, there are a multitude of different perspectives. To think that we can eliminate the multitude and agree on a truth is unrealistic.

For Nietzsche, *perspectivism* means that our reality does not consist of facts and objective truths but only interpretations of the world. These interpretations come through the eyes of individuals and groups (Best and Kellner 1991, 22). Individuals and groups have to make sense of their worlds. Interpreting the world around us is largely a social act. When we try to make sense of things (i.e., the act of interpretation), we try to understand them within a particular worldview. The development of language and consciousness emerged in the process of communal living. Both communication and language, therefore, are social products. Communication only becomes necessary when the individual gives up solitary life and freedom for the belonging and security of group life. At this stage, language is essential for the well-being of the group. The development of language corresponds to the development of the individual's consciousness of himself or herself (Nietzsche 1974, 297-300).

The group, however, shapes a person's consciousness. Nietzsche concludes that most people only know themselves as part of communities (i.e., what is average). In his view, human thinking is always controlled in part at least by the nature of awareness; this thinking is always "translated back into the perspective of the heard" (Nietzsche 1974, 299). Of course, the *Übermensch* can rise above the crowd or herd. He or she can choose how to live, but even the *Übermensch* cannot escape the limitations associated with perspectivism.

Accordingly, Nietzsche contends that humans can only be conscious of the "common world." What he drives home is that

> we simply lack any organ for knowledge, for 'truth,': we 'know' (or believe or imagine) just as much as may be useful in the interests of the human herd, the species; and even what is here called 'utility' is ultimately also a mere belief, something imaginary, and perhaps precisely that most calamitous stupidity of which we shall perish someday (Nietzsche 1974, 300).

Here Nietzsche hits upon the major problem. How can we know anything with certainty? How could Kant know that his reason has discovered the moral law? How can the utilitarian know the consequences that determine the rightness or wrongness of an act? Alternatively, how can the religious person know that God exists and provides us with knowledge from above? Why should one agree with the ethical relativist's claim that whatever a society deems to be right is right? Regarding the last position, one might argue that the relativist lives by values that preserve society; these values are pragmatic. Yet, what about societies where leaders adopt values harmful to the general population or to a minority?[3] Since we have no "biological organ" for determining truth or morality, how can we judge?

Perspectivism, therefore, recognizes and imposes limits on all value judgments. Time, location, and the act of interpretation determine the limits of what is possible. As a result, all moral systems of thought whether they are utilitarian or deontological (i.e., duty based), fall within different worldviews or perspectives. The best we can do is to develop our moral perspective realizing that it competes with other perspectives.

The advantage of perspectivism is that it allows a person the room to grow, experiment, think, and listen without having to pronounce final judgment upon those with whom he or she disagrees. It also allows one room to argue for his or her own views and even try to reform society without the delusion that he or she has the corner on truth. Such an approach could lead to mystery and humility, knowing that total understanding of the world is far beyond us and that it is unrealistic to believe we can capture the Truth in our limited concepts.

This approach can also allow one to make claims that some views of truth and reality are more humane, caring, considerate, and fair than other views without claiming that our views are final. I concur with Nietzsche's assertion that everything we do derives from our interpretations of the world and reality. If one adopts the premise that societies should be fair and look after their own people, then there can be meaningful dialogue over how to achieve such goals.

All we have is a particular perspective of our world. Social and psychological forces shape and color this perspective. We live in our little "corner" of the world at a particular moment in history, in a particular social context. Our perspectives or interpretations derive from a variety of experiences.

Even our most basic way of understanding the world, which one gains through oral or written communication, derives from a taken-for-granted faith that we can understand the thoughts of another person. Sociologist, Alfred Schutz, has described this view as the "reciprocity of perspectives." We assume that the person with whom we are conversing shares similar life experiences with us. We assume that our experience of a particular object and another person's experience of the same object are the same and so communication is possible (Schutz 1967, 11-12). Without such assumptions, communication and social life would be impossible. Still this "reciprocity of perspectives" may often hide differences and give the impression that we are more alike than we actually are. Ethnomethodology, another school of social thought related to Schultz, examines what happens when problems occur in communication. Those individuals who work in this field carried out experiments where they intentionally disrupt the communication process. These studies discover that subjects find a way to mend, overcome, and repair the problems in communication.[4] Yet it also demonstrates that the reality, which we accept as true or beyond question, is really a subjective reality. This view indicates that ultimately we can never know the mind of another person.

Moreover, Nietzsche tells us that we cannot even fully know ourselves much less the intentions of another person. At best, knowledge of the world and nature is incomplete, and as we grow and develop as a species, we discover errors and new truths. The possibilities for new understandings or perspectives are infinite (Nietzsche 1974, 297-302, and 336-337).

From a perspectivist position, therefore, one could develop an ethic. However, this ethic could never be absolute or universal. One individual or group may have a better perspective than another, but even such a value judgment is open to dispute and debate. We may value the scientific or moral perspective that makes sense to us and helps us make more sense of the world around us. Perspectivism has the value of recognizing diversity without sacrificing the belief that there is a right or wrong. It may be my perspective, but I think slavery is wrong regardless of what society thinks. I hold that view even if the universe is cold and completely indifferent to the plight of the slave. Therefore, I would have none of the problems Durkheim has with the notion of reforming a slave society into a non-slave society even if it caused other problems. This aspect is to me what distinguishes relativism from perspectivism.

I offer this notion of perspectivism as a possible alternative to relativism. It allows flexibility, and it moves the focus away from the notion of "Truth." Perspectivism as I define it draws upon the views of Nietzsche and Schutz, and it allows room for discussion and disagreement. It does not insist that all values are equally right. It can only articulate a perspective or interpretation of things. There is no illusion that this interpretation is final or absolute. Views can change indefinitely. As societies change, our understandings of the world and our place in it also change. Who can imagine what worldviews will be in 20, 30, or 100 years from now?

Perspectivism is primarily a social phenomenon. Social and psychological forces shape our views of the world and our place in it. The views we espouse are a patchwork. They are mediated or come to us through ideas, language, books, teachers, or other experiences. Now we can see how these views work in three different postmodern perspectives on ethics. These three share similarities and differences.

Edith Wyschogrod

Postmodernism calls modern ethical theories into question since they depend upon modern modes of thought. Wyschogrod desires an ethic redefined in postmodern terms. As she defines it,

> A postmodern ethic must look not to some opposite of ethics [i.e., nihilism] but elsewhere, to life narratives, specifically those of saints defined in terms that both overlap and overturn traditional stipulations and that defy the normative structure of moral theory (Wyschogrod 1990, xiii).

For her, ethics occupies the realm of activity between oneself and the other person. This ethic is not dependent upon rules or norms of conduct coming from modern moral theories (Wyschogrod 1990, xv).

Since one cannot depend upon moral theory, Wyschogrod attempts to find another means for developing an ethic. As a result, she looks to narratives or stories about the lives of saints as a way toward an ethic. These stories are concrete expressions that can give guidance and direction for life. They inspire and motivate us to become something more than we are now. By saints, she does not mean individuals from particular religious communities, but individuals we find "across a broad spectrum of belief systems and institutional practices. A saintly life is defined as one in which compassion for the Other, irrespective of cost to the saint, is the primary trait" (Wyschogrod 1990, xxii-xxiii and 34).[5] The saint, therefore, is

> one whose adult life in its entirety is devoted to the alleviation of sorrow (the psychological suffering) and pain (the physical suffering) that afflicts other persons without distinction of rank or group or, alternatively, that afflicts sentient beings, whatever the cost to the saint in pain or sorrow (Wyschogrod 1990, 34).

Wyschogrod endeavors to develop her ethic based upon the narratives about saints. Saintly narratives are important because they recount a story, and in the process, the readers or hearers of the story feel its imperative force (Wyschogrod 1990, 6). By narratives, however, she does not mean that an ethic depends upon a so-called "master narrative," (i.e., narratives that have normative value for the larger community) (Wyschogrod 1990, xvii).[6] Saintly narrative tells about a saintly individual who lives at some point in the past. This narrative also tells about the time of the one who is telling the story (i.e., the narrator) and the audience one is addressing (i.e., the addressees) (Wyschogrod 1990, 9-10, 29). Wyschogrod resists the view that a saintly narrative simply serves to legitimate already existing customs or theological views. She, however, contends that the lives of saints often conflict with dominant theological views. Rules of thumb and not norms or laws provide legitimacy and guide saintly practices (Wyschogrod 1990, 12-14, 29-30).

Wyschogrod also describes her ethic in terms of several different aspects. The discussion below focuses on differentiality, eclecticism, otherness, and empowerment. These tendencies come from postmodern thought, and they define ethics in a way that resists boundaries and limitations (Wyschogrod 1990, xvi-xxii). Differentiality pertains to the critique of modernism. I have already discussed this aspect. It contrasts modern thought that seeks to establish a unified discourse as a means of establishing reality and truth with postmodern thinking that stresses differentiality or difference. Eclecticism and the otherness of persons are terms that express postmodernism's commitment to inclusion and openness to what is different (Wyschogrod 1990, xvi-xx). As the reader might recall, inclusion is a key aspect of modern instrumental values as described by Parsons. In that discussion, I note that this ideal of inclusion carries over into the postmodern perspective. Yet postmodernism adds the notion of difference to it. Inclusion includes everyone not in a unity of thought but in diversity.

Empowerment relates to the dynamic of power. Life involves a struggle over power. This struggle is inevitable. Life always entails a struggle over power between competing forces. Often this struggle results in a situation where my gain is someone else's loss. Wyschogrod, on the other hand, seeks power *for the other* and not power to be used against the other. The saint can empower others to become something other than what they are at present, something better (Wyschogrod 1990, xx-xxii, 56).[7] This brief description shows the proclivity of postmodernism to understand the complexity of life without squeezing phenomenon into universal structures (Wyschogrod 1990, xvi-xxii).

Wyschogrod intentionally capitalizes the "Other" when referring to the other person. It is this Other who provides the reference point of moral existence. The Other is a living force, not a cold concept. Moreover, the Other is unlike oneself in that the Other's existence carries compelling moral significance (Wyschogrod 1990, xxi). Her ethic encourages compassion, and embracing of the Other's pain. The saint's life and the moral life are a labor, and its completion, the alleviation of another person's needs, lies in the future (Wyschogrod 1990, 63-86, and 95-99). Saints have a *desire* to aid the "Other" in relieving his or her suffering and promoting his or her joy (Wyschogrod 1990, 227-229, 257). Saints express moral values in a way that can motivate us and show us how we can transform or change our life. The saint's body is a signifier. It signifies or embodies love, compassion, and generosity in human form. These values are binding not because of some abstract rule but because of influence on us (Wyschogrod 1990, 52). They draw us toward the Other.

The saint's work has "always already belonged to the Other" (Wyschogrod 1990, 105-122). In contrast to ordinary work that is always oriented toward a future goal or purpose, saintly labor is distinctive. As described in saintly narratives, the saint renounces the self. She notes that "powerful persons of royal birth have been canonized in Western Christianity" for their deeds. Yet, saintly work has a particular characteristic. "Saintly work across a broad range of religious traditions typically abandons self-empowerment and wealth" for the sake of the Other (Wyschogrod 1990, 96). For the saintly life, therefore, there is a decentering of the "I" or subject. The "I" of the saint is replaced and speaks with the voice of another (Wyschogrod 1990, 122-123). Therefore, the Other takes center stage for the saint.

Another aspect of her ethic seeks to bypass propositional moral language to find a way for promoting or encouraging moral action. From her perspective, moral actions do not depend upon propositional statements or moral theories. Moral actions come out of an encounter with the Other. At this point, she draws from Emmanuel Levinas who argues that we have a responsibility for the Other. For Levinas, there is a moral dimension in human beings. This dimension carries with it a responsibility at the very moment when we encounter the Other *face-to-face* and enter into dialogue.

Levinas' notion of *face* is important. The face, not the person, places a claim on us. By person, Levinas means the mask or persona that one wears. We all play various roles in society. The parental role entails various sub-roles such as teaching our children or providing for their safety and well-being. At work, we also play various roles. These roles are the masks we wear at appropriate times. These masks hide the face. It is the face, therefore, and not the person, that makes claims on us. The face refers to the self without mask or covering. This face-to-face dialogue "calls me to account for my attitude. It is here that Levinas believes one finds the source and the ground of our moral obligations" (Kockelmans 1992, 125-126).

In such an encounter between the Other and myself, I see and understand the Other in relation to myself. I assume that the Other person is sufficiently enough like myself to make communication possible. The body of the saint, therefore, becomes a signifier or a general image; it communicates a message to the Other. This saintly message can also move or inspire the rest of us to respond to the Other (Wyschogrod 1990, 49-52). She does not attempt to legitimate this message in the guise of moral theories, which have been unsuccessful in leading one to moral action (Wyschogrod 1990, xxii, xxiv-xxvi). Instead, the saintly narrative most effectively communicates this message.

Altruism is a particularly distinctive characteristic of the saint and the ethical life. She does not necessarily claim that altruism is an "*a-priori* given" or that altruistic acts derive from completely unselfish motivation (Wyschogrod 1990, 161-162). Neither does she believe altruism to be a universal trait of human beings. She limits her claims concerning altruism to the view that we all have a basic sensitivity to others, but "not everyone yields to the pressure of this primordial encounter" (Wyschogrod 1990, 150).[8] Putting ourselves in the other person's place may help us understand what the Other person needs and thinks, and this knowledge may even produce a "cognitive conviction." Nevertheless, this "cognitive conviction generally fails to *motivate* altruistic action" (Wyschogrod 1990, 39-40).

Altruism comes through saintly practice. Saints are those who are "uniquely sensitive" to the Other. Therefore, saintliness is "never be fully realized" (Wyschogrod 1990, 149-150, 161-162). We can understand saints as examples of particular types of behavior motivated by compassion or courage. Examples or fair samples refer to the notion that the part can also tell us something about the whole. Acts of compassion of a particular person are parts, and they may tell us something about the larger context out of which these acts emerge. They are dependent upon views of *equity* or *fairness*. These views depend upon particular social contexts (Wyschogrod 1990, 155-162).

Additionally, the Other's *lack or need of something* is what matters. Proximity is not a factor for saints. It is true that we tend to act more benevolently toward those people with whom we are in close contact (e.g., family members) than people who are more distant from us. However, the saint acts with compassion not toward the closest but toward those in need. For the saintly figure, one could say that the greater a person's need, the greater the claim that person has on the time and energy of the saint (Wyschogrod 1990, 242-243).[9]

The suffering of the Other is what guides the saint's desire. Still, it is an excessive need. From the viewpoint of the saint, the Other is the one whose need always exceeds the saint's ability to make things tolerable. Since the need of the Other never completely disappears, the Other always imposes upon the saintly life. The saint's desire is "unconstrained and excessive yet guided by the suffering of the Other" (Wyschogrod 1990, 256).

Positively, her ethic embraces difference and diversity. She makes a compelling argument that the power of saints and their lives can inspire and empower us to become something more than what we are now. It is also helpful because it causes us to reflect or perhaps rethink how we should relate to the Other. Yet, the person with reservations or the cynic might ask why one should choose to follow the example of saints. Her response to such a person is not overly compelling. Yes, those few individuals who always seem to have the other person's interest at heart may inspire us. However, I wonder if her ethic can muster a great deal of support.

The basis of her argument centers on the saint who attracts us because of the extraordinary character of his or her life. We can find this extraordinary character in the saint's extremism (Wyschogrod 1990, 243).[10] Moreover, she maintains that a "rudimentary sensitivity" exists for everyone. Even though the impulse exists, we often resist it (Wyschogrod 1990, 150). However, if this impulse does exist, her arguments gain plausibility. If we have this "rudimentary sensitivity", the example of the saint would appeal to us on a rather basic level.

Moreover, we can view certain aspects of modern social life as the dulling or even the silencing the altruistic voice within us, a view similar to Bauman's view on moral impulse. In this light, those who read or hear these narratives about saints may respond in any variety of ways, some positive and others negative. The power of these narratives may be considerable. I share Wyschogrod's belief that moral theory has failed to motivate altruistic actions, but I have doubts about whether the power of narrative can succeed where theory fails. It is in my judgment an improvement. However, does the saintly narrative have the power to motivate our actions? It is one thing to admire a saint and another to respond by following the saint's example.

Her book leaves me with questions. Do saintly lives and the narratives about saints move us beyond admiration to action? The lives of people who inspire us can have a great deal of influence over the individual, but does that influence spill over into one's life, work, or everyday existence? For those people favorably disposed to such narratives of saintly lives, the stories may shape their own moral perspectives. Nevertheless, her ethic calls one to rethink the relationship between the self and the Other.

The view that she draws from Levinas concerning our obligations to the Other seems to offer justification for moral obligations toward the Other. In agreement with Levinas, she acknowledges that the demands of the Other derive out of concrete interactions with the Other, and these interactions put one under an obligation that is prior to "propositional language or moral theory" (Wyschogrod 1990, 49). For Levinas, the face of the Other "both commands one not to harm and solicits one's aid; to acknowledge the other's face is to bear responsibility to the other and for the other" (Schroeder 1992, 531). According to Levinas, such responsibility is not reciprocal. My responsibility for the Other is of concern instead of some expected return for my actions. Wyschogrod concludes that since saints experience the need of the Other more radically than anyone else, they serve as our paradigm because they respond to the Other with generosity and compassion (Wyschogrod 1990, 229).

Still her account leaves some additional questions. Does she ever really give a clear justification of why people ought to act altruistically? What has she said to convince the "cynic" that altruism lays a claim upon his or her life? Foucault's brief treatment of ethics moves in a different direction.

Michel Foucault

Foucault has influenced many different disciplines. In the field of ethics, he prefers to focus on technologies of the self instead of technologies of domination. His writings relating to ethics come late in his career, and they center on the "care of the self." This work differs from his earlier writings, which merely "interpreted [human subjects] as an effect of language, desire, and the unconscious" (Best and Kellner 1991, 42). In his earlier account, human subjects are passive and the product of various forces. In his work on ethics, however, Foucault comes to see human subjects as capable of some freedom, autonomy, and creativity, not merely a result of other forces. At this point in his work, he recognizes the necessity of studying both the technologies of domination and technologies of the self (Best and Kellner 1991, 60-61).

Ethics tend to take the first path, the technologies of domination. Deontological (i.e., nonconsequentialist) ethics, teleological or consequentialist ethics, and even relativistic ethics have many difficulties when taken as a complete system of ethical thought. To a large degree, these ethical systems of thought are inadequate. Some may contend that all we need to do is just improve these ethical systems and eliminate the problems as Ross and Habermas attempt to do with Kant. Such thinkers seem to have faith in the ability of moral theory to motivate correct behavior, a faith that lacks conviction among many today. Foucault views ethics based on the technologies of domination as potentially dangerous. Caputo says ethics and "piety unbroken by laughter spills blood" (Caputo 1993, 65).[11] Foucault explains that his "point is not that everything is bad, but that everything is dangerous, which is not exactly the same thing as bad" (Foucault 1984, 343).[12]

The source of this danger derives from our tendency for creating divisions and hierarchies. We find such tendencies in divisions such as "sane and insane, the laudatory and mean, elevated and low, [and] . . . the normal and abnormal . . . as well as divisions of men and women and authority and subject" (Scott 1990, 55). Modern ethical systems distinguish divisions or pairs. These pairs correspond to good/bad, desirable/undesirable, and ruler/ruled. The danger is that an ethical subject may fail to dominate the self, and instead he or she may seek to dominate others. One may do this by attempting to make his or her own values the norm for the larger society. People may act to enforce their values thinking that they have the best interest of the other at heart. In this way, there is always a lure for those in positions of power to enact policies that are to their own advantage and that exploit others. This description could apply to deontological, teleological, and relativistic ethical systems.

On Kant's view, I cannot only legislate for myself but for everyone else as well. Moreover, I can justify my act by saying that any rational person ought to agree with me. Consequentialists do the same by demanding that we should only consider the consequences of an act in making moral decisions. Relativistic ethical positions may simply justify the existence of domination by requiring individuals to accept and conform to the views of the larger community. The other person may find himself or herself at the mercy of someone else's ethical system. Following such an ethical system, one may attempt to impose his or her values on others. Such an imposition is an attempt to manage the life of others, thinking all the time that we can determine what is best not just for a particular other, but for all others through some impersonal abstract moral theory.

Foucault sees danger in any type of ethic that tries to universalize a course of action or a way of deciding right or wrong in an absolute sense. He is not saying that one should avoid involvement in ethical issues, but that ethics is a present and ongoing task in that "we always have something to do" (Foucault 1984, 343). It is never finished, and there is no point at which one now reaches completion.

Foucault draws from the Greeks to develop an ethic based on the care of the self. Yet, care of the self is not an egoist position. It involves consideration for the other. The care of the self involves a creative endeavor where one tries to make oneself a work of art. Art is something that ought to relate not only to objects but also to life. Like Nietzsche, Foucault sees ethics as an individual's attempt to "create himself or herself" free of the delusion that the self can have completely correct knowledge concerning universals or Truth. One should actively mold one's self and give one's life character and meaning (Foucault 1984, 351).[13]

Part of his study deals with pleasure in relation to sex. In sexual activities, for example, Greek males consider their own pleasure and not the pleasure of women and boys. Therefore, no reciprocity characterizes these relations. Only men receive pleasure. Foucault raises the question about the nature of pleasure, which also relates to our previous discussion concerning the conflict between one's personal interests versus the interests of others. Foucault asks:

> Are we able to have an ethics of acts and pleasures which would be able to take into account the pleasures of the other? Is the pleasure of the other something that can be integrated in our own pleasure, without reference either to law, marriage, to I don't know what? (Foucault 1984, 346)

Foucault recognized that if Greek men had tried to take the pleasure of the other person into account, it would have entailed more than minor changes in Greek society. Such consideration would have resulted in the destruction of a *hierarchical and patriarchal system*, where men did not have to consider the feelings of women or boys.

For Foucault, therefore, taking the pleasure of the other into account is important for ethics. There is no system for determining how to do this. He clearly states that one person's pleasure is just as important as the other person's pleasure. Therefore, Foucault's ethic could be more than a personal ethic concerning the care of the self. Ethical action should consider the other person as well as the self. So his ethic extends to the social realm.

According to Foucault, ethics can exist without resorting to types of coercion (Foucault 1984, 348). He does not accept a necessary connection between "our ethics, our personal ethics, our everyday life, and the great political and social and economic structures" (Foucault 1984, 350). Instead, he proposes an ethic with no necessary connections to these structures. Creating the self as a work of art entails avoiding being bound to other things, not even to the self as it is at present or to the nature of the self (Foucault 1984, 351). We may seek to live authentic lives, for instance. Being true to oneself is important.

Yet can or should one go beyond this sense of authenticity? Creating the self may carry us beyond our true self for good reason. We may see our limitations and desire to be more than what we are. We may never be able to change who we are at our core, but we can strive to create ourselves to be what we desire.[14] Our desire also says something important about us. What we want to be, regardless of who we are, relates to authenticity as well.

The care of the self or the relationship to oneself has four major aspects (Foucault 1984, 352). The first aspect of this inquiry tries to identify the part of oneself or one's behavior interested in moral conduct. For some it is "feelings." For Kant, it would be one's "intentions," the intention to act according to the moral law and do one's duty. For Christians, the concern is over the kind of desire one has. In one instance when Saint Augustine remembers a boyhood friend, his real concern is over the type of desire he has for his friend. For some Christians, one should eliminate desires. For example, one should act only to produce children and not for pleasure (Foucault 1984, 352, 359).[15] This first aspect, therefore, concerns the ethical substance.

Part two of his inquiry considers the "mode of subjection." The mode of subjection concerns the manner in which a person is called upon to see and comprehend their "moral obligations." In the Christian and Jewish faiths, for instance, the Hebrew Bible or Old Testament tells one how to live and act. It tells the Jew or Christian what his or her obligation is to God and to other human beings. The Ten Commandments address both of these issues. For Christians, the New Testament is authoritative and provides information on one's obligations. For others, natural law or rationality may provide the way of knowing and understanding our obligations. For Foucault, obligation might be conceived as a way to make one's existence as beautiful as possible (Foucault 1984, 353).

Each one of these ways can provide legitimation for moral thought and action. Groups and individuals can subordinate themselves and their actions to one of these modes. The mode of subjection, therefore, determines the type of moral obligations one feels. The Muslim feels a moral obligation when he or she believes the Koran calls him or her to a particular action.

The third aspect of his ethical study treats the ways in which one can change or shape oneself to become an ethical subject. It has to do with how one regulates his or her acts to become the type of person he or she wishes to be. In other words, to become a good father or a faithful spouse, one has to moderate his or her acts to become that sort of person. The fourth and final aspect of his ethical study considers the individual's goal. What kind of person does one aspire to become? It concerns the *telos* (i.e., goal or end) to which we aspire (Foucault 1984, 354-355). To become a good parent, for example, one has to develop certain traits. The goal of being a good parent also depends upon the individual's views of the model parent.

Foucault studies ethics by means of these four aspects. He demonstrates these four aspects in connection with classical Greek ethics. (1) The *ethical substance* was *"aphrodisia"* (i.e., acts, desires, and pleasure). (2) The *mode of subjection* was "politico-aesthetic choice." For instance, there is no obligation for a man to be truthful with his wife. (3) However, if one wants to have a beautiful existence (i.e., the good life) or a good reputation or to rule others, then one has to *shape or moderate* his or her actions in certain ways; so, the husband will be honest with his wife. (4) Finally, the *goal or teleology* for Greek ethics is self-mastery.

This approach is especially interesting from a historical point of view. Foucault sees both positive and negative aspects in Greek ethics. On the negative side, Greek ethics tends to be nonreciprocal. It means that men who are dominant in this society seek only their own pleasure. Even self-mastery is negative so long as it concerns ruling others. The classical Greek perspective says that one must be able to master the self before ruling others. However, this view changes over time. Self-mastery becomes

> something which is not primarily related to power over others: you have to be master of yourself not only in order to rule others . . . but you have to master yourselves because you are a rational being. And in this mastery of yourself, you are related to other people, who are also masters of themselves. And this new kind of relation to the other is much less nonreciprocal than before (Foucault 1984, 357-358).

Foucault finds a positive ethic in the Hellenistic or Greco-Roman culture, which he identifies as the care of the self. The Greek words that express this idea mean that a person works on something. The care of the self, therefore, implies that one continually works on oneself. This work is not an ethic that the state or anyone else imposes on the individual. It is a self-imposed ethic not in conformity with Kant's moral law. On the contrary, it is part of the creative life.

Foucault appears to prefer the view that ethics involves self-control. Self-mastery involves mastering one's desires and establishing oneself as a free self. This process of self-mastery is an ongoing one. Freedom, therefore, is "mastery of and power over oneself." We should, according to Foucault, gain power and domination over ourselves and not others. In practical terms, this view would require that individuals set their own ethical standards and take personal responsibility for their actions (Best and Kellner 1991, 62-68). It would also seem to entail that we should consider the other when we act. The standards we set undoubtedly derive in large part from the morals taught to us as a child. However, it may go far beyond parental or societal instructions. An individual may form or shape his or her ethical self in agreement with many different and varied influences and experiences.

Therefore, Wyschogrod's ethic focuses on the Other. Foucault's ethical perspective focuses both on the self and other. Foucault's views are also consistent in many ways with the work of Nietzsche. Like Foucault, Caputo draws upon and responds to the work of Nietzsche although in a different way. Caputo's perspective on obligation also has significant similarities to Wyschogrod's views on ethics. In Caputo's work, we can find a view that values both the thought of the Greeks, which inspired Nietzsche and Foucault and the moral perspective of the Jews. Caputo refers to this mixture as "jewgreek."

Jewgreek contains a little of the Jewish rabbi who can weep and laugh and a little of Dionysus[16] who dances but who can also entertain suffering. Caputo's love for Jewish rabbis and Dionysus and his mixing of the two may cause lovers of Greek thought some discomfort. How could Dionysus possibly include within his circle those who impede the dance and ecstatic joy? Chapters four, five, and six above prepare for the discussion of Caputo's views. Chapter four discusses the ethical perspective of the Judeo-Christian tradition as well as the views of important Greek philosophers. Chapter six focuses partly on the thought of Nietzsche and his approval and disapproval of certain aspects of Jewish thought. Nietzsche's attitude is often elitist, and this elitism partly reflects the Greek tradition. He only responds negatively toward the priestly Jewish and Christian thought related to his view of slave morality. Caputo, on the other hand, loves the prophetic passion for justice one finds in Jewish and Christian thought, for the least of these, for the widow and orphan. This love compels him to find a way to hold on to and listen to both his rabbi and Nietzsche.

John D. Caputo

Caputo confides to the reader that his opposition to ethics keeps him up at night. Whatever his objection is to ethics, therefore, it must be serious. His love for Nietzsche and Kierkegaard, but especially for Nietzsche, has led to this insomnia. He notes Kierkegaard's description of the terrible despair that would exist without God who provides life with purpose and meaning. Since this situation would be so unbearable, Kierkegaard concludes it cannot be true. Caputo then recalls a quote from Nietzsche who says in essence that no one would accept an idea as true just because it would bring him or her pleasure. Caputo cannot merely wish his uneasiness away and fall into a restful slumber (Caputo 1993, 15-16). Just because one might want an ethic that makes everything safe by disclosing to us our obligations to ourselves and others does not mean such an ethic exists.

What if, on the other hand, we live in a world where things just happen, and there is no explanation? A child dies with AIDS (Caputo 1993, 36-39). We want to know why. Yet what if there is no answer. The child dies because the child dies. Obviously, the child has a physical defect that leads to death, but that does not answer the deeper question of why this could happen. How can this event or disaster fit into an ethical or moral universe? What if there is no answer to this why? It happens. There is nothing beyond to give it purpose or meaning. There is no thing that transcends the everyday world from which we can get a better view. Maybe we can appreciate Caputo's difficulty when we contemplate what happens without ethics or some ruling principle from which we can make sense of our world. We are cut loose from a safe world where good is rewarded and evil punished.

Caputo has accepted the most difficult truth of life. It is not difficult because it is complex or hard to comprehend; it is difficult because it interrupts our days and nights. Things are not so just because we want them to be so. This simple statement is true but hard to accept. We want things to be true; we need things to be true. We cannot live if they are not true. Unfortunately, the universe does not care about what we need or want. This indifference is the cold hard truth that Caputo faces up to. Not all the wishing in the world can change things. While Kierkegaard describes the possibility that there is nothing beyond the finite in profound language, he could not bring himself to consider it as a real possibility. Nietzsche could, and he expresses it in an equally eloquent fashion (Caputo 1993, 15-16). Caputo contemplates life and obligation without the Transcendent or Infinite that goes by different names: the "Voice of God, or of Pure Practical Reason, or of the Social Contract we have all signed, or a trace of the Form of the Good stirring in our souls, or the trace of the Most high" (Caputo 1993, 15). Now I follow his thought to see what might fill the void of a world without ethics.

Caputo is not happy about losing ethics; he just sees it as facing up to the truth. His book, *Against Ethics*, is simply and straightforwardly an expression of his concerns about ethics. Still, his account can be complex, and it can move us to think in ways we are not accustomed to think. He is addressing among others professional philosophers. In contrast to modern philosophical approaches, Caputo wants to keep metaphysics to a minimum. Metaphysics comes from two Greek words. *Meta* means after or behind, and physics means nature. Consequently, metaphysics is a search for principles or a principle that explains all fundamental reality. Now for those like me who may have little interests, patients, or aptitude for metaphysics, his argument that we should keep metaphysics to a minimum is good news. Still better, why not dismiss it altogether? It is here that one can see the practical side of Caputo's point about metaphysics, and so I discuss his views on this topic in a minimal way (Caputo 1993, 220-223).

He wants to keep metaphysics at a minimum; well I am all for that. Although, why can we not just ignore it? The problem is that we cannot. It is so much a part of how we think and the language we use that we cannot possibly dismiss it altogether. Metaphysics is part of the language or grammar that provides meaning and purpose to life. We cannot think or communicate without it.

For instance, a subject or agent (i.e., the name of what performs an action or acts upon or toward an object) is part of all human communication whether written or oral. This agent in a grammatical sense often stands behind much of our ways of thinking and supplying meaning. Ethics can be an agent. Ethics as an agent implies that we live in a world where there is right or wrong. Moral law as an agent suggests that rules exist, and we must obey them or punishment may result. God as agent could function or take the place of the moral law and along with God's predicate can provide a long list of rules that require human obedience. Agents or subjects such as God or the moral law or whatever, therefore, are products of language, and language is a human creation. Subjects, predicates, and objects constitute a way of speaking; this way of speaking structures our lives, thoughts, and actions. How could one possibly step outside of this box?

It is part of the human situation, therefore, that we find ourselves caught in a world without wings to fly above it all and see things in the brilliant light of the world of Being. Caputo's view implies that we cannot escape the cave or its murkiness. The world of Being or the world above us is not a world we can get to even if it exists. What seems to be an excessive concern for a small point, therefore, is not so small. To reduce metaphysics to a minimum is to keep it as down to earth and practical as possible without reference to the Transcendent, whatever that might be, of which we have no certain knowledge.

I must confess before continuing that I enjoy Caputo's writing style and his honesty. I share his love for Kierkegaard and Nietzsche, and I am intrigued by his articulation of "jewgreek." I must also admit that I find his views attractive and compelling in many ways. His rejection of ethics is not as bad as it sounds if one needs my reassurances. It opens a space for obligation not ethics. Obligation does not come to us after hours of ethical analysis. Like Bauman, he says it just happens. It happens without a why. It is not based on rationality and cannot produce the moral law. It is a simple feeling or emotion, and it cannot be made secure (Caputo 1993, 5). It is certainly not something metaphysical ethics can endorse. With that out of the way, I now try to present his main ideas in succinct fashion.

Caputo is a philosopher or as he prefers a poet or clerk of obligation. His work is a "deconstruction" of ethics. I briefly discuss deconstruction below. For now, I can provide a brief description. Deconstruction is like pulling on a lose thread of cloth that seems well made only to have the garment unravel. This unraveling is what Caputo does with ethics. It cannot deliver what it promises. It cannot make obligation safe, absolute, rational or reduce it to a calculation. Obligation simply happens, a scandal to the good name of ethics. In short, "ethics contains obligation, but that is its undoing (deconstruction). Ethics harbors within itself what it cannot maintain, what it must expel, expectorate, or exclude" (Caputo 1993, 5). In this fashion, Caputo rejects the ethical enterprise for the sake of simple obligation.

Another important aspect of postmodern or deconstructive thought concerns difference. Modernism as we have seen longs for unity. It would like nothing better than to crush difference, to end it. A foundation needs to be strong so it can support any structure built upon it. Difference is too indecisive, too weak. Differences more likely lead to the end of unity, the same, the one, or the foundation. So postmodern prefers difference to the same. Yet what kind of difference might it value? Caputo identifies two types: heteromorphism and heteronomism. The first has to do with different forms and the second with a different law (i.e., a law from outside not at all the same as Kant's moral law produced by autonomous individuals) (Caputo 1993, 55-62).

The first type is the difference of Nietzsche and Dionysus, the love for many forms, the free spirit that responds to the other out of his or her gratitude for life (i.e., the Greek of the jewgreek relationship). The direction is important. It begins with the individual and proceeds outward to the other. On this view, Nietzsche feels that great individuals act out of an obligation to oneself and not the other. I do not mean he endorses ethical egoism, but that one does for others out of a generous spirit. It is not that the sense of obligation comes from the other but from the self. He believes that suffering or disaster could be good for the individual. How we respond to our own suffering defines our character whether good or bad. What good one does should proceed from within. It is about creating ourselves as a certain type of person that really counts. He recognizes the play of forces or forms. His will to power entails the overcoming of opposing forces or the being overcome by such forces. Therefore, he recognizes diversity and plurality. He recognizes the need for different perspectives and interpretations of life. Some are good and others bad. Some go under and some win out. The good person knows that life is a battle with numerous forces and the will to power involves self-overcoming. The good person, therefore, is not enslaved by the other (heteronomy); instead he or she acts for others because it is a part of what he or she wishes to do (i.e., autonomy).

The second type of difference or otherness comes to the individual from the other. The direction here is reversed. The law of the other imposes itself on me. Obligation is not the obligation one imposes on oneself to become a certain type of person. Obligation comes from outside the self. This law of the other (i.e., heteronomist) is the Jew part of the jewgreek. It imposes itself on me. I perceive a law or obligation in the "face" of the other to use Levinas' word. Caputo identifies with this law of the other. While Nietzsche wants a distance between himself and the masses or ordinary folk, Caputo expresses his desire for proximity, closeness, for being in the midst of masses and misery. Relief of misery for Caputo is a "happy science *par excellence*" (Caputo 1993, 54).

Yet is it an easy matter of an "either or" decision, of choosing one type of difference over the other? Is it a matter of choosing the law of the other over the valuing of diversity or the other way around? For Caputo, it is not an "either or" proposition. The jewgreek way is the way of both kinds of difference. The term used in deconstruction is undecidability. One might view heteromorphism and heteronomism as opposites valuing one and subordinating the other. However, Caputo shows how the two interact. Heteromorphism or many forms is open to diversity so how could it possibly exclude *any form*? How could it exclude the somber individuals who answer to the law of the other, those who feel an obligation to ease the misery of the other, or not to turn away from the face of the other? On the other hand, heteronomism is too considerate in its relation to the other. It could not shut out or exclude from its gatherings those who want to dance and celebrate the diversity of forms. Both Dionysus and the Jewish rabbi love diversity and newness (Caputo 1993, 64). Neither one needs to exclude the other.

As previously discussed, keeping metaphysics to a minimum is an important concern for Caputo. This point may seem abstract and a subject for philosophers, but it affects the very nature of thinking from the philosopher to the young child. We have probably all experienced someone offering us comforting words that should reassure us that life is not random and that if we do things a certain way we can expect to have a good life. The child who looses a grandmother might be comforted that grandmother is now in heaven and one day he or she will see her again. The older child who sees a television show about an innocent man executed for a crime he did not commit might be comforted by being told that if one lives right that cannot happen. Perhaps the man is involved in unlawful behavior leading to his disastrous end. In other words, we tell ourselves that if we follow the rules written in the stars or in a Book of Scripture, things will go well. Kant tells us that if one suffers for doing right in this world there must be another where justice and moral actions are rewarded. In other words, there is an agent or an instrument of some kind whether a personal God or an impersonal guiding principle that can settle accounts, rule and guide our lives, and keep us safe from ultimate harm. The world makes sense in one way or another. People may differ on how that occurs, but we desperately want it to be true. Something is there to guide us, perhaps a guiding star. If we follow this guide, we may feel that it leads to happiness, contentment, and safety.

Such thinking, however, is not keeping metaphysics to a minimum. Along this line, Caputo discusses the German words *es gebt*, which means, "it is" or "they are." Caputo says things happen, and they happen simply "because they happen." This is the minimal way he describes obligation. When the practice of metaphysics reaches beyond the minimal way of thinking, the "it" of *es gebt* comes to stand for an agent outside that directs or causes. To say that it is raining should not cause one to ask who or what is responsible for the rain (Caputo 1993, 223-227). It does not refer to someone. It is just a way of saying rain happens.

The same is true with obligation. Obligation comes from Caputo's deconstruction of ethics. He is against ethics because of its ties to metaphysics. Metaphysics is looking for something, a personal God, Principle, Truth, *Telos* or goal, and this something can therefore provide a foundation for ethical judgments. Obligation is a "scandal" to ethics (Caputo 1993, 5). To keep metaphysics to a minimum is simply to acknowledge that obligation happens. It happens to me without a why. It happens because it happens. "Obligations happen for the while they happen and then fade away" (Caputo 1993, 237). It comes and goes. I feel bound. It demands my response, but I cannot master it (Caputo 1993, 8).

Caputo does not claim to know or be able to reason his way to obligation. It simply imposes itself on him. He feels it, an embarrassment to someone like Kant who sees no moral worth in such feelings. Obligation is the call of justice. It is a "call we receive to which we must respond" (Caputo 1993, 26). This call is for Caputo an earthbound call.

A religious version of this call can be found in the thought of Levinas. Levinas says that obligation happens in face-to-face interactions. Obligation comes from the Infinite and not the finite as Caputo maintains. For Levinas, obligation has the trace of God. Levinas says he does not know the source of obligation. So why, asks Caputo, does he identify it as the trace of God? (Caputo 1993, 226) If, however, one is willing to provide metaphysics with a little more importance, the other or the face of the other may, as Levinas maintains, contain the trace of God.

Yet this objection to Levinas' love of ethics is not to say that Caputo is without religion. He cannot dismiss it, and he can never claim to know this life is all there is. In fact, knowing is the point. How could we know? That is where faith may come in for the religious person. I cannot know if there is any beyond, I must rely on faith. Faith does not, however, provide certainty and so one may ultimately find oneself in the same place. Obligation happens. I feel it. I do not know where it comes from. I may have faith that it comes from God. I just know it happens.[17] Beyond that, I have faith there is one who loves justice for all, who loves all people and has an appreciation for difference. In another place, Caputo expresses his passion and love for God. He poses the question of Saint Augustine as his own question, "what do I love when I love my God?" (Caputo 2001, 134) Nonetheless, this religion is based on faith not certainty or metaphysics. This God cannot be proven to exist; it is a passion for a God defined by love and zeal for the impossible. Passion for the impossible is a passion for justice, a concern for the poor and needy, the widow, the orphan, and the stranger. It is a call for us to lend a helping hand to those in need of our help (Caputo 2001, 126-127).

In the movie, *Contact*, Ellie Arroway makes a trip through a wormhole to meet the aliens who made the trip possible. The alien who greets her says human beings are "capable of such beautiful dreams and such horrible nightmares. You feel so lost, so cut off, so alone, only you're not. See, in all our searching, the only thing we've found that makes the emptiness bearable, is each other." This sums up part of Caputo's views on obligation. Obligation creates links between us; it brings us together in the dark cold night. The bond between human beings offers a space where warmth, shelter, and hospitality can be shared (Caputo 1993, 247). We are not alone. For so long as the earth continues, obligations happen, and our fates are intertwined.

Deconstruction of Binary Opposites and Différance

The work of Derrida has provided a good bit of momentum for postmodern thought. His work opposes modern thought that tries to produce an overarching or transcendent principle to judge everything else. Foucault's views on the danger of ethics fit well with Derrida's concerns. Modern thought is about control and domination. It gives some people an advantage over others. It values some people at the expense of others. It creates a situation where violence can occur. Violence does not have to refer to wars or gang activity; it can refer to systems of thoughts or principles that bully us into conformity. How does this coercion come about? In many cases, it comes about because of binary opposites.

So why should one fear something that sounds so academic and distant from everyday life. In fact, it is not far removed; it affects our thought and behavior on a daily basis. After a brief description, we can see how such oppositions affect modern life.

Modern ethical theories generally tend to divide the world into binary oppositions that value one thing at the expense of the other. For example, many philosophers and other professionals in the past have thought that reason guides men whereas emotion governs the behavior of women. Oppositions like this one are numerous in our world. These types of oppositions are hierarchical in nature making one trait preferable to another. This practice derives from human bias and prejudice.

Before Derrida, Nietzsche calls oppositions into question. In his book, *Beyond Good and Evil*, Nietzsche asks, "How can anything originate out of its opposite? for example, truth out of error? or the will to truth out of the will to deception? or selfless deeds out of selfishness?"[18] Metaphysicians view these opposites as having their foundation in the eternal world of Being and not in this world, which is always changing or becoming to use Platonic language. As Nietzsche notes, however, truth and error, will to truth and deception, selfless and selfishness are not opposites at all. In *Genealogy of Morality*, Nietzsche describes how even our faith in science derives from an older metaphysical faith, a faith that fails to question its own assumptions regarding opposites. If the will to truth avoids the temptation to be deceptive, then it will ultimately bring about its own demise (Nietzsche 1994, 117-127).[19]

Recently, poststructuralism has directed an attack on such oppositions. Derrida has demonstrated how these oppositions always value one object or idea at the expense of the other. There are several oppositions associated with modern thought such as mind/body, subject/object, white/black, male/female, ruler/ruled, reality/appearance, speech/writing, nature/culture just to name a few. In these examples, the former term always carries a greater value than the second one. Derrida also recognizes, as did Nietzsche, that one term is not opposite of the other, but that it relies and resides in the other term (Sarup 1993, 32-44; Best and Kellner 1991, 21).

Truth is not something that is absolute and free from error, but it is a creative act and a process. Nietzsche says that "truth is therefore not something there, that might be found or discovered—but something that must be created and that gives a name to a process . . . that has in itself no end" (Nietzsche 1967a, 298). Each generation generates its own truth. The truth of one generation, for instance, becomes an error for a later one, but this latest version of the truth develops out of the earlier supposed truth. For example, burning witches is based on the truth of certain religious people in the past. Opposites are human constructs; they create order and confer value on things while at the same time devaluing or undermining other things.

Since we will discuss gender bias in the next chapter, I look ahead for a moment. Steven Best and Douglas Kellner cite four oppositions related to gender bias. They incorporate

> ⍊ dichotomies between rational/emotional, assertive/passive, strong/weak, or public/private. These are strategic oppositions which privilege men in the superior position of the hierarchy and women in the inferior position, as the second sex. Such ideological discourses, which go back as far as Plato and Aristotle, justify the domination of women by men, enslaving women in domestic activities, and excluding them from public life and the voice of reason and objectivity (Best and Kellner 1991, 207).[20]

Additionally, these oppositions define categories and concepts to which society expects the individual to conform. Historically, going against such oppositions have caused women a great deal of trouble even leading to physical violence (e.g., witch burning).

Besides binary oppositions, Derrida also emphasizes "différance" in opposition to unity. To be brief, I just note that différance is actually an intentional misspelling of the word difference. He uses différance with a special sense that, among other things, incorporates the notion of difference and deferral or postponement.[21] Modern philosophical systems attempt to uncover the foundation or the basis of truth. This view, which Derrida calls the *metaphysics of presence*, would in theory allow direct or unmediated access to reality. Derrida demonstrates through his readings of philosophers such as Edmund Husserl, Jean-Jacques Rousseau, Claude Lévi-Strauss, and others that philosophical structures or systems only end up undermining or deconstructing themselves. In other words, moral theories are mediated through prior experiences, and these experiences are filtered through such things as culture, language and desire. In short, he attempts to show how the writings of Husserl, Rousseau, and Lévi-Strauss, falter by their own standards.

For example, the philosopher Rousseau values nature over culture. On his account, human beings originally live in an innocent state of nature. In this state, humankind is happy and self-sufficient. He views culture, on the other hand, as an addition or supplement to nature. In this way, Rousseau values nature over culture. Derrida points out, however, that there is never a pure unsupplemented state of nature. According to Rousseau, pure unmediated speech belongs with nature and writing is a supplement that belongs to the realm of culture. Therefore, he would value speech (i.e., primary) above writing (which is a derivative of speech). Derrida's reading of Rousseau, however, shows that Rousseau in his written communication depends upon writing (i.e., the supplement) to convey his ideas, a supplement that he himself has judged as inferior. In essence, his assumptions regarding nature and culture undermine his work (Sarup 1993, 39).

Deconstruction is a way to counteract certain negative tendencies associated with the metaphysics of presence and the binary opposites resulting from such philosophical systems. In general, deconstruction attempts to expose a "concept as ideological or culturally constructed rather than natural or a simple reflection of reality" (Patricia Hill Collins 1990, 14). For instance, Sojourner Truth, an early black feminist, exposed the notion of woman to such a critique. There are certain expectations that accompany what it means to be a woman. Society can then judge particular women by certain standards and expectations. If a woman lives up to such standards then she fits the general category of woman. Differences between a particular woman's actions and this category (i.e., expectations based on binary oppositions) can cast aspersions upon her femininity. Patricia Hill Collins says that Sojourner Truth's

> life as a second-class citizen has been filled with hard physical labor, with no assistance from men. Her question, 'and ain't I a woman?' points to the contradictions inherent in blanket use of the term *woman*. For those who question Truth's femininity, she evokes her status as a mother of thirteen children, all sold off into slavery, and she asks again, 'and ain't I a woman?' Rather than accepting the existing assumptions about what a woman was and then trying to prove that she fit the standards, Truth challenged the very standards themselves (Patricia Hill Collins 1990, 14).

In summary, traditional philosophical movements as well as modern ethical theories have worked on certain assumptions. These assumptions are informed by the ideology of opposites, and this has led them to take a dim view of difference. I would conclude that any adequate ethic has to reject the notion of rigid dichotomies or opposites. Men and women, for instance, may be different in some important respects, but we can no longer value what is masculine at the expense of the feminine. In my judgment, we can evaluate any ethical perspective by the way it deals with difference.

Promise of an Emerging Pluralistic Society

Taking pluralism seriously in heteromorphistic and heteronomistic forms would create a better society. Until recently, educational and political institutions reflect only the views of white educated males who control the work place as well as most if not all the institutions both sacred and secular. Their voices decide public and private policy, define right and wrong, and decide what is important and is not important. Whether intentional or not, they could effectively silence voices of dissent.

Along these lines, there have always been liberals who champion the cause of those without a voice in government. Unfortunately, they also feel entitled to speak for the voiceless. They, the enlightened ones, know what the excluded others need. For that reason, leaders like Malcolm X or Martin Luther King Jr., are so important for young Afro-Americans shut out of the system.[22] According to Cornel West, Malcolm X calls on black people to love and to affirm themselves and to stop viewing themselves through the eyes of white people (West 1994, 136-137). Adopting a positive view would lead to Afro-Americans taking a more active role in shaping their own political and social institutions, and these institutions would reflect their own concerns. Fear of course is an obstacle to difference and diversity. Foucault's statement about the danger of ethics is a relevant warning. The moral values of the larger society or the majority can have a devastating impact on the minority or on those who desire to do things differently.

People like Malcolm X have had a cumulative influence on our society. Without reformers, we still might live in a world where women have little say in the world outside the home and minorities would have to be content to live by the rules of others. The current public climate regarding openness to all people reflects a new attitude. That is not to say that this attitude of openness is the majority view. This attitude reaches many phases of our society from the political domain to public education. Still the old forces who preach fear and hatred are very much alive.

The problems of establishing an ethic or moral perspective that values difference and pluralism are significant. Many forces would resist such openness with every tool at their disposal. Perhaps such a society is idealistic and unrealistic. On the other hand, perhaps it is impossible, which interestingly enough is Caputo's name for religion. The impossible in fact recommends a special kind of religion to us. Religion for him would be a call for justice or a call for us to love and fulfill our obligation to the other (Caputo 2001, 7-8). Impossible for him simply means unforeseeable. We cannot know ahead of time how justice or love might break into society. [23]

One other possible barrier for viewing difference positively is an easy acceptance of it. I mean an acceptance that leads to a sort of unity, where no differences matter, where what one has to say is nice but has no chance of claiming any special attention. Tolerance in this context is nothing more than indifference. Here, difference is not appreciated but given a nod of indifference.

Even if change occurs, one should not forget that as groups make gains and move from the disrespected to the respected, they also try to change society often by employing the same kinds of intolerance that they once abhorred. Human nature at its worst seeks to eliminate difference. It is fearful and seeks to hide behind castle walls. There is always the danger of one set of standards being forced on others, and the source of this danger is not limited to conservative or religious fundamentalists.

CONCLUSION

Many of the ethical perspectives in this chapter can provide positive guidance for one seeking an ethical perspective as a guide for life. Ross' view that rules can have exceptions clears up one of the major objections to Kant's moral theory. Habermas' notion of discourse ethics further strengthens Kant's moral views by giving "affected parties" a voice. Postmodern ethical perspectives or those that share certain postmodern concerns have also made many contributions. For example, an ethic of care makes the case for an ethic based on our natural ability to care for others. Our own good often relates to the good of others. Ethical views that recognize and value diversity are also crucial for any discussion of ethics today.

Furthermore, Foucault's work is vitally important. To begin with, he remarks that all ethical systems or models have limits and are always potentially hazardous. He prefers the ethics of the Greco-Roman world that value self-mastery. One should merely try to control oneself and not others. This view is quite useful. He draws upon Nietzsche and argues that one should make oneself a work of art or create oneself as an ethical subject in this case. The practice of ethics or engaging in ethical behavior, therefore, requires self-discipline; an individual has to be able to abide by his or her own set of principles. His concern also extends to the other person as well. The ethics of Wyschogrod and Caputo focus on the other. At this point, I would just note that there are many ways of defining morality and pursuing a moral life.

In the next chapter, I take a brief look at the issue of gender in relation to power and control. I focus on the issue of sexual equality. As much of our discussion has shown, control and power are prevalent in moral issues. These forces pervade almost every aspect of life. The danger is that many people are not so much concerned with controlling their own lives but wish to control the lives of others. Consequently, I have decided to discuss an issue that relates to power and domination. A great deal has been written about this topic in recent years. Sexual equality primarily belongs to the area of social ethics although it also involves personal ethics.

NOTES

1. For a concise description of his communication theory, see Collins and Makowsky 1989, 260-265.

2. Niebuhr's discussion of the pride of knowledge could serve as an excellent description of certain postmodern ideas. The pride of knowledge is gained by forgetting. What one forgets is that our knowledge is limited.

3. Should members of that society follow these values regardless of whom they harm? Is there not a time when members should work to reform society?

4. For instance, Emanuel A. Schegloff found that when problems occurred there were certain mechanisms at work that tended to restore and repair the communication. See Emanuel A. Schegloff 1992, 1296.

5. Edith Wyschogrod capitalizes the "Other" when referring to another person.

6. A master narrative in this context would refer to a story or a text that sets norms or standards by which one is to live. The Bible would be an example of a master narrative. Such master narratives have value, but if a society considers them normative, then there is a danger that the stories of individuals would be suppressed or made to fit into the larger story. See the comments of K. Anthony Appiah, in his essay, "Identity, Authenticity, Survival: Multicultural Societies and Social Reproductions," 1994.

7. For a further discussion of Wyschogrod's notion of power, see Valantasis 1995, 786-787.

8. This view would be consistent with Bauman's notion of the moral impulse.

9. Lack is not necessarily a deficiency, but something we all share to varying degrees. See Newman Robert Glass 1995, 310-311.

10. Also see the response of Larry May in his review of her book (May 1992, 183-184). For Wyschogrod's pragmatic critique of moral theory, see page xxv of *Saints and Postmodernism.*

11. A one sided view that ignores plurality and only concentrates on piety is not healthy, and it is incomplete. I discuss this further in relation to Caputo's views on ethics.

12. This chapter comes from an interview with Foucault concerning his current work on ethics.

13. Also, see Nietzsche 1974, 232-233.

14. Foucault briefly discusses the work of existentialist philosopher, Jean-Paul Satre, and his concern for authenticity.

15. He does note that there may be a change in the Christian's ethical substance by the seventeenth century.

16. Dionysus is important for Nietzsche, and it provides a balance to the critical and rational thought. Dionysus is a Greek god of wine who might be associated with frenzy and dance, creativity and excitement. For Caputo, Dionysian can perhaps unhappily include the darker side of life and in turn, the Jewish rabbi can rejoice, laugh, and dance in a grand Dionysian spirit.

17. Caputo does not actually tell how to determine what our obligation requires us to do. Bauman's point out that knowing we should help does not eliminate ambiguity.

18. Also see Nietzsche 1967a, 298-299.

19. Kaufmann points out that Nietzsche defines the will to truth as the will not to deceive. See Kaufmann 1974, 357-361. The will to truth has often perhaps unconsciously led to the will to deceive. Many people actually desire deception under the banner of truth.

20. In relation to feminism and hierarchical oppositions, see the discussion of Hélène Cixous and Luce Irigaray in chapter 5 of Sarup 1993.

21. This term means "presence" or "fullness of meaning is always deferred from one sign to another in an endless sequence. Thus if one looks up a word in a dictionary, all it can give is other words to explain it" (Baldick 1990, 58).

22. See Cornel West 1994, 132-151.

23. Caputo distinguishes between the "relative or present future" and the absolute future. In the relative or present future, we can see, anticipate, plan for, and predict with some degree of accuracy what is going to happen. In the "absolute future," we cannot know or foresee what is to come.

Chapter Ten
Men, Women, and Power

INTRODUCTION

Women have served all these centuries as looking-glasses possessing the magic and delicious power of reflecting the figure of man at twice its natural size. (Virginia Wolff 2005, 35)

Gender is just one area where inequality occurs. Class and race are two other areas. Gender is an ascriptive category. Modernity has not eliminated discrimination based on gender. Its ideal of achievement remains unrealized.

Part of the reason for this failure comes from the power of primary socialization. It continues to create people who accept traditional or ascriptive values. Regardless of legislation trying to eliminate inequality, certain attitudes persist. A good amount of advertising still depicts men and women in traditional ways to sell products. In the educational world, much of our literature reflects traditional gender roles. History tells students about a past where only men are kings and presidents. The world's great religions and their scriptures are filled with men who are leaders and important figures with women typically filling the traditional roles of having children, nurturing them, and taking care of the household. Those writings reach over the years and continue to have their effect.

In the Christian tradition, for example, women have played vital roles in the church and have kept it viable. Yet women have traditionally been excluded from the highest positions in the church such as priests or ministers. Daphne C. Wiggins in her book, *Righteous Content: Black Women's Perspectives of Church and Faith*, comments that if one enters the majority of African American churches one would probable see "male pastors standing before predominantly female audiences" (Wiggins 2005, 1). This situation is also true of Black congregations in the late 1800's. It is not unique to the Black Church either since one can find the same state of affairs in New England Puritan churches around the middle of the 1600s. All through the 1700's, female membership continues to rise in the "mainline" Protestant churches. Wiggins cites the work of historian Ann Douglas. She notes that the separation of church and state causes Christianity to lose some influence. As a result, fewer men become ministers since there is also a loss of money in churches. This loss of money results from the separation of church and state due to the loss of state money. In this setting, the role of women diminishes as well. Theology becomes more limited to the domestic realm where women are central rather than the public arena where men are dominant. As a result, men increasingly stay away from an active involvement in the life of the church. This tendency continues through the 1800s in American Protestantism. She says that the "Black Church would manifest the same phenomenon of male absenteeism throughout the twentieth century, albeit for different reasons" (Wiggins 2005, 1).

This story documents the ongoing power of traditional socialization along gender lines. In the religious studies courses I teach, the discussion of gender reveals that many students want to separate the religious world from the everyday world. Many men and women defend equality in the work place, but they are not as willing or eager to do so in the religious arena. This double standard may also be found in Islamic traditions where women in some countries can progress in secular fields, but they are limited in their roles and influence in the religious world. As a result, the ascriptive or traditional side of life continues to exercise power over gender issues not just in the private sphere but also in the public one as well. Traditional forces still impede the move toward equality.

DIFFERENCES

Unfortunately, the push for equality has the unintended effect of devaluing difference. While the women's movement rightly wants equal opportunity, the emphasis on being as good as men has not left room for the appreciating differences between men and women. Focusing on the differences between men and women has often been the first step in gender discrimination. It assumes that a woman's difference from her male counterpart is what makes him more qualified. Individuals differ, and the main issue for me is how to deal with difference. Men differ from other men and women from other women. My concern is how to avoid putting people into special categories and giving preference to people in one particular category over those in another.

The issue of differences between men and women is complex and still a matter of debate. Are differences due to nature or nurture or both? Deborah Tannen identifies two false assumptions associated with the nature/nurture controversy. These false assumptions have caused a storm of controversy. First, there is the assumption that differences between men and women are biological in origin, and they assume that if this is the case then women must naturally be subordinate to men. From this assumption, one might contend that there is no need to change society. A second view assumes the opposite. It says that differences between men and women are cultural in origin, and they assume that society can easily change this situation through additional education. Tannen rejects both views (Tannen 1994, 12-14).

In response to the former position, we might say that nothing is more human or natural than trying to overcome the limitations that nature has placed upon us. It is human nature to strive to become more than we are at present. What we are and what we aspire to be is often not the same thing. While one may not be able to break away completely from certain natural traits, he or she may seek to overcome his or her nature to embrace a new one. One may have to choose to act in a particular way. For example, Tom may desire to be outgoing. While he may never overcome his shyness, he may be able to act consistently with his desire to be outgoing. In short, we are not completely defined or determined by our nature.

Regarding the second group, one must realize that it is not so easy to change society or culture. A good example is traditional gender roles. These traditional roles have existed over thousands of years, and they show no signs of disappearing any time soon. Consequently, it is not either nature or nurture when it comes to gender. Gender differences are surely natural and social in origin. Nevertheless, since our nature changes over time as part of the natural evolutionary process, I would argue that neither of these positions, nature or nurture, really resolves anything.

Perhaps, it is impossible to identify the differences as resulting from nature or nurture alone. It is not a choice of either nature or nurture, but a combination of both. The reason for the difficulty is that males and females enter into different worlds from the moment of birth based on their sex (Lorber 1994, 40). Parents do not treat baby boys in the same way they treat baby girls. The different ways of responding to male children versus female children are so ingrained that they usually operate below a conscious level. Parents may cuddle female infants keeping them close to their bodies while bouncing male infants on their knees and keeping them at a further distance. Even though there are some differences between males and females, knowing their exact nature is problematic.

Turning now to the issue of sexual equality, the remainder of this chapter explores this ideal from different angles. There are many aspects involved in sexual equality that make it a rather difficult issue. Some people feel compelled to define equality as giving everyone equal opportunity regardless of sex or race. The notion that women can compete with men on even terms is an example of this kind of thinking. From this perspective, fair and impartial treatment would bring about a society based on equality. This view as stated does not consider that the standards of judgment retain a male bias. Putting off the discussion of impartiality for the moment, the question arises, why do women want to define and accept masculine standards as the basis for sexual equality? It implies that typical male attributes are better than typical female attributes, and it adopts male standards as the norms for which women should strive. This attitude is hostile to differences that may distinguish men and women.

SEX AND GENDER

While sex is biological in nature, gender is social. There are observable differences that derive from both sex and gender. Sex differences between boys and girls are biologically innate and essential for reproduction. These biological traits help to determine gender roles. Biological differences are differences in (1) sexual organs, (2) genes, and (3) hormones. Researchers have linked the hormone testosterone, for instance, to aggressiveness and even the tendency for violence in boys and men. This has led Camille Paglia, for instance, to justify masculine aggressive behavior. On her account, men are driven by their so-called "male energy." Getting involved with men is a risk. She says that

> We cannot regulate male sexuality. The uncontrollable aspect of male sexuality is part of what makes sex interesting. . . . What feminists are asking for is for men to be castrated, to make eunuchs out of them. The powerful, uncontrollable force of male sexuality has been censored out of the white middle-class homes (Paglia 1992, 63).

On her account, men in this country are either weak because "feminists" seek to make men "eunuchs," or they are merely slaves to their sexual drives. Steven Goldberg makes the argument that because of hormones men are going to be more aggressive, which gives them a competitive advantage.[1] Due to biological differences women should play the roles that nature has endowed them to play, which is primarily homemakers. In contrast to biological differences, gender differences stem from the social environment. These differences do not derive from one's biological sex. The extent to which differences relate to gender rather than biology, however, continues to be a disputable point.

Gender refers to the cultural definitions of what it means to be masculine or feminine. Gender roles develop over time and relate to societal views. This process is social construction. Gender roles reflect the different expectations and experiences in relating to one's sex. These gender roles define who we are, what we should do, and how we should act. We come to know these expectations so well that we cease to be aware of them. Many people, for instance, would never debate whether they should dress their baby daughter in pink; they just know that it is the appropriate thing to do. It is only when we see these expectations being ignored that we become aware that something is inappropriate. Seeing a boy dressed in pink would stand out.

Stereotypes about what men should do versus what women should do still have an impact. For instance, it is a common view that men cannot really nurture their children, and even if they could, mothers can do it much better. Some may argue that this view has scientific support.[2] Women develop the ability to nurture their young due to their role as primary care givers in hunter-gather societies. Since mothers have to nurse their children for some time after their birth, it is natural for them to fulfill this obligation. Again, it is difficult to distinguish between nurturing as an aspect of one's nature versus nurturing as a response one learns. For whatever reason, women do become better nurturers, since society considers it their primary tasks. As time passes, these differences become institutionalized, and they establish norms and expectations for proper behavior.

Even today, we might be able to say that women are on the average better nurturers than men. However, it would be better to say that some people are better nurturers than others. Are all women good mothers by virtue of being a woman? Stereotypes such as this one taint our thinking and help to maintain our modern division of labor based on gender. These divisions have been instrumental in maintaining inequality. Gender roles and expectations fuel the view that mothers cannot be good employees since they have to care for their children. Traditionally, men were able to create a standard that entails putting one's job first. This attitude is possible for men, however, because the mother is at home taking care of all the domestic jobs, which in turn frees her husband to concentrate on his profession.

If gender is social, then it is also a "human invention, like language, kinship, religion, and technology" (Lorber 1994, 6). In this statement, Judith Lorber sees gender as something humans invent. She maintains that gender is a social institution that develops from human culture and not from biology or procreation. Therefore, societies decide what is masculine and feminine (Lorber 1994, 1). Gender is not a passive or static category; conceptions of gender do not remain constant. As societies change, notions about gender can also change. In Lorber's words, "gender is constantly created and re-created out of human interaction, out of social life, and is the texture and order of that social life" (Lorber 1994, 13). Moreover, humans keep these roles and expectations alive by living them out in their daily activities.

Gender is also an organizing force. It tends to order our relations in daily life and in such social structures as "the hierarchies of bureaucratic organizations" (Lorber 1994, 6). Still, gender roles and expectations may differ from culture to culture. In patriarchal societies, males traditionally possess the higher status positions in society. However, there are some exceptions where these patriarchal roles do not apply. Margaret Mead was the first anthropologist to study sex roles in non-Western societies (Mead, Margaret 1963). Her purpose is to show that the men and women do not inherit the occupational roles, norms, and conduct, but that they learn them. She also attempts to show that norms tend to vary from group to group. Anthropologist William A. Haviland observes that

> Other social scientists who have studied the personality and temperament of men and women tended to make the common characterization of women as nurturing, supportive, emotionally dependent, passive, and more verbal; whereas men are depicted as dominant, competitive, positively sexed, innovative, and stronger (Haviland 1974, 369).

Mead wonders whether such stereotypes are universal, which leads her to study three tribes in New Guinea.

From these three tribes (the *Arapesh*, the *Mundugumor*, and the *Tchambuli*) Mead concludes that sex roles are not universal. In the *Arapesh* tribe, men and women "were trained to be 'cooperative, nonaggressive, [and] responsive to the needs and demands of others.' Sex was not a powerful driving force for either men or women" (Haviland 1974, 369). The *Mundugumor* are quite different from the Arapesh. In the Mundugumor tribe, "both men and women developed as 'ruthless, aggressive . . . with the maternal cherishing aspects of the personality at a minimum'" (Haviland 1974, 369-370). The attitudes about sex in the *Tchambuli* tribe, Mead says, are a reversal of Western attitudes about sex. Women are "dominant, impersonal, and managing partners," whereas men are "'less responsible and emotionally dependent persons'" (Haviland 1974, 370).

Having carefully observed the different patterns of child rearing in each of these societies, Mead concludes that

> many, if not all, of the personality traits that we have called masculine or feminine are as lightly linked to sex as are the clothing, the manners, and the form of head-dress that a society at a given period assigns to either sex (Haviland 1974, 370).

Mead's conclusions alert us to the danger of assuming that traditional roles derive from nature. If roles are not universal, then they must at least partially depend upon particular societies and socialization. These findings imply that men can play roles that are generally considered feminine in most societies, and women can perform roles considered masculine (Haviland 1974, 369-371).

Another anthropologist, Jo Fleeman, has suggested that men may have come to dominate in societies where great physical strength is necessary for survival. For example, in societies where hunting and warfare play an important role, males have the advantage, and this leads to their preferred status (Haviland 1974, 370-371). Yet as these types of societies change to where that is no longer the case, then there would be no reason why gender roles would not change or evolve as well unless traditional expectations deriving from socialization have become so powerful as to halt any further change.

Also in a society where physical strength is necessary and men gain a favored status, this higher status probably leads to a division of labor based on sex. This higher status would likely continue even after the threat passes. This situation would likely result in a widespread belief of male superiority. Therefore, this attitude would become part of the society's value system impeding females from doing certain types of prestigious work. Consequently, people might tend to rank automatically a woman's job as less important (Haviland 1974, 371; and Lorber 1994, 34-35).

In ancient hunter-gather societies, Lorber says that hunting is not necessarily restricted to just men (Lorber 1994, 126-130). According to Lorber's description of the Paleolithic period, humans are primarily food gatherers. The primary sources of food would be "wild vegetables, nuts, fruits, and grass-eating animals" (Lorber 1994, 126). Humans would have taken meat from predators. Men, women, and children would have cooperated in obtaining larger quantities of meat, bones, skins, and furs by herding animals off "cliffs or into swamps or pits" (Lorber 1994, 126). Therefore, the only individuals who would be unable to go on hunting raids would be mothers who are nursing infants or minding young children. The division of labor in these early societies may have distinguished between those who cared for the young children and those who do not. Those who mind the children probably gather and process fruits and vegetables (Lorber, 127).

This division of labor was a cultural solution that enabled the group to provide for its needs (Lorber 1994, 128-129). In time, this division of labor, by means of continual repetition, became a matter of routine. From this routine, these societies came to expect and then required these arrangements. Moreover, certain rituals came to legitimize this division of labor, and eventually what once related to usefulness became a matter of *norms* and *mores*. This society had to train male and female children for the roles they played in the community (Lorber 1994, 130). According to Lorber, in both Paleolithic and Neolithic times, women had at least an equal status as men because they produced food and children.

From this perspective, however, the question remains, why does society typically accord men a higher status than women? Why do the Paleolithic and Neolithic times of a social egalitarianism not continue?[3] Lorber suggests that the status of women depends upon food production and distribution of surplus. If a society's continued well-being is harmonious with minding of children and the woman distributes the surplus, then her prestige is high. On the other hand, if the society's well-being is not harmonious with rearing children then the opposite is the case. Lorber identifies the shift in the status of women from high to low in agricultural societies about 5,000 years ago. With agricultural societies, there is a change in the division of labor that favors men over women. As people settle down and begin to raise their food, the population of these communities increases, and eventually they move into less fertile areas. These farmers have to sow their seeds deeper in such a land, and over time, there is the invention of the iron plow. Additionally, certain animals are domesticated instead of being hunted. Some animals provide milk and others wool (Lorber 1994, 141).

In these agricultural societies, the division of labor also changes. Men go from hunters to herding and domesticating animals as well as clearing land for farming. This type of work is inconsistent with nurturing and raising children. Men gain control of the land in this type society; women concentrate on food processing. This division of labor leads to a gap between men and women. The technology that allows for better farming techniques and the increasing value of domesticating animals give men an advantage.

Increase in property and wealth leads to a stratified society valuing men more highly than women. It is also during this time that patrilineal decent (i.e., inheriting or determining decent through the male line) becomes dominant. The status of women decreases in agricultural societies because women do not contribute as much to production as they did in the hunter-gatherer societies. As men gain ownership of property, they are able to distribute the surplus (Lorber 1994, 18-143). Male dominance, therefore, goes back to the emergence of agricultural societies around 3,000 B.C.E.

Not only did women have status in some of the earliest human societies, they also have power. Helen E. Fisher says that women have a certain amount of power in ancient societies because they control certain valuable resources and they have the "right to distribute this wealth outside the home" (Fisher 1992, 214). Remember that power is typically distributed in society and does not always reside in the hands of just one person or group. One may possess power in one area of life and not in another. Women in some ancient societies may have possessed some wealth or economic power. This power may have also provided them with a considerable "informal influence." Power would not necessarily mean they are leaders of the group (Fisher 1992, 218). Lorber and Fisher show us that it is not true that all past societies are strictly speaking patriarchal in nature.

A SELECTIVE HISTORY OF SEXUAL EQUALITY

I now turn attention to a more recent history of this issue. This history is selective. It begins with Plato and continues to the present. This historical sketch helps clarify some of the major concerns relating to the issue of gender. Following this historical sketch, I discuss sexual equality in relation to certain themes covered in previous chapters. The discussion leads us to respond to the following three questions: (1) Can we maintain our differences and still have equal opportunities? (2) Can we be different without turning those differences into oppositions that value one trait at the expense of its supposed opposite? (3) Can society value the differences between the sexes and perhaps even find creative ways for those differences to make life richer? I would frame the issue of sexual equality in a way that allows differences to be appreciated and not used against women.

Sexual equality is a concern for Plato. He advocates sexual equality in the sense that women should have the same rights as men. To create a society where this equality would be possible, Plato outlines a new family structure for the Guardian and the Auxiliary classes (Plato 1987, 182-195). Recall that the Guardians are the rulers responsible for the well-being of the state. The Auxiliary class is responsible for the protection of the state. In *The Republic*, Plato is describing how a society ought to operate. His proposal describes what the perfect state would look like. Many of his ideas may surprise modern readers; Plato's notion regarding women goes against the norms of his own day. Plato's reluctance, in *The Republic*, to reveal his plan for equality illustrates the extent to which it differs from prevailing attitudes. He anticipates laughter and ridicule from his audience.[4]

Plato begins from the premise that men and women have only one main difference, women can bear children and men cannot. Plato anticipates the typical response that there are natural differences between men and women and the corresponding argument that men should play roles consistent with their nature and likewise women according to their nature. Plato, on the other hand, says that if men and women can do the same jobs then any difference based on sex is irrelevant. As a result, a woman can have great intellectual capacities qualifying her to be a philosopher just as any man can possess such qualities. In this case, he says that the two share the same nature. He concludes that

'There is therefore no administrative occupation which is peculiar to woman as woman or man as man; natural capacities are similarly distributed in each sex, and it is natural for women to take part in all occupations as well as men, though in all women will be the weaker partners' (Plato 1987, 234).

The latter part of this statement does reveal that Plato has not made a complete break with traditional thinking on gender. Yet his views are a step away from the traditional views on gender or sexual differences. Women in the upper two classes should have the same opportunities as men. Women should share a common education and enjoy the same occupations and opportunities including going to war (Plato 1987, 252). For this to occur, he even devises a way of freeing women from the task of raising their own children. Child rearing would become the concern of the state. Plato then put forth the view that

our men and women Guardians should be forbidden by law to live together in separate households, and all the women should be common to all the men; similarly, children should be held in common, and no parent should know its child, or child its parent (Plato 1987, 237).

Still, he recognizes that the Guardians would have to satisfy their sexual instincts and that the state has to take care of the children. He devises a system whereby children are the result of selective breeding. Note his comments on this subject:

'We must, if we are to be consistent, and if we're to have a real pedigree herd, mate the best of our men with the best of our women as often as possible, and the inferior men with the inferior women as seldom as possible, and bring up only the offspring of the best. And no one but the Rulers must know what is happening, if we are to avoid dissension in our Guardian herd' (Plato 240).

The mating would take place at marriage festivals. The goal is to produce children from the best couples in society. The state should reward those individuals who have rendered distinguished service by giving them more opportunities to mate, therefore, ensuring better offspring. The state would raise the children produced through these unions in state nurseries. These nurseries would care for the children leaving the Guardian parent free to look after the interests of the state. According to Plato, "the children of the inferior Guardians [or] any defective offspring of the others, will be quietly and secretly disposed of" (Plato 1987, 241).

Plato's statement regarding the "quite and secret disposal" of children born to the inferior Guardians probably refers to the distribution of children among the third class who would then raise these children as their own. On Plato's view, the state can transfer the children from the upper classes to the third class. The state can also promote children from the third class to the upper two classes (Plato 1987, 182). However, he also favors infanticide of defective children and other illegitimate births.[5] In short, Plato envisions a society where the rulers of the state carefully plan a particular kind of family structure. This type of society would seek the most gifted without regard to sex. In effect, this type of social structure would break down traditional family ties along kinship lines. Plato feels private affairs associated with the family would distract the Guardians from their duty to the community as a whole. With child rearing responsibilities taken care of by the state, women could compete with their male counterparts on a more level playing field. In short, the state as pictured in *The Republic* endeavored to eliminate those things that would distract one from his or her duties to the larger community (Lee 1987, 44-45).

Still, the standards for achieving in Greek society are those established by male elites. Those jobs traditionally associated with women are not highly esteemed. A very different view on women derives from Aristotle. Aristotle focuses on households and their proper structure. The proper structure requires wives to be subordinate to their husbands. This structure is just part of the larger structure where the household is a smaller segment of the state. Aristotle identifies three hierarchal structures that should be present in the household. First, husbands are heads of the household. Wives are subordinate. Next, slaves are subordinate to their masters. Finally, children are to be submissive to their parents.

The Roman leaders, in particular, insist on the maintenance of this household code. Rome expects Jews and Christians as well as all other groups to abide by it. Jewish and Christian literature of the time defends itself against charges that it might violate this code. The Christian church may have come under suspicion when the church accepts a woman whose husband has not converted. This situation puts the early church leaders in a difficult position. There are New Testament texts that instruct women to be submissive to their husbands and slaves to their masters. There are those in first century Rome who debate the role and status of women. Nevertheless, the household code continues to have great influence on the Western world through the influence of the Judeo-Christian tradition.

By the end of the first century and continuing until the present, many churches adopt and defend the view that wives are to be submissive to their husbands. Many Christians today affirm male dominance. For some brides, the marriage vows still obligate them to obey their husbands. Christian fundamentalists do not see male dominance as a continuation of earlier ideologies rooted in the Greco-Roman political world. They see it as a divine command that wives should obey their husbands.

Many churches resist any change that would allow women to fill the same positions as men in the church. In response to pressure, many Christian fundamentalists attempt to paint an exalted view of women and their importance in the church. They may stress the importance of a woman's role as mother, teacher of her children, or *homemaker*. In the August 10, 2007, my local Newspaper (The Athens News Courier) ran an article with the title "Southern Baptist Seminary to Offer an Academic Program in Homemaking." The seminary in question is Southwestern Baptist Theological Seminary in Fort Worth, Texas. This event should make it clear that equality is not a goal for everyone. It makes clear that many people today still believe that women should play traditional roles consistent with the household code.

Yet, many denominations have made changes, and they support the equality of women in the work place and in the church. They base their interpretation of the Bible on a firmer academic footing that avoids literalistic readings. Mainstream biblical scholarship recognizes that some passages in the Bible support the fundamentalist interpretation. Yet, it also recognizes that certain New Testament writers and writings support gender equality in the church. More moderate faith traditions realize that the Bible reflects the time and place in which it is written. They are more open and able to accommodate views that are more enlightened. These faith traditions provide women with the same opportunities for ministry as men enjoy.

In Western societies, the issue of equality has taken on considerable importance in the last two hundred years. Engels, a close associate of Marx, identifies family, private property, and the state as institutions that lead to the subordination of women. The development of monogamous marriages, for instance, allows men to pass on their wealth to their own children. Women are to be faithful to their husbands, but Engels cites prostitution and adultery as ways that men avoid monogamous marriages. Another facet of monogamous marriages is that the management of the household loses its public status and becomes a private matter. Women become head servants of the household. According to Engels, the modern family still exists in the hidden or private "slavery of the wife." Engels maintains that with the coming social revolution, the economic basis for monogamy vanishes since private wealth is transformed into social property. Moreover, the education and care of children should take on a social character (Engels 1969, 57-73). The connecting of exploitation with the family and economy continues to be a theme among feminists in the Marxist tradition. According to some current theories, "patriarchy, the ideological dominance of women by men, is located both in the family and in the workplace" (Lorber 1994, 2).

One of the first major hurdles for equal rights concerns the right to vote. In the last century, society denies women many of the legal rights they have today. Society does not allow women to vote, own property, enter into contracts, or serve on juries. In addition, women find themselves excluded from certain male-dominated professions. They receive the right to vote in England in 1918 and in the United States in 1920. This right only occurs after a long and bitter struggle (White 1985, 212).

In the late 1960's and early 1970's, the feminist effort to gain sexual equality wins other important victories. The *Equal Pay Act* of 1963 says that men and women must receive equal pay for equal work. *Title VII* of the *Civil Rights Act* of 1964 is important. This act prohibits any discrimination based on race, color, religion, sex, or national origin. The struggle for sexual equality continues. Women still receive less pay than men. James E. White writes as follows:

A study of college teachers shows that the average salary for women is still about 5,000 dollars less than the average yearly salary for men. Despite improvements, there are still very few women in the male-dominated professions of professor, lawyer, physician, and engineer (White 1985, 212).

Only a few percent of women have actually made it into upper positions in major firms. The controversy over the ERA (i.e., Equal Rights Amendment) continues. This Amendment states, "Equality of rights under the law shall not be denied or abridged by the US or by any state on account of sex." Alice Paul introduces this Amendment in 1923, and Congress does not pass it until 1971. However, the Amendment is "not ratified by three fourths of the state legislatures" (White 1985, 212). ERA has now been introduced as S.J. Res. 10 by Senator Edward Kennedy and H.J. Res. 40.

Alison Jaggar in her essay, "Feminist Ethics: Some Issues for the Nineties," sketches the history of feminism during the 1960's to the beginning of the 1980's. The issue of sexual equality in the late 1960's requires sexual equality. Jaggar says, "By the end of the 1960's, most feminists in this country had come to believe that the legal system should be sex-blind, that it should not differentiate between women and men" (Jaggar 1993, 81). In practical terms, this means that both men and women should receive equal opportunity and pay for equal work.

With this brief historical sketch in mind, we can now look at four views of sexual equality from the 1970's and early 1980's. Together these four views highlight several key issues involved in the discussion of sexual equality.

FOUR VIEWS OF SEXUAL EQUALITY

I begin with an article written by Marilyn Frye first published in 1975 when the term "chauvinism" is a popular word in the feminist vocabulary. Frye rejects this term as a correct description of men's attitudes toward women. She begins her essay with a definition and description of sexism. According to Frye, sexists consist of those individuals

who hold certain sorts of general beliefs about sexual differences and their consequences. They hold beliefs that would, for instance, support the view that physical differences between the sexes must always make for significant social and economic differences between them in any human society, such that males and females will in general occupy roles at least roughly isomorphic to those they now occupy in most extent human societies. In many cases, of course, these general beliefs might more accurately be represented by the simple proposition: Males are innately superior to females (Frye 1985, 216).

Her essay identifies three types of sexists: doctrinaire sexists, primitive sexists, and operational sexists. The *doctrinaire sexists* believe that men are superior to women and offer some type of theoretical justification for such beliefs. Doctrinaire sexists believe that one can prove these general theories of male superiority through empirical testing. Goldberg, who I will discuss below, fits into this category. The second type is a *primitive sexist*. The primitive sexist adheres to the same views as the doctrinaire sexist. The difference is that the primitive sexist believes such propositions to be a matter of metaphysical truth instead of focusing on empirical data as a way of legitimating his or her position. They would justify their views on philosophical foundations. The primitive sexist could contend that certain "value-laden" male/female dualisms turn up in the thinking of many different cultures (Frye 1985, 216). The existence of such value distinctions must be significant in determining the roles of males and females.

The third type is the *operational sexists*. These sexists do not have either a thought out theory of male superiority or a metaphysical or religious justification. They simply hold the view that men are superior. She says that both the primitive and operational sexists may have a stronger sexist view if they have heard of or been educated in the doctrinaire position. Generally, operational sexists just seem to operate on the basis that men are superior to women.

What is more important, however, is Frye's discussion of certain key attitudes of so-called male chauvinists. She says that the term "male chauvinism" is misleading. Instead of chauvinism, she defines the attitudes of male superiority as *phallism*. The term "chauvinism" may refer to a number of different things and not just a male attitude toward women. For instance, chauvinism can allude to a rather blind patriotism. Phallism, however, is a more specific term that tends to deny women a place in the so-called "conceptual community."

Phallism refers to the self-deceptive denial that females are full persons. As a society, we

> tend to think of distinctively human characteristics as distinctively masculine and to credit distinctively human achievements like culture, technology, and science to men, that is, to males. This is one element of phallism: a picture of humanity as consisting of males. . . .
>
> Identifying with the human race, with the species, seems to involve a certain consciousness of the traits or properties one has qua member of the species. . . . We [as human beings] generally focus on those specific differences that we can construe as marking our elevation above the rest of the animal kingdom (Frye 1985, 219).

This sort of arrogance, which one might call humanism, is the same type of arrogance that characterizes the phallist. The phallist assumes a position of superiority based on sex. Such an attitude regards a woman with contempt and condescension. For the phallist, females need the help of men because they are inferior to men. Frye does not believe that all men treat women in this way out of malice. For many, it is a *self-deceptive* practice.

The most important point is that males have defined what it means to be a person, and therefore, they have seen themselves as making up the conceptual community. They are reluctant to grant women access. She concludes that men who exclude some human beings from personhood are only deceiving themselves. The male oriented conceptual community has no power or authority to "make a person not a person." The way in which this conceptual community has maintained its masculine character is still a concern for feminists. Frye contends that females do make up part of the conceptual community, and society should hear their voices in all areas of life. The ethic of care, for instance, constitutes a case of feminism defining an alternative ethical system based on care for particular persons instead of the abstract masculine notion of impartiality.

Goldberg takes an opposite viewpoint. In "The Inevitability of Patriarchy," Goldberg expresses a view that Frye identifies as doctrinaire sexist. Goldberg argues that there are important biological differences between men and women. It is his view that men naturally achieve a higher status than women. He refers to the work of anthropologist Margaret Mead who notes that even if men perform duties such as cooking or weaving in a society, both men and women of that society consider these jobs more important than the jobs performed by women. Statistically, he maintains that men fill the higher status roles in any society. He considers particular instances where this is not the case as aberrations from the norm and insignificant.

Further, Goldberg argues that the male hormone testosterone provides men an aggressive advantage over women. This fact gives men the advantage and allows them to obtain the higher status positions. Women, therefore, are unable to compete successfully against men for these higher positions. According to Goldberg, society should socialize their children to respect and fill traditional gender roles in conformity with biological reality. He comments that

> if society did not teach young girls that beating boys at competitions was unfeminine (behavior inappropriate for a woman), if it did not socialize them away from political and economic areas in which aggression leads to attainment, these girls would grow into adulthood with self-images based not on succeeding in areas for which biology has left them better prepared than men, but on competitions that most women could not win (Goldberg 1985, 229).[6]

Goldberg concludes that women should accept male dominance and play traditional female roles involving helping and nurturing, since these are the roles that nature prepares women to play. He assumes, therefore, that whatever is should be. This view is consistent with what we might identify as the "naturalistic fallacy." Such an attitude does not account for the fact that human nature is always changing.

Joyce Trebilcot responds to this sort of argument. In an article concerning sex roles and nature, Trebilcot examines sex roles. Trebilcot identifies three arguments often used to support sexism. To begin with, some sexists argue that certain so-called *psychological differences* between the sexes automatically lead to different sex roles. These differences, in turn, make *male dominance inevitable*. She counters that what is inevitable is not "that every woman will perform a certain role and no man will perform it, but that most women will perform the role and most men will not" (Trebilcot 1985, 233). In other words, roles are open to variation.

Second, some sexists maintain that *each sex is happier playing these traditional sex roles*. However, this statement is not true. Trebilcot argues that everyone ought to have the freedom to choose what they wish to do. If a woman is happy doing what society has traditionally labeled as a job for men, then she should be free to pursue that job.

Another argument that supports sexism derives from the notion of efficiency. This argument justifies traditional sex roles because they engage men and women in the roles for which they are best suited. This is the argument of Goldberg. Trebilcot concedes that this argument may be true. Men may be able to do certain tasks better than women. The question is, however, should society exclude men and women from certain roles on this basis? For Trebilcot, the notions of liberty, justice, and equal opportunity outweigh the argument from efficiency.

She concludes that even though there may be psychological differences between men and women, sex roles are not preordained. People should be free to choose roles that suit their own personal interests or needs. There should not be any sanctions, which attempt to force a correlation between roles and sex. In short, she maintains that we should not focus on what "men and women naturally are, but what kind of society is morally justifiable" (Trebilcot 1985, 235). To answer this question we must appeal to the notion of justice, equality, and liberty.

The final article comes from Ann Ferguson. Ferguson recommends androgyny as an ideal for human development rather than traditional sex roles. Androgynous means having the characteristics or nature of both male and female. In this article, she supports

> androgyny as an ideal for human development. To do this I shall argue that male/female sex roles are neither inevitable results of "natural" biological differences between the sexes, nor socially desirable ways of socializing children in contemporary societies. In fact, the elimination of sex roles and the development of androgynous human beings is the most rational way to allow for the possibility of, on the one hand, love relations among equals, and on the other, development of the widest possible range of intense and satisfying social relationships between men and women (Ferguson 1985, 247).[7]

In heterosexual love relationships, women have been vulnerable in the area of production. In production, the socialization process has adversely affected women. Since women usually have lower paying jobs than men, they are at an "economic disadvantage when it comes to supporting themselves. If they leave their husbands or lovers, they drop to a lower economic class" (Ferguson 1985, 255). In addition, women often have children and households they have to manage; often they have two jobs and not one. Recently, this predicament has led to the conclusion that women are less reliable than men because women are typically the ones who are absent from work or leave work to care for their children or take care of other household obligations.

She concludes that we should strive to be an androgynous person. Only this type of person can have an ideal love relationship, and only this type of person can reach his or her full potential. The ideal androgynous person would transcend the traditional masculine/feminine categories. They would be active and independent, with a desire to do socially meaningful work, and they would desire equal and loving relationships with others. According to Ferguson, we should not limit these relationships to traditional heterosexual relationships. In her view, heterosexuality, bisexuality, and homosexuality can all be legitimate expressions of this type relationship. What she rejects is the traditional divisions of labor associated with one's gender.

The essays by Frye, Goldberg, Trebilcot, and Ferguson address different aspects of the sexual equality issue. They reflect the attitudes of the 1970's and early 80's. These articles raise a number of important issues. Frye's argument concerning the conceptual community is still a concern although things are slowly changing. In my own field of biblical studies, for instance, scholars are much more concerned about issues of gender and class now than forty years ago. Barriers remain, however. Therefore, Frye's issue is still relevant. Distinguishing between gender differences that result from nature from those that derive from nurture is still a relevant topic. Finally, Ferguson's article on androgyny may raise several questions: How should we raise our children? Should we avoid teaching them traditional male or female roles? Should we try to transcend these traditional sexual roles as Ferguson suggests?

FEMINIST ETHICS TODAY

To these questions and concerns, we can add additional ones raised by recent work. Jaggar identifies several current issues that are of concern for feminists such as equality and difference, impartiality, moral subjectivity, autonomy, and the views of morality based on the Enlightenment. Many feminists are now attempting to dispel erroneous distinctions between men and women perpetuated by Western philosophy. As we discussed earlier, Western philosophy has constructed a view of men and women based on binary opposites. For instance, men are strong, rational, assertive, and public whereas women are weak, emotional, passive, and private. Here I am not denying that there are real differences between boys and girls or men and women. These differences create stereotypes firmly rooted in the minds of most people. As a result, we assume that men and women should act in compliance with certain expectations informed by such stereotypes. These stereotypes also go into defining norms and standards. We teach boys to be aggressive and not show their emotions, and these qualities are frequently sought out by employers.

The problem is not the differences, but the valuing of the one at the expense of the other. Men may have an advantage at getting a high level job in the firm because employers feel he will be more aggressive and stable. A woman, on the other hand, may have children or she may become pregnant, which may interfere with her work. This possibility can harm her chances of upward mobility. Modern arguments calling for equality based on impartiality bring these dualisms to the front of the debate.

Many feminists today have rightly rejected the notion of impartiality. Men have traditionally defined ideas such as justice, impartiality, moral rules, and judgments. We may be quick to agree that if two people go for a job the best qualified should get it. If this occurs, we might say that he or she deserves to get the job. The employer is, therefore, just and impartial. Nevertheless, we might question the requirements for the job. Are they fair? Did they require more than what is necessary? Is it logical to accept masculine standards and biases for job performance and give them a higher status while devaluing or rejecting feminine qualities? These questions, however, do not call for the abandoning of impartiality as an ideal. One could respond that companies must only make requirements that are relevant to doing the job in question.

A somewhat different objection to impartiality comes from a feminist *ethic of care*. Manning argues that the notion of impartiality "assumes that we need to repress our natural motives and requires that we ignore merit, loyalty, and affection. . . . Impartiality requires that we 'treat friends as strangers'" (Manning 1992, 23-24). The problem becomes rather clear in Manning's illustration:

> One can imagine the reaction of the drowning wife who, upon being rescued by her husband, asks, 'What took you so long?' If he tells her, 'I was trying to see if I could justify rescuing you rather than the stranger drowning with you. When I realized that I could apply an impartial rule impartially and still save you, I immediately proceeded to do so' (Manning 1992, 24).

Jaggar notes that feminists today are beginning to challenge the notions of *equality and impartiality* (Jaggar 1993, 83-84). In the modern Western tradition, there has typically been recognition of impartiality as a fundamental value. Impartiality relates to achievement as described by Parsons. In education, for instance, Parsons believes that a teacher has to treat all students the same. This relationship between teacher and student should be impartial. Nevertheless, Manning acknowledges that there are times when teachers must relate to a student in his or her particularity (Manning 1992, 98-99). Particularity means that the teacher considers the student as an individual and not as part of an abstract whole. Impartiality requires weighing the interests of each individual equally and permitting differentiation only based on differences that one can show to be morally relevant.

Along a somewhat different line, impartiality requires one to treat other individuals as morally interchangeable. This principle requires one person to look at another individual in an abstract fashion. Elizabeth, for instance, is not a special person with special abilities, but she is a white female with a college degree and four years of work experience. This approach does not allow us to see the special characteristics of particular individuals who may have abilities that would make them a better choice for the job than someone who may have better qualifications on paper.

Another issue Jaggar raises concerns moral subjectivity. Feminists and nonfeminists alike have criticized the neo-Cartesian model of moral selves. This portrayal understands all human beings as disembodied, separate, autonomous, unified, and rational selves.[8] All moral selves are similar. This position assumes that human beings can be disinterested and objective. However, we are all part of different social communities and networks, which affect the way we see the world. We are not exactly alike. There are real differences that may cause us to reason or see the world differently (Jaggar 1993, 84-85).

The whole focus on the self leads naturally to a focus on autonomy. Simply put, autonomy means self-rule. Autonomy, like impartiality, has been a continuing ideal of modern moral theory. The autonomous view, as espoused by Kant, holds that reason alone is sufficient for determining morality. The rational or moral self is the ultimate authority in matters of morality and truth. According to this view, the moral self is unattached and disinterested in personal attachments. This self, they say, is free from prejudices and self-deception. Postmodernism has rejected this view of the self. Postmodernism has not as a whole rejected autonomy in every sense. Nietzsche and Foucault focus on the self. Morality should proceed from the self as a creative act. Some modern feminists have pointed out the impossibility of separating oneself from particular attachments (Jaggar 1993, 85).

Jaggar notes that the modern moral view has come under suspicion. The modern point of view defines morality as universal in scope. That is in effect the absolutists' position; moral claims are universally valid for all times and all places. Many feminists are skeptical about human ability to discover any universal moral code. Relativists and postmodernists simply reject this notion. Ethical relativism says that right depends upon the society to which one belongs. Feminists, however, would not simply accept the dictates of society. A feminist could not accept the relativistic view that one should not try to change society. In other words, feminists, unlike relativists, seek to reform society.

Finally, Jaggar identifies two categories of feminists in relation to moral epistemology. Feminists in the first category do not explicitly challenge or reject the modern conception of morality as consisting primarily in a system of rationally justified rules or principles. They would build on the Enlightenment or modern tradition. Those feminists in the second category deny that morality is reducible to rules, and they emphasize the impossibility of justifying the claims of ethics by appeal to a universal, impartial reason (Jaggar 1993, 85-87). This latter approach is in line with postmodern moral thinking.

Another aspect of this debate emerges when one considers women who not only suffer discrimination based on gender, but also due to class and race. Women of color have advanced a school of thought known as womanist theology and ethics. The term derives from Alice Walker who is the author of *The Color of Purple*. For her, a womanist is a feminist but with a difference. Feminists are understood as emerging out of a "white woman's culture." Feminism does not reflect the experiences of all women. Neither does *womanist* include the experiences of all women, but specifically refers to the experiences of black women or other women who suffer discrimination due to sex, race, and class. Women's experiences are not universal. Walker says, "Women of all races and classes should take the initiative to search out the truth for themselves. Nothing short of contributing to the ongoing development of full personhood is accomplished when this is done" (Burrow 1998, 161).[9]

I conclude by providing a summary of Walker's definition of the term "womanist." This summary comes from an article written by Rufus Burrow Jr., entitled "Womanist Theology and Ethics." Burrow offers a brief description of Walker's use of the term womanist. A womanist is one who "loves women and women's experience. She is self-determined and thinks for herself. She is a feminist of color" (Burrow 1998, 162). Second, a womanist is one who takes responsibility, acts maturely, and one who is in charge. She is independent and does not allow "White women nor men of any race to rule and control her life. She is self-determined and capable of thinking and speaking for herself whenever she deems it necessary" (Burrow 1998, 162). Third, a womanist is one who is particularistic in that her primary concern is with Black women and other women. Her concern is not devoid of a universal concern with the "welfare and wholeness of all persons regardless of gender, race, class, sexual orientation" (Burrow 1998, 162). However, her primary concern is for particular women. The fourth part is about being courageous and persistent. A womanist supports the family and church always working out a way to accomplish important goals even in the face of resistance and problems (Burrow 1998, 163). Therefore, this movement is in part an attempt to find a voice separate from the voice of the feminist movement, which has been controlled by the interests of middle class white women. There needs to be dialogue between different women's groups. Again, this is an instance where difference could play a positive role. The particular can hinder the universal (one size fits all).

Sexual Equality, Women, and Power

This brief sketch of the issue and different positions brings us back to the beginning. It shows the number of different views on sexual equality. The issue of difference has often been used as a way to argue that men should play one set of roles and women another. We have also raised the question of nature versus socialization. Are differences due to nature or socialization? Can males and females be different and have access to equal opportunities? Moreover, just what does equality mean? I conclude my discussion by offering a brief response to these questions.

Clearly, there are differences between males and females. Some of these are due to nature. David M. Buss has argued that in early human societies men attempt to control their mate's sexual behavior because they want to make sure the children are their own and not the children of another man. Out of this situation, men develop a tendency to become extremely jealous and treat women more as a possession. In some cases, this situation leads to the problems of "sexual coercion and violence." Women, on the other hand, select successful mates. This preference leads "women to favor men who possess status and resources and to disfavor men who lacked these assets" (Buss 1994, 212). This is another explanation for why things are the way they are now.

Buss also notes that human nature changes; human nature is not something written in stone. According to Buss, human action is inexorably a product of both [biology and environment]. Every strand of DNA unfolds within a particular environmental and cultural context. Within each person's life, social and physical environments provide input to the evolved psychological mechanisms, and every behavior without exception a joint product of those mechanisms and their environmental influences. Evolutionary psychology represents a true interactionist view, which identifies the historical, developmental, cultural, and situational features that formed human psychology and guide that psychology today (Buss 1994, 17).

Arguments for playing traditional gender roles based on the belief that what is should be, therefore, are not sufficient. As times change, men overall are likely to become more nurturing as they take a larger part in their children's upbringing, and women may become more assertive. Who we are and what we want to be is always going to change as cultural and social conditions change. Differences based on traditional sex roles are likely to hang on in some circles for the unforeseeable future. Because gender and its corresponding roles and expectations are so embedded in our way of living, change may be slow.

Another concern I have with this discussion is casting the talk of difference into difference between the sexes. To say that all men are rational and that all women are emotional is clearly incorrect. Likewise, to judge reason as desirable and emotion as undesirable is equally a problem. Reason and emotion have their place. We need to realize that some men are more sensitive than others and some women are less emotional than others. One way to value differences is to stop judging people based on certain binary oppositions. This breaking down of binary oppositions would also make it more difficult to exclude women from higher management positions because they have family responsibilities. It would also encourage employers to see that both fathers and mothers deserve time with their families.

Finally, how should we define the meaning of equality? Does equality mean that males and females are generally alike in that they can do the same things equally well? Much of the logic for determining sexual equality rests upon the premise that if men and women are the same (i.e., equal), treating one differently than the other results in inequality. However, if men and women are not the same then it is acceptable to treat one differently than another (Lorber 1994, 282). For this reason, women have felt it necessary to argue that they can perform at or above the level of men.

This type of reasoning values similarity over difference. Some have seized on the differences between men and women as a way to discriminate against women. Some might reason that giving birth represents an indisputable natural difference between men and women; it is not a legal problem to differentiate on this basis (Lorber 1994, 282-302).[10]

The belief that men and women are not equal because men are stronger than women is a common contention, and as a result, men are more capable of doing certain jobs than women. I do agree that there are jobs that might favor men over women because they require physical strength. Still there is no need to prevent women from obtaining these jobs. If requirements for the job are not inflated as a way of discriminating, then it may be that men overall have a better chance at meeting the requirements than women.

There are cases where differences of strength are relevant to doing the job. Nevertheless, physical strength may often be an excuse. In an increasingly automated world, machinery does the work that once required brute strength (Lorber 1994, 49). If strength is a *legitimate requirement for performing a job*, one should look for a qualified person and not merely assume that males are stronger. Strength may be a biological difference due to our evolutionary development, but this difference is not as significant now as in the past. In other areas, it seems likely that women can do just as well as men if given the opportunity.

In theory, therefore, it does not seem that the biological differences between men and women are that great. It would seem that human nature is a result of an interaction between social and biological influences. If so, who and what we become is not written in stone. Yet, there are differences even if these differences are largely a product of our social environment. Again, I would say that we should respect these differences as opposed to judging people by them. In a sense, this would require setting traditional gender roles and expectations aside. Regardless of how much we are similar, we are never identical or interchangeable. For instance, children will always differ; some children may prefer the sciences and others take up artistic pursuits. The question becomes, can we learn to affirm rather than discourage difference?

CONCLUSION

So, how should society deal with the issue of sexual equality? Individual responses may depend upon one's social location, which can include such things as one's gender, geographical location, class, educational level, age, religion, and job experiences. A religious fundamentalist may have a different attitude about sexual equality than persons who are secular minded or from a more mainline religious tradition. For those who support equal opportunity and sexual equality in the home and in the work place, the issue becomes one of how we can bring about sexual equality in a way that respects differences. In the final analysis, we may have to struggle with some ambiguity concerning sexual equality. Abstract rules or notions of impartiality are not sufficient and may cause more problems than they solve. The ambiguity always leaves us with some questions as to what sexual equality would entail and how society should go about trying to obtain it.

So, what would it take to do away with sexual inequality? First, it would take some agreement on the part of experts as to what constitutes sexual inequality. It would entail a commitment on the part of all involved parties to tackle this problem. On a more individual level, however, parents and educators would have to work to equip children so that they can succeed. Churches would need to incorporate practices that are nondiscriminatory toward women. Some already do, but fundamentalist groups continue to practice discrimination when it comes to what roles women can play in the church. This also would include the

Catholic Church as well. Some might argue that the current worldview favors equality, but much advertising and movies still perpetuate prevalent stereotypes. Finally, society as a whole must change. There is no way to undo what has been done. We cannot rewrite history or the world religious scriptures. Only the passing of time can lessen the grip of these forces. However, we can educate a new generation who is not bound by traditional ideas and expectations about gender roles. Schools would often have to be the force to counteract attitudes passed on in traditional settings such as the home.

NOTES

1. We will discuss his views below.

2. See for example Fisher 1992 196-199.

3. The use of the word egalitarian may be an over statement.

4. In the *Republic*, Plato is reluctant to discuss the issue of sexual equality because he knows that it will be unpopular.

5. See Plato 1987, 244-259 for specific details. Also, note the comments by Aristotle 1981, 443-444.

6. This article was taken from his book by the same title published in 1973.

7. This article is an excerpt from a book published in 1981.

8. This view depends upon René Descartes (1596-1650) discussed earlier.

9. In theology, womanist offers a necessary completion to liberation theology, which is written largely by males and out of male experiences of oppression. Liberation did not really address the experiences of women suffer oppression due to class, race, and sex.

10. For a more detailed discussion of this issue, see chapter 12 in Lorber. She argues that this differential treatment is political and not biological. Leave for childbirth is seen in the same way as male disability, and *"women* are still discriminated against because their time off for pregnancy or childbirth."

Chapter Eleven

The Moral Life: Obligation and Affirmation

For everything there is a season, and a time for every matter under heaven ...a time to weep, and a time to laugh; a time to mourn, and a time to dance. (Ecclesiastes 3:1, 4)

In the preceding chapters, I have attempted to produce a clear and readable account of moral thinking in ancient, modern, and postmodern societies. Rather than just rehashing all the views covered in a brief summary, I would rather suggest some conclusions I have drawn from this journey. In this concluding chapter, I offer my own views, and I would be pleased if the reader has also developed some of his or her own as well. As a result, most of what follows derives from my own personal experiences and reflection.

I have struggled with this issue for some time. I have always been uneasy or reluctant to adopt modern ethical systems of thought. I have been shaped by modernism and understand the need for foundations upon which one can build solid structures. In my experience, however, most of these foundations are not so solid. For better or worse, I lay out my own ideas on morals and ethics.

At the beginning of this book, I define ethics as what societies characteristically endorse or reject. Often acting unethically in this sense leads to sanctions. I am in agreement with Caputo in my reluctance to embrace the word ethics in a metaphysical sense. Ethics for me is simply what a person or a society approves of or what they reject. According to this definition, ethics is only useful as a descriptive term, not as a prescriptive one. It tells us what individuals or groups believe about right and wrong and what behavior they expect from others. That is all it does. The ethics of past societies may attempt to prescribe since one who violates an ethical standard may be punished by the group or tribe. I have simply tried to describe various ethical or moral views.

In my judgment, metaphysical approaches to ethics cannot provide a secure ethic with rules and guidelines for behavior. I do not think that a universal ethic is possible or desirable. Universal rules provide a means to an end; they attempt to enact a certain type of morality. From the modern view, these rules must be universal and blind. They are blind in that they treat everyone the same, the modern view of impartiality. Avoiding ethics in this sense is avoiding the need for force or domination, avoiding the violence and danger of ethics.

The attempt to legitimate ethics or ethical systems based on some Transcendent principle whether it is a divine will or a moral law is also inadequate in my judgment. One does not have to possess an ethical system grounded in the moral law or pure practical reason or the Good beyond Being (Plato 1987, 309) to act with compassion toward others. For me, compassion and respect for others are key components for any moral view. Justice and fairness should encourage acting with compassion and respect. Yet even the concepts of fairness and justice should not be seen as abstract concepts. We should not turn them into abstract rules. Justice, compassion, fairness, and respect take place in particular settings with respect to particular people and groups. These traits call for a judge who can consider each particular case. There is not an abstract all encompassing definition of justice that can guarantee justice in a universal sense. One could program a computer to act as judge and determine justice if justice depends simply on following universal rules that have no exceptions. Justice of any merit or degree only occurs when a judge makes a judgment or decision in a particular case after considering the particulars of a case.

Still many see the need for universal rules as a necessity. What would life be like if we do not have a set of ethical rules to tell people how to live? What would society be like without the notion of treating people impartially? Surely, we need ethics to rid society of nepotism and bias. I also want to eliminate bias and prejudice. I want to live in a society that values equality. I fully agree that we must have laws to prevent discrimination. Still, one could ask how much modern ethical systems such as deontological ethics or utilitarian ethics have really contributed to a better society. They may be helpful as means of thinking through ethical issues. On the other hand, one may find feeling and impulse a better guide in many cases. Acting from feelings based on compassion or concern for all of humanity is in my mind not inferior to ethics based on rational thought. This kind of ethic does not lack moral worth. Still, there is a place for analysis. As Bauman says, a moral impulse may tell us to do something, but one must still decide what the best course of action is. Rational thought may help in most cases. Caputo says to lend a helping hand, but we are not equipped to know what that entails without thought and consideration, and then we still cannot know it with certainty. That is why he says we feel obligation.

Consequently, I do not think ethics in a metaphysical sense is necessary or helpful. I rather would say that ethics in a minimal everyday sense is useful in many situations. By ethics in a minimalist pluralistic vein, I am not advocating relativism. Every society may have its version of ethics, but the ethics of a society may not be just or fair. I would add that justice and fairness are not things we can determine in an absolute or unconditional way. They are judgment calls; they are decisions that allow us to do the best we can in a given situation.[1]

Some sort of ethic is necessary for societies. It is like traffic laws; a certain amount of order is necessary to prevent unnecessary harm to others. I admit it; I do have an inclination for some order. I recognize the need for some order; I also recognize that too much order is dangerous. I do understand that human nature is not all good. Often it brings people to do the most unimaginable things. Love of self or self-preservation or looking out for one's own pleasure without concern for others is a recipe for problems in society. On the other hand, I would agree that human beings now and then do the right thing, as they understand it, regardless of how it affects their own personal happiness. On this basis, I would argue that we must have a minimal ethic, which means there is a potential for one person to impose his or her will on another. Any ethic, however, that provides guidance for life should be informed by a moral impulse or feelings of obligation.

So what would a minimal ethic be like? It needs to be practical, flexible, and it should come from one's sense of obligation to others. Considering others does not exclude a consideration of self either. In short, ethics should consider the well-being of all people. I do not have a principle upon which this statement can rest secure. It is part of what I feel as an obligation. I feel an obligation to fairness and justice. That does not mean that I always know what it is or what it requires. Still, it is the assumption upon which many of my personal views rest.

In social interaction, people have to make decisions about proper behavior and practice. They have to make these decisions because order to some degree is necessary for the practical life. The purpose for order is not so much to limit difference as to give it a place where it can operate and have a say. A limited order does not have to rule out dialogue, disagreement, or difference. It can provide a space for all of that. If it does not provide such a space, then the order needs to be disturbed, challenged, opposed, and changed through responsible means.

In this book, I have discussed social and personal ethical perspectives. I begin here with the notion of order in the public world. I limit my comments to professional ethics, ethics as routine guidelines, and ethical standards that also have the backing of legal force. Professional ethics would refer to a code that provides guidelines for behavior in a particular profession. Some may be more serious than others. Medical ethics, for instance, may involve much more serious matters than ethics related to a small business that sets down guidelines for the treatment of customers. Still, both professions need ethical guidelines. In both cases, these guidelines should promote behavior that is fair and just.

Ethical guidelines or customs should also be shaped by a sense of fairness for all people. People can work to make their communities better by looking out for everyone who needs help. Church and community organizations can play an important role. On this level, however, there is the danger that ethics can become distorted and oppressive. Individuals and groups who are committed to a notion of openness and hospitality must do their best to keep the community ethic from becoming narrow and exclusive. Communities often need to be reformed or their vision needs to be broadened. Ideally, ethics in this context could create better communities that try to create a space where everyone is important and all life can flourish.

Concerning areas where legislation is involved to protect the rights of workers or citizens, again they should be based on a concern for the welfare and well-being of everyone involved. Laws preventing discrimination are necessary because without them some people would not receive a fair chance to make a living, to support a family, or just to have a productive life. In my mind, a concern for justice should be at the heart of our public life.

I have spent a good deal of time discussing consequentialist and nonconsequentialist ethics in the preceding pages. Both have value even if they cannot produce the right or correct answer to what I should do in every situation. Obligation happens. I often feel obligations that have nothing to do with making utilitarian or egoistic calculations. Still considering outcomes can be helpful in deciding what I need to do. They do not provide answers, but they do help one think through the issue. Rational analysis of the situation is also helpful. Nevertheless, one must ultimately decide. Decision means there are no hard and fast answers. I weigh the information and my obligation; afterwards, I make a judgment call. It is never more than that. There is no way to know if it is right in an absolute sense because I only have eyes for the present, for what I see; I only have a mind for what I know and experience; I have no ability to see things as God sees them nor stars to guide the way in these matters.

Some may respond that such admissions undermine ethics to which I agree; they undermine ethics on the larger metaphysical scale. Others may say that such views provide no real authority and so are doomed to failure. Perhaps this dark assessment is right. Perhaps calling people to follow their sense of obligation is doomed to failure because humans are simply evil. Consequently, has ethics in a *normative sense* created a Garden of Eden? Has it led in a steady progress toward a morally superior society? Modernity cannot really claim that we have continually made progress in the direction of a better and more moral society. Maybe much of the good in the world has come from good people who have acted more on an impulse to do the right thing than on the findings of ethical theory. It may very well be as Wyschogrod says that narratives or stories are more effective in promoting the good than theory.

Before moving on to the private or individual sphere, I would clarify one point. Ethics in the public arena are necessary. Again, I mean ethics in the sense of what is customary. Every society needs guidelines in the public arena to order life, to prevent harm to people who are part of the community. A rigid community may do harm to its members if it attempts to control every individual by taking away his or her freedom to be different. There is also another problem with this type of communal ethic. It might be communal, but what about the stranger, the one outside the gate or the border? I would argue that our sense of obligation to the other should help us to provide shape to public ethics so the community might be enlarged, opened up to the point where it may even lose much of its original identity. This openness may even lead to a redefining of the community as it responds to the other. So ethics may be practical, but it can be informed by the very best humanity has to offer. This may sound too idealistic for the one who fears that human nature is more selfish than good.

What about ethics associated with the individual? This discussion is not just a discussion of the individual. It is a discussion of the individual and the individual's relations to others. It also has a social dimension. I prefer to talk about moral impulse and obligation here rather than ethics. In one sense, ethics has a relativistic feel to it. I love the plurality it implies, but I am not comfortable with relativism. A Nietzschean perspectivism is much better (Nietzsche 1974, 336). The affirmation of difference, diversity, and multiplicity of forms is healthy. It keeps things open and alive. Pluralism is necessary for a healthy and productive society. An order that suppresses difference is not desirable. Still, something seems to be missing. What is missing in Nietzsche's thought is *heteronomism* or law of the other.

Like Caputo, I do not simply accept Nietzsche's heteromorphism and reject heteronomism. Both have their place. I appreciate Nietzsche's view of doing for others out of a sense of gratitude or because I want to be a generous person or I want to be a loving person, and, as a result, I decide to give my life to the other. Again, I would not be *enslaved* by the other, but I would embrace the other out of a desire to make myself that kind of person. Yet, I cannot escape the feeling that Bauman and Caputo are also right. Since childhood, I have felt obligation and in this feeling, I am sure I am not alone. I have often felt that the other calls me to account for my actions. I have often felt a sense of guilt. Guilt is not only related to feeling bad about not following the herd (i.e., Nietzsche), it often seems that the struggle is with the self. I feel guilty not because others disapprove, but because I disapprove with my actions or thoughts. Where does this come from?

Ultimately, I do not know where it comes from; there is a difference between knowing and faith. I do not know why I feel guilt or why I feel obligation. I just do. So guilt may be the feeling we have in disappointing the herd, but it may also come from somewhere else. Feeling obligation or a moral impulse makes sense. As Bauman says, it does not tell us exactly what we should do; it tells us we should do something. Again, this seems true. There may always be an element of doubt for the individual who rejects ethical systems as a way of making moral decisions. We may ask ourselves the following questions. "Did I do the right thing?" "Did I do enough?" "Did I do too much?" The answers to such questions represent an internal struggle.

The person of faith might ask why I would not simply rely on Scripture as a way of deciding issues of right and wrong. Certainly, I have been guided by the Hebrew Bible and the New Testament along with Christian theology and other types of religious literature. The parables of the Good Samaritan and the Prodigal Son have captivated me since childhood. The Golden Rule of doing unto others has always served as a faithful guide. Still, neither the Hebrew Bible nor the New Testament provides one with an unmediated word from the divine.

Commandments, rules, prophetic warnings, and parables have to be interpreted. Our interpretations reflect our abilities, our personal experiences, and our educational level. Even if one accepts the view that God reveals divine Truth to us, we are still in the position of interpreting that word from within "a human, all too human context." The receiver of the revelation is situated in a particular social and historical context. The revelation is mediated through human language, experience, and culture. We cannot simply bypass interpretation. Moral decisions must be made by individuals based on their interpretations of any number of factors.

The title of this book and chapter is the *Moral Life: Obligation and Affirmation*. The title reflects the influence of Nietzsche and Caputo. Caputo's term "jewgreek" is reflected in obligation and affirmation. The moral life is not something grim and sad. The Greek tradition sees the moral life as the good life. Plato's *The Republic* presents a plan or blueprint for the good life. Therefore, the moral life should be the good life. Moreover, as Nietzsche tells us affirming life is affirming not just the good but it affirms what is necessary. Life is about being a free spirit, but one cannot escape suffering and pain. Can we embrace that too as part of life? Can it possibly make us better and more able to live a full and enriching life? This life is not a life free of cares and responsibility. This life calls for one to improve oneself.

In addition, affirmation of life involves having the courage to affirm life in the face of ambiguity. For the Christian theologian Paul Tillich, one can even be courageous in the face of despair, doubt, and the possibility of meaninglessness.[2] The affirmation of life focuses on living this finite life in agreement with one's own principles, and living in agreement with these principles entails self-mastery. Ethics from this perspective is a creative exercise on the part of the individual.

Charles E. Winquist's discussion of self-becoming provides a bridge between obligation to the other and affirmation. Individuals cannot live in total isolation from other human beings. Winquist points out that "self becoming is always relational (communal), always contingent, and always unfinished" (Winquist 1995, 141). We can only become human in some sort of community. Our individual development participates in a larger reality that highlights our dependence on others. Human interdependence on each other implies certain mutual responsibility. Individual freedom without any limits does damage to such communities. Drawing upon Nietzsche's notion of "making things beautiful," Winquist contends that life is less beautiful when institutions, ideologies, groups, or individuals oppress, exploit, or take advantage of other individuals or groups (Winquist 1995, 142, 146-147). This relational element comes at the point where the acts of affirmation and the creation of the moral self encounter the obligation coming from the other. It is not a matter of a one-way street, but traffic moving back and forth.

The Jewish-Christian side of this ethic at its best is a call to the other, to justice for the other. It is an obligation to the poor and needy, to the orphan, to the widow, and to the stranger. It is a call to help those who need help. It is a call to be on the side of those who need us, and it is a call for us to join in their struggle. It is often more than I can handle, and to be honest it is not a call that I always welcome.

However, defining obligation as obligation to others who are part of my community or tribe is not at all sufficient. Community often defines itself in relation to those outside the community. The metaphor of community often functions on the level of "us" versus "them".[3] A community would cease to be a community if there are no boundaries, or if there are no outsiders. Community may seem like a good thing, but it can also come up very short in how it deals with others outside its walls. In some cases, communities may cause as much or more harm than individuals. Communities that are fearful of the other, of difference, may act violently with respect to others rather than feeling any obligation to them.

So if community is not a completely satisfactory metaphor for social ethics or obligation to the other, is there another option? Hospitality, a very biblical notion is perhaps a better candidate to describe a relational life open to the other, to difference and diversity. Hospitality sounds more accepting, more open, more responsible, and more just. There is a limit to hospitality since the host is in charge and some hosts may be more gracious than others.[4] Still it is a good metaphor. I personally do not begrudge my host for not turning over the keys of the house to me. Instead, hospitality should elicit feelings of gratitude, and it may leave us feeling a sense of debt to our host.

This sense of being in debt produces the need to repay the kindness of the host.[5] Caputo points to the connection of gift giving and altruism (Caputo 1997, 148). A pure gift like pure altruism is impossible. We inhabit the space between pure gift and economy—the economy of the gift. Gift giving always entails reciprocity. The gift puts the receiver under a debt and when the debt is repaid, the gift is canceled. Likewise, there are only degrees of altruism. Thus, a feeling of indebtedness is appropriate. It is a human response to a kind gesture and a good response to that gesture is the feeling of gratitude. In our lives, I would guess that most of us have experienced the kindness of a host and have extended hospitality to others.

Therefore, hospitality suggests a warm welcome, openness, a helping hand, an appreciation of the other and his or her differences. Hospitality or openness to the need of the other should replace fear, hatred, and inhospitable reactions toward the stranger or the one in need. The host is not, as we said a selfless person, a saint. The host finds some return on his or her investment whether it is the joy of one's company or the peace of mind or good feeling that comes with being there for another. The other is also likely to feel a debt whether he or she ever attempts to repay the kindness. In short, I am no saint, and a sense of obligation does not make one a perfect altruistic person who gives without return. In addition, love of self is not bad, because it helps us to know what the other needs. They need the kinds of things we need. Love of self can guide and lead one to a love of the other. Jesus says we should love others (i.e., our neighbor) as we love ourselves (Caputo 1997, 148). It is this love or connection that might help us imagine what we can do to help the other. We can try to put ourselves in the other person's place as a way of seeing how we might act responsibly toward others.

Finally, all the structures we once relied on for certainty in the modern world no longer yield that certainty. How can one learn to live in an age where truth is not a fixed and certainty seems impossible? How can we learn to adapt to a situation where ethics or beliefs are not absolute? Is it possible to develop a moral view that would give one peace of mind in the face of change and uncertainty? I have suggested an approach that bids farewell to certainty and ventures into the world of uncertainty. It does not depend on ethics as a metaphysical enterprise; it depends upon ethics or obligation. It does not trust in rationality or human ability to construct systems of thought that can lead us to the Promised Land. Instead, it trusts in a feeling, an impulse for guidance. The day to day business of deciding how to respond or if to respond can be aided by human reason and rationality, by calculations, by analyzing the need and our ability to respond to that need. My point is not that reason or calculations are bad, but that they are incomplete and always will be incomplete. In the end, we have to decide in the face of incomplete knowledge often with no assurance that our decisions are the right ones.[6]

In my judgment, the moral life can be lived between obligation and affirmation. It would be a life that helps but does not harm the other, at least not intentional and never just for the sake of causing pain. Morals ought to function to create a better society more accepting of differences, more accepting of all others, open to and welcoming of difference rather than leading a charge against it. Morals or obligation can help guide our actions in meeting both our own needs and the needs of others. A moral perspective or outlook that recognizes our interconnectedness and need for each other as well as a sense of hospitality or openness to the other would promote cooperation and good will.

No perfect society has ever existed, and I am enough of a skeptic to believe that one never will exist. We live among a sea of people some good, most are capable of both good and bad, and others not so good. We go through periods of highs and lows. Moral progress is an illusion; in reality, things get better and worse all the time. Our alternatives are to throw up our hands and give up, or keep trying.

Perhaps, a principle similar to the Golden Rule provides the proper attitude for making moral decisions. Treating people the way I want to be treated if I am in a similar situation is a starting place for deciding what my obligation is. From this point, we are on our own. We must decide. The feeling of obligation leaves us with ambiguity and doubt. Nevertheless, it provides a place for one to begin the decision making process.

NOTES

1. Caputo in his book *Deconstruction in a Nutshell*, discusses Derrida's view of justice. He says that the judge is not one who legalistically follows the law, but who makes

judgments about the law and persons in specific situations. If it is just a matter of enforcing the law, a computer could dispense justice (Caputo 1997, 125-140, 149-155).

2. See Paul Tillich 1952, 26-31, 171-178. Tillich draws upon Nietzsche's notion of the will to power, and he interprets it as self-affirmation of life. Tillich embraces meaninglessness as part of faith. He says that "the act of accepting meaninglessness is itself a meaningful act. It is an act of faith" (Tillich 1952, 176).

3. For deconstruction of the notion of community, see Caputo's *Deconstruction in a Nutshell: A Conversation with Jacques Derrida* (Caputo 1997, 107-109, 124). The only acceptable community would be a completely open one exposed to the *"tout autre"* (i.e., every other or wholly other) (Caputo 1997, 124).

4. Caputo describes Derrida's deconstruction of the word hospitality. The word comes from two Latin words. *Hospes* refers to the stranger. This word "came to take on the meaning of the enemy or 'hostile' stranger (*hostilis*)" (Caputo 1997, 110). The second word is *"pets (potis, potes, potentia)* to have power" (Caputo 1997, 110). The point is that the word does reflect a line between the stranger and the host. The host does not give away his or her right as the master of the house when extending hospitality. A host is one who owns a place of his or her own in which he or she can determine the limits of his or her openness. Hospitality, however, only begins or exists when one presses on further beyond this limit and offers his or her property as a gift, where absolutely no return is expected or felt, which is never completely possible (Caputo 1997, 110-111). This kind of impossible hospitality, the kind that is "neither real nor ideal, neither present nor future present, neither existent nor idealized" is *undeconstructible*. The *undeconstructible* does not become something outside or transcendent. It motivates or incites a desire for deconstruction and what is to come that cannot be seen or predicted (Caputo 1997, 128).

5. Derrida has also discussed gift. A pure gift as he describes it is impossible (Caputo 1997, 140-151).

6. Who are we responding to when we respond to the other? On some occasions, we feel an obligation to respond to the other at a very basic level. Levinas calls this level face-to-face. The face is not a persona or role we play. It is the person stripped of all defenses completely vulnerable and needy. It is who we are at our core. The face is not the social self. This self is stripped of all pretenses. This self is the part of our being that calls out even in the darkest hour hoping for aid and comfort, but fearing there is no one to give it. It is this presocial sphere of life.

Works Cited

American piety in the 21st century: New insights to the depth and complexity of religion in the US http://www.baylor.edu/content/services/document.php/33304.pdf.

Anderson, William L. 1991. Introduction. In *Cherokee removal: Before and after*, ed. William L. Anderson, vii-xvi. Athens and London: Brown Thrasher Books, The University of Georgia Press.

Ansell-Pearson, Keith. 1992. Who is the Übermensch? Time, truth, and woman in Nietzsche. *Journal of the History of Ideas*: 53: 309-331.

———. 1994. Introduction: Nietzsche's overcoming of morality. In *On the genealogy of morals*, ed. Keith Ansell-Pearson, ix-xxiii. Cambridge Texts in the History of Political Thought. Cambridge University Press.

Appiah, Anthony K. 1994. Identity, authenticity, survival: Multicultural societies and social reproductions. In *Multiculturalism: Examining the politics of recognition*, ed. Amy Gutmann. 149-163. Princeton: Princeton University Press.

Aristotle, 1976. *Ethics*. London: Penguin Books.

———. 1981. *The politics*. London: Penguin Books.

———. 1993. Happiness, function, and virtue. In *Social and personal ethics*, ed. William Shaw. 35-42. Belmont CL: Wadsworth Publishing Company.

Aschheim, Steven E. 1997. Nietzsche, anti-Semitism and the Holocaust. In *Nietzsche & Jewish culture*, ed. Jacob Golomb, 3-20. New York: Routledge.

Ayer, A. J. 1946. *Language, truth, and logic*. New York: Dover Publications.

Balch, David L. 1974. 'Let wives be submissive. . . . the origin, form, and apologetic function of the household duty code (Haustafel) in 1 Peter.' Ph.D. diss., Yale University.

Baldick, Chris. 1990. *The concise oxford dictionary of literary terms*. New York: Oxford University Press.

Baron, James N. 1994. Organizational evidence of ascription in labor markets. In *Equal employment opportunity: Labor market discrimination and public policy*, ed. Paul Burstein, 71-83. Sociology and Economics: Controversy and Integration. New York: Aldine De Gruyter.

Barry, John M. 1997. Rising tide: the great Mississippi flood of 1927 and how it changed America. New York: Simon & Schuster.

Bauman, Zygmunt. 1993. *Postmodern ethics*. Cambridge, Mass.: Blackwell Publishers.

Beck, Lewis White. 1956. Translator's introduction. In *Critique of practical reason*. ed. vii-xix. The Library of Liberal Arts. Indianapolis: The Bobbs-Merrill Company, Inc.

Berger, Peter L., and Thomas Luckmann, 1966. Social construction of reality: A treatise in the sociology of knowledge. New York: Anchor Books.

Berger, Peter L. 1963. *Invitation to sociology: A humanistic perspective*. New York: Anchor Books.

———. 1969. The sacred canopy: Elements of a sociological theory of religion. New York: An Anchor Press Book.

Best, Steven, and Douglas Kellner, 1991. *Postmodern theory*. The Guilford Press: New York.

Beyerlin, Walter ed., 1978. *Near eastern religious text's relation to the Old Testament*. The Old Testament Library. Philadelphia: The Westminster Press.

Bordo, Susan. 1987. *The flight to objectivity: Essays on Cartesianism and culture*. Alanny: State University of New York Press.

Borg, Marcus J. 1994. *Meeting Jesus again for the first time*. San Francisco: Harper.

Bové, Paul A. 1986. Intellectuals in power: A genealogy of critical humanism. New York: Columbia Press.

Brandt, Richard B. 1993. The morality and rationality of suicide. In *Social and personal ethics*, ed. William Shaw, 90-99. Belmont, CA: Wadsworth Publishing Company.

Brested, James H. 1954. *The dawn of conscience*. New York: Charles Scribner's Sons.

Brueggemann, Walter. 1993. Texts under negotiation: The Bible and postmodern imagination. Minneapolis: Fortress Press.

Burrow, Rufus Jr. 1998. Toward womanist theology and ethics. *Encounter* 59: 157-175.

Burstein, Paul. 1994. Discrimination against minorities and women: Some historical background. In *Equal employment opportunity: Labor market discrimination and public policy*, ed. Paul Burstein, 1-4. Sociology and Economics: Controversy and Integration. New York: Aldine De Gruyter.

Buss, David M. 1994. The evolution of desire: Strategies of human mating. New York: Basic Books.

Butler, Joseph. 1964. Sermons and dissertation on virtue. In *British moralist*, vol. 1. Indianapolis: Bobbs-Merrill.

———. 1975. Man isn't always selfish. In *Classic philosophical questions*, ed. James A. Gould, 2d ed. 122-132. Columbus, OH: Charles E. Merrill Publishing Company.

Caputo, John D. 1987. *Radical hermeneutics: Repetition, deconstruction, and the hermeneutic project*. Studies in Phenomenology and Existential Philosophy. Bloomington, IN: Indiana University Press.

———. 1993. *Against ethics: Contributions to a poetics of obligation with constant reference to deconstruction*. Studies in Continental Thought, ed. John Sallis. Bloomington and Indianapolis: Indiana University Press.

———. 1997. *Deconstruction in a nutshell: A conversation with Jacques Derrida*. Edited with Commentary by John D. Caputo. New York: Fordham University Press.

———. 2001. On religion: Thinking in action. London: Routledge.

Cohen, Warren. 1995. *Ethics in thought and action: Social and professional perspectives*. New York: Ardsley House, Publishers, Inc.

Collins, Patricia Hill. 1990. *Black feminist thought: Knowledge, consciousness, and the politics of empowerment*. Perspectives on Gender, ed., Kay Deaux. New York: Routledge.

Collins, Randall, and Michael Makowsky. 1989. *The discovery of society.* 4th ed. New York: Random House.

Collins, Randall. 1971. Functional and conflict theories of educational stratification. *American Sociological Review* 36: 1002-1019.

———. 1979. The credential society: An historical sociology of education and stratification. New York: Academic Press.

Crenshaw, James L. 2010. *Old Testament wisdom: An introduction,* 3d ed. Louisville: Westminster John Knox Press.

Cross, Frank Moore. 1973. The song of the sea and Canaanite myth. In *Canaanite myth and Hebrew epic.* Cambridge, MA: Harvard University Press.

Crossan, John Dominic. 1992. The historical Jesus: The life of a Mediterranean Jewish peasant. San Francisco: Harper Collins.

Cuzzort, R. P., and E. W. King. 1989. *Twentieth-century social thought.* 4th ed. Fort Worth: Holt, Rinehart, and Winston, Inc.

Derrida, Jacques. 1985. *The ear of the other: Otobiography, transference, translation.* Ed. Christie McDonald. Lincoln, NE: University of Nebraska Press.

Day, Willard 1977. Ethical philosophy and the thought of B. F. Skinner. In *Behaviorism and ethics,* eds. by Jon E. Krapfl and Ernest A. Vargas, 7-28. Kalamazoo: Behaviordelia, Inc.

De Beauvoir, Simmone. 1994. *The ethics of ambiguity.* New York: A Citadel Press Book.

Derrida, Jacques 1995. *On the name.* Stanford: Stanford University Press 23: 140-141.

Durkheim, Émile. 1933. *The division of labor in society.* New York: Free Press.

———. 1993. *Ethics and the sociology of morals.* Translated with an introduction by Robert T. Hall. Great Minds Series. Buffalo: Prometheus Books.

Elkind, David. 1994. *Ties that stress: The new family imbalance.* Cambridge, MA: Harvard University Press.

Engels, Friedrich. 1969. *The origin of the family, private property, and the state.* New York: International Publishers.

Epicurus, 1975. We should seek our own pleasure. In *Classic philosophical questions,* ed. James A. Gould, 161-169. 2d ed. Columbus, OH: Charles E. Merrill Publishing Company.

Ferguson, Ann. 1985. Androgyny as an ideal for human development. In *Contemporary moral problems,* ed. James E. White, 247-262. St. Paul: West Publishing Company.

Fiorenza, Elizabeth Schüssler. 1983. *In memory of her.* New York: Crossroads.

———. 1984. Bread not stone: The challenge of feminist biblical interpretation. Boston: Beacon Press.

Fisher, Helen E. 1982. *The sex contract: The evolution of human behavior.* New York: William Morrow and Company, Inc.

———. 1992. Anatomy of love: The natural history of monogamy, adultery, and divorce. New York: W. W. Norton and Company.

Fisher, Roger and William Ury 1981. *Getting to yes: Negotiating agreement without giving in.* New York: Penguin Books.

Fletcher, Joseph. 1966. *Situation ethics: The new morality.* Philadelphia: The Westminster Press.

Foucault, Michel. 1984. On the genealogy of ethics: An overview of work in progress. In *The Foucault reader,* ed. Paul Rabinow. 340-372. New York: Pantheon Books.

Frank, Stephen P. 1994. Peasantry. In *Encyclopedia of social history.* ed. Peter N. Stearns, 555-557. vol. 780. New York: Garland. Garland Reference Library of Social Sciences.

Frankena, William K. 1973. *Ethics*. 2d ed., Foundation of Philosophy Series. Englewood, NJ.: Prentice-Hall Inc.

Frankfort, Henri. 1961. *Ancient Egyptian religion: An interpretation*. New York: Harper & Row, Publishers.

Frye, Marilyn. 1985. Male chauvinism: A conceptual analysis. In *Contemporary moral problems*, ed. James E. White, 214-224. St. Paul: West Publishing Company.

Garbarino, Merwyn S. 1977. *Sociocultural theory in anthropology: A short history*. Basic Anthropological Units, eds. George and Louise Spindler, New York: Holt, Rinehart and Winston.

Gilligan, Carol. 1982. *In a different voice*. Cambridge, Mass.: Harvard University Press.

Glass, Newman Robert. 1995. Splits and gaps in Buddhism and postmodern theology. *Journal of the American Academy of Religion* 63: 303-319.

Gnostic Society Library The Nag Hammadi library—The Gospel of Thomas http://www.gnosis.org/naghamm/gthlamb.html.

Goldberg, Steven. 1985. The inevitability of patriarchy. In *Contemporary moral problems*, ed. James E. White, 224-230. St. Paul: West Publishing Company.

Gunkel, Hermann. 1984. The influence of Babylonian mythology upon the biblical creation story. In *Creation in the Old Testament*, ed. Bernhard W. Anderson, 25-52. Issues in Religion and Theology, 6. Philadelphia: Fortress Press.

Haas, Peter J. 1994. The quest for Hebrew Bible ethics: A Jewish response. *Semeia*: 66: 154-155.

Habermas, Jürgen. 1975. *Legitimation crisis*. Translated by Thomas McCarthy. Boston: Beacon Press.

———. 1990. Moral consciousness and communicative action. Cambridge: MIT Press.

Hall, Elizabeth, Marion Perlmutter, and Michael Lamb, 1982. *Child psychology today*. New York: Random House.

Haviland, William A. 1974. *Anthropology*. New York: Holt, Rinehart and Winston, Inc.

Heilbroner, Robert. 1993. *21st century capitalism*. New York: W. W. Norton & Company.

Heller, Peter. 1997. Freud in his relation to Nietzsche. In *Nietzsche & Jewish culture*, ed. Jacob Golomb. 193-217. New York: Routledge.

Helsel, Paul R. 1950. Early Greek moralists. In *A history of philosophical systems*, ed. Vergilius Ferm. 82-82. New York: The Philosophical Library.

Hinde, Andrew 2003. *England's population: A history since domesday*. Survey. New York: Oxford university Press.

Hobbes, Thomas. 1970. Natural conditions of mankind and the laws of nature. In *Morality and rational self-interest*, ed. David P. Gauthier. 133-150. Englewood Cliffs, NJ: Prentice-Hall, Inc.

Homans, George C. 1978. The general propositions of exchange theory. In *Contemporary sociological theories*, ed. Alan Wells. 131-146. Santa Monica: Goodyear Publishing Company.

Honer, Stanley M., and Thomas C. Hunt. 1978. *Invitation to philosophy: Issues and options*, 3d ed. Belmont, CA: Wadsworth Publishing Company.

Jaggar, Alison. 1993. Feminist ethics: Some issues for the nineties. In *Social and personal ethics*, ed. William Shaw. 78-88. Belmont, CA.: Wadsworth Publishing Company.

James, William. 1975. Man is free. In *Classic philosophical questions*, ed. James A. Gould, 150-158. 2d ed. Columbus, OH: Charles E. Merrill Publishing Company.

Johnstone, Ronald L. 2007. *Religion in society: A sociology of religion*. 8th ed., Englewood Cliffs, NJ: Prentice Hall.

Kalin, Jesse. 1970. In Defense of egoism. In *Morality and rational self-interest*, ed. David P. Gauthier. 64-87. Englewood Cliffs, NJ: Prentice-Hall, Inc.

Kant, Immanuel. 1952. The science of right. In *Great books of the Western world*, ed., Mortimer J. Adler, 397-460. vol. 42. Chicago: William Benton, Publisher Encyclopædia Britannica, Inc.

———. 1956. *Critique of practical reason*. The Library of Liberal Arts, ed., Oskar Piest. Indianapolis: The Bobbs-Merrill Company, Inc.

———. 1964. *Groundwork of the metaphysic of morals*. Translated by H. J. Paton. New York: Harper & Row Publishers.

Kaufmann, Walter. 1974. *Nietzsche: Philosopher, psychologist, antichrist*. 4th ed. New Jersey: Princeton University Press.

Kierkegaard 1954. *Fear and trembling*. Garden City: Doubleday Anchor Books Translated with introduction and notes by Walter Lowrie.

King, Martin Luther Jr., 2000. *Why we can't wait*. Signet Classic New York: Penguin Group.

Kockelmans, Joseph. 1992. Twentieth-century continental ethics, part I. In *A History of Western ethics*, ed. Lawrence C. Becker, 118-128. vol. 1. New York & London: Garland Publishing, Inc.

Lankford, George E. ed., 1987. Native American legends, southeastern legends: Tales from the Natchez, Caddo, Biloxi, Chickasaw and other nations. American Folklore Series. Little Rock: August House.

Lawson, Hilary. 1985. *Reflexivity: The post-modern predicament*. Problems of Modern European Thought, ed. Alan Montefiore. La Salle: Open Court.

Lee, Desmond 1987. Tanslator's introduction. 11-58. In *Plato: The republic*. London: Penguin Books.

Lenski, Gerhard E. 1966. Power and privilege: A theory of social stratification. New York: McGraw-Hill.

Lindzey, Gardner, Calvin S. Hall, and Richard F. Thompson, 1978. *Psychology*, 2d ed. New York: Worth Publishing Inc.

Locke, John. 1975. Epicurus, 1975. Knowledge is ultimately sense knowledge. In *Classic philosophical questions*, ed. James A. Gould, 238-254. 2d ed. Columbus, OH: Charles E. Merrill Publishing Company.

Lorber, Judith. 1994. *Paradoxes of gender*. New Haven: Yale University Press.

Loubère, Leo A. 1994. *Nineteenth-century Europe: The revolution of life*. Englewood Cliffs: Prentice Hall.

Lukes, Steven. 1985. *Marxism and morality*. Oxford, Clarendon Press.

MacIntyre, Alasdair. 1966. A short history of ethics: A history of moral philosophy from the Homeric Age to the twentieth century. New York: Macmillan Publishing Company.

Mandeville, Bernard de. 1975. Man is always selfish. In *Classic philosophical questions*, ed. James A. Gould, 2d ed. Columbus: Charles E. Merrill Publishing Company.

Manning, Rita C. 1992. *Speaking from the heart: A feminist perspective on ethics*. New Feminist Perspective Series, ed. Rosemarie Tong. Lanham: Rowman & Littlefield Publishers Inc.

May, Larry. 1992. Review of *Saints and postmodernism: Revising moral philosophy*, by Edith Wyschogrod, In *Ethics* 103: 181-184.

McCarthy, Thomas. 1990. Introduction. In *Moral consciousness and communicative Action*. ed. vii-xiii. Cambridge: MIT Press.

McGrath, William J. 1997. Mahler and the Vienna Nietzsche Society. In *Nietzsche & Jewish culture*, ed. Jacob Golomb. New York: Routledge. Pp. 218-232.

Mead, George Herbert. 1934. *Mind self and society.* Chicago: University of Chicago Press.

Mead, Margaret. 1963. *Sex and temperament in three primitive societies.* New York: William Morrow.

Medlin, Brian. 1970. Ultimate principles and ethical egoism. In *Morality and Rational Self-Interest,* ed David P. Gauthier. 56-63. New Jersey: Prentice-Hall, Inc.

Meeks, Wayne. 1983. The first urban Christians: The social world of the Apostle Paul. New Haven: Yale University Press.

Mill, John Staurt. 1957. *Utilitarianism.* The Library of Liberal Arts, ed Oskar Piest. The Bobbs-Merrill Company Inc.

———. 1975. Man is determined. In *Classic philosophical questions.* ed. James A. Gould 136-149. 2d ed. Columbus, OH: Charles E. Merrill Publishing Company.

Neidert, Lisa J. and Reynold Farley. 1994. Assimilation in the United States: An analysis of ethnic and generational differences in status and achievement, In *Equal employment opportunity: Labor market discrimination and public policy,* ed. Paul Burstein 27-37. Sociology and Economics: Controversy and Integration. New York: Aldine De Gruyter.

Niebuhr, Reinhold. 1964. *The nature and destiny of man.* New York: Charles Scribner's Sons. Volume I Human Nature.

Nietzsche, Friedrich. 1967a. *The will to power.* Translated by Walter Kaufmann and R. J. Hollingdale and ed. Walter Kaufmann, New York: A Vintage Book.

———. 1967b. *The birth of tragedy and the case for Wagner.* Translated by Walter Kaufmann New York: Random House.

———. 1974. *The gay sciences: With a prelude in rhymes and an appendix of songs.* Translated by Walter Kaufmann. New York: Vintage Books.

———. 1978. *Thus spoke Zarathustra: A book for none and all.* Translated by Walter Kaufmann. New York: Penguin Books.

———. 1982. *Daybreak: Thoughts on the prejudices of morality.* Cambridge: Cambridge University Press.

———. 1984. *Human all too human.* Translated by Marion Faber. Lincoln: The University of Nebraska Press.

———. 1989. *Beyond good and evil: Prelude to a philosophy of the future.* Translated by Walter Kaufmann. New York: Vintage Books.

———. 1990a. Twilight of idols. In *Twilight of idols/The anti-Christ.* Translated by R. J. Hollingdale. New York: Penguin Books.

———. 1990b. The anti-Christ. In *Twilight of idols/The anti-Christ.* Translated by R. J. Hollingdale. New York: Penguin Books.

———. 1992. *Ecce homo: How one becomes what one is.* Translated by R. J. Hollingdale. New York: Penguin Books.

———. 1994. *On the genealogy of morality,* Cambridge Texts in the History of Political Thought, ed., Keith Ansell-Pearson. Cambridge University Press.

Noddings, Nell. 1984. *Caring: A feminine approach to ethics and moral education.* Berkeley: University of California Press.

———. 1989. *Women and evil.* Berkeley: University of California Press.

———. 1995. A morally defensible mission for schools in the 21st century. *Phi Delta Kappan* 76: 364-368.

Noss, David S., and John B. Noss, 1974. *Man's religion,* 5th ed. New York: Macmillan Publishing Company.

———. 2008. *A history of the world's religions,* 12th ed. New Jersey: Pearson Prentice Hall.

Olson, Robert. 1967. *A short introduction to philosophy*. New York: Harcourt, Brace & World, Inc.

Paglia, Camille. 1992. The rape debate, continued. In *Sex, art, and American culture*, New York: Vintage Books.

Parsons, Talcott. 1967. The school class as a social system. In *The study of society*, ed. Peter I. Rose. 647-666. New York: Random House.

Paton, H. J. 1964 Analysis of the argument In *Groundwork of the metaphysic of morals* 13-52. New York: Harper & Row Publishers.

Pierce, Jessica. 2005. *Morality play: Case studies in ethics*. Boston McGraw Hill.

Plato, 1987. *The republic*. New York: Penguin Books.

Pojman, Louis P. 1990. *Ethics: Discovering right and wrong*. Belmont: Wadsworth Publishing Company.

Pritchard, James B. ed., 1958. *The ancient near east: Volume I an anthology of texts and pictures*. New Jersey: Princeton University Press.

Rad, Gerhard von. 1972. *Genesis*. The Old Testament Library, ed., G. Ernest Wright. Philadelphia: The Fortress Press.

Redfield, Robert. 1956. Peasant society and culture: An anthropological approach to civilization. Chicago: The University Press.

Richelle, Marc N. 1993. *B. F. Skinner: A reappraisal*. Hillsdale: Lawrence Erlbaum Associates, Publishers.

Ross, W. D. 1975. We have obligations independent of our happiness. In *Classic philosophical questions*, ed. James A. Gould, 189-197. 2d ed. Columbus: Charles E. Merrill Publishing Company.

Ruse, Michael. 2004. Evolutionary ethics past and present. In *Evolution and ethics: Human morality in biological & religious perspectives*, eds. Philip Clayton and Jeffery Schloss. 27-49 Grand Rapids: Wm. B. Eerdmans Publishing Company.

Sahakian, William S. 1974. *Ethics: An introduction to theories and problems*. Barnes and Noble Outline Series. New York: Barnes and Noble Books.

Santaniello, Weaver. 1997. A post-Holocaust re-examination of Nietzsche and the Jews: Vis-à-vis Christendom and Nazism. In *Nietzsche & Jewish culture*, ed. Jacob Golomb. 21-54. New York: Routledge.

Sarup, Madan. 1993. An introductory guide to post-structuralism and postmodernism. Athens: The University of Georgia.

Schegloff, Emanuel A. 1992. Repair after next turn: The last structurally provided defense of intersubjectivity in conversation. *American Journal of Sociology* 97: 1295-1345.

Schrift, Alan D. 1990. Nietzsche and the question of interpretation: Between hermeneutics and deconstruction. New York: Routledge.

Schroeder, William R. 1992. History of Western ethics: II. twentieth-century continental, Part II. In *Encyclopedia of ethics*, ed. Lawrence C. Becker, 758-765. Vol 1, New York & London: Garland Publishing, Inc.

Schumacher, E. F. 1993. Buddhist economics. In *Social and personal ethics*, ed. William Shaw. 461-466. Belmont, CL.: Wadsworth Publishing Company.

Schutz, Alfred. 1967. Common-sense and scientific interpretation of human action. In *Collected papers I: The problem of social reality*, ed., Maurice Natason. 3-47. The Hauge: Martinus Nijhoff.

Scott, Charles E. 1990. *The question of ethics: Nietzsche, Foucault, and Heidegger*. Studies in Continental Thought, ed. John Sallis. Bloomington and Indianapolis: Indiana University Press.

Shanin, Teodor. 1990. Defining peasants: Essays concerning rural societies, expolary economics, and learning from them in the contemporary world. Oxford: Basil Blackwell.

Shaw, William H. 1993. An Introduction to ethics. In *Social and personal ethics*, ed. William Shaw. 2-34. Belmont, Cl.: Wadsworth Publishing Company.

Sinnott-Armstrong, Walter. 2009. *Morality ~~without God?~~* New York: Oxford University Press.

Sjoberg, Gideon. 1960. *The preindustrail city: past and present*. New York: The Free Press.

Skinner, B. F. 1971. *Beyond freedom and dignity*. New York: Alfred A. Knopf.

Spencer, Herbert. 1899. *Principles of sociology*, vol. II. New York: D. Appleton and Company.

———. 1971. On society as a system. In *Sociology: The classic statements*, ed., Marcello Truzzi. 71-80. New York: Random House.

Stambaugh, John E., and David L. Balch, 1986. *The New Testament in its social environment*. Library of Early Christianity, ed. Wayne A. Meeks. Philadelphia: The Westminster Press.

Sumner, Graham. 1975. Ethics are relative. In *Classic philosophical questions*. ed. James A. Gould, 82-96. 2d ed. Columbus, OH.: Charles E. Merrill Publishing Company.

Tannen, Deborah. 1994. *Gender & discourse*. New York: Oxford University Press.

Taylor, Charles. 1992. *The ethics of authenticity*. Cambridge, MA.: Harvard University Press.

Thornton, Russell. 1991. The demography of the trail of tears period: A new estimate of Cherokee population losses. In *Cherokee removal: Before and after*, ed. William L. Anderson. 75-95. Athens and London: Brown Thrasher Books, The University of Georgia Press.

Tillich, Paul. 1952. *The courage to be*. Yale University Press: New York & London.

Tönnies, Ferdinard. 1971. On Gemeinschaft and Gesellschaft. In *Sociology: The classic statements*, ed., Marcello Truzzi. New York: Random House.

Toulmin, Stephen. 1990. *Cosmopolis: The hidden agenda of modernity*. New York: Free Press.

Trebilcot, Joyce. 1985. Sex roles: The argument from nature. In *Contemporary moral problems*, ed. James E. White, 230-236. St. Paul: West Publishing Company.

Valantasis, Richard. 1995. Constructions of power in asceticism. *Journal of the American Academy of Religion* 63: 775-821.

Voltair. 1919. Voltaire in his letters. Translated by S. G. Tallentyre with a preface and forward. New York: The Knickerbocker Press.

Wallace, Ruth A., and Alison Wolf, 1986. *Contemporary sociological theory: Continuing the classical tradition*, 2nd ed. Englewood Cliffs, NJ.: Prentice-Hall Inc.

Wallbank, Walter T., Alastair M. Taylor, and Nels M. Bailkey, 1976. *Civilization past and present*. 7th ed. vol. 2. Glenview: Scott, Foresman and Company.

Watson, J. B. 1926. What the Nursery Has to Say about Instincts. In *Psychologies of 1925*, ed. C. Murchison. 1-35. Worcester: Clark University Press.

Weber, Max. 1962. *Basic concepts in sociology*. Translated by H. P. Secher. New York: Philosophical Library Inc.

———. 1964. The sociology of religion. Translated by Ephraim Fischoff. Boston: Beacon Press.

———. 1971. The three types of legitimate rule. In *Sociology: The classic statements*, ed., Marcello Truzzi. New York: Random House.

West, Cornel. 1994. *Race matters*. New York: Vintage Books.

Westermann, Claus. 1971. Zum Geschichtsverständnis des Alten Testaments. In *Probleme biblischer Theologie: Gerhard von Rad zum Geburstag*, ed. H. W. Wolff, 611-619. München: Chr. Kaiser, 1971.

White, James E. 1985. *Contemporary moral problems*, ed. James E. White, 212-214. St. Paul: West Publishing Company.

Wiggins, Daphne C. 2005. *Righteous content: Black women's perspectives of church and faith*. ed. Peter Paris Religion, Race, Ethnicity. New York: University Press.

Wilson, John A. 1951. *The culture of Ancient Egypt*. Chicago: The University of Chicago Press.

Wilson, Robert R. 1994. Sources and methods in the study of Ancient Israelite Ethics. *Semeia*: 66: 61-62.

Winquist, Charles E. 1995. *Desiring theology, religion & postmodernism*, ed. Mark C. Taylor. Chicago: University of Chicago Press.

Wolf, Eric R. 1966. *Peasants*. Foundations of Modern Anthropology Series, ed. Marshall D. Sahlins. Englewood Cliffs, NJ: Prentice-Hall.

Wolman, Benjamin B. ed., 1973. *Dictionary of behavioral science*. New York: Van Nostrand Reinhold Company.

Woolf, Virginia. 2005. A room of one's own. With an introduction by Susan Gubar. Orlando: Harcourt Inc.

Wyschogrod, Edith. 1990. *Saints and postmodernism: Revising moral philosophy, Religion and Postmodernism*, ed. Mark C. Taylor (Chicago: The University of Chicago Press.

Yovel, Yirmiyahu. 1997. Nietzsche and the Jews: The structure of an ambivalence. In *Nietzsche & Jewish culture, ed. Jacob Golomb*. 117-134 New York: Routledge.

Index

About the Author

Tony L. Moyers is associate professor of religion and department chair of humanities, social science, and political science at Athens State University, Alabama. Dr. Moyers has a Ph.D. from Baylor University, Texas.